Fernando Alonso

UNIVERSITY PRESS OF FLORIDA

Florida A&M University, Tallahassee
Florida Atlantic University, Boca Raton
Florida Gulf Coast University, Ft. Myers
Florida International University, Miami
Florida State University, Tallahassee
New College of Florida, Sarasota
University of Central Florida, Orlando
University of Florida, Gainesville
University of North Florida, Jacksonville
University of South Florida, Tampa
University of West Florida, Pensacola

Fernando Alonso with Cuballet student Arielle Smith. Photo by Vladimir Smith.

Fernando Alonso

The Father of Cuban Ballet

Toba Singer

University Press of Florida

Gainesville

Tallahassee

Tampa

Boca Raton

Pensacola

Orlando

Miami

Jacksonville

Ft. Myers

Sarasota

Library of Congress Cataloging-in-Publication Data
Singer, Toba.
Fernando Alonso : the father of Cuban ballet / Toba Singer.
p. cm.
Includes bibliographical references and index.
ISBN 978-0-8130-4402-6 (alk. paper)
1. Alonso, Fernando, 1914– 2. Ballet dancers—Cuba—Biography. I. Title.
GV1785.A634S56 2013
792.802'8092—dc23 [B]   2012031969

The University Press of Florida is the scholarly publishing agency for the
State University System of Florida, comprising Florida A&M University,
Florida Atlantic University, Florida Gulf Coast University, Florida
International University, Florida State University, New College of Florida,
University of Central Florida, University of Florida, University of North
Florida, University of South Florida, and University of West Florida.

 University Press of Florida
15 Northwest 15th Street
Gainesville, FL 32611-2079
http://www.upf.com

Dedicated to
Fernando González
René González
Antonio Guerrero
Gerardo Hernández
Ramón Labañino

Dance not only with the muscles of your body,
also work with the muscle of the heart.

Fernando Alonso

Contents

Part III. Recuerdos (Recollections)

Prologue with Letter from Alicia Alonso

It was intermission. Ninety-three-year-old Fernando Alonso sat alone in his customary mezzanine seat in Havana's García Lorca Theater. During the Sixtieth Anniversary Festival of the Cuban National Ballet, he would see perhaps twenty performances by an array of his former students, who danced either with the Cuban National Ballet or with world-class companies that had welcomed them as ranking members. Earlier in the day he had presided over rehearsals and ballet class at the company-affiliated academy. He was seated in the same row and just a few seats away from two important Cuban personalities: his former wife, the ballerina assoluta Alicia Alonso, and the prime minister of Cuba, Raúl Castro. At intermission, friends, international celebrities, and admirers, most of them former students, would arrive to greet him. He would respond warmly, offering words that captured a shared and meaningful moment in the past. The story that brought him to his special place in a theater he played no small role in helping come to life concludes with his having won, through his exceptional contribution to the art and science of teaching ballet, the hearts, minds, and deepest respect of his Cuban *compañeros*, as well as dance figures the world over. It is studded with rich experiences, brilliant moments, unstinting inventiveness, and his personal insistence on the highest caliber of effort, performance, attitude, and comportment. In Fernando Alonso there is also an auxiliary motor generating a boyish ebullience harboring an insouciant weakness for the charms of young women. He has indulged his fancies, but not for free: he and others have paid a price, both personally and professionally.

I decided to write about Fernando Alonso's work based on two exchanges. The first took place during an interview with the London Royal Ballet star Carlos Acosta, who credited Alonso as a brilliant teacher who brought science into the ballet studio. The second occurred during a conversation with the ballet teacher Lupe Calzadilla and her daughter, San Francisco Ballet principal dancer Lorena Feijóo, both of whom are Cuban-born. While I was interviewing Calzadilla for *Dance Magazine*, Lorena generously agreed to take time between rehearsals of William Forsythe's *Artifact Suite* to help with translation. During a lively conversation in two languages, Lorena demonstrated how Fernando Alonso trained the corps de ballet to achieve a precision for which there is no equal. As she traced a diagonal to show that it was the *second* dancer in that line who determines their spacing, she suddenly stopped and said, "*You* should write a book on Fernando! Nobody has written anything about him in English, and he is ninety-two years old!"

About a decade earlier I had seen a video of an unfinished documentary film about Alicia Alonso, made by a team of filmmakers led by my friend Frank Boehm. I remembered Fernando's observations in the documentary as having been among the most insightful. I decided to e-mail Fernando's daughter, Laura, whom I had met, to propose that I write a book about her father. Several weeks later, an e-mail arrived in which Laura pronounced the book proposal "brilliant!" By the following July, I was on my way to Querétaro, Mexico, where Fernando Alonso would be the guest of honor at the First Ibérica Contemporánea Dance Festival, initiated by Centro ProArt, a visionary dance center dedicated to Iberian and classical dance traditions, including those originating in Cuba.

Fernando Alonso has devoted a lifetime to his work; for him, the words "life" and "work" are strands of a double helix. As the details of both emerged during hours of interviews and time spent with Fernando, his family, colleagues, the youngest and oldest of students and teachers who are his direct beneficiaries, and the artistic staff of the Cuban National Ballet and National Ballet School, I came to realize that his story has become refracted through a prism in which the National Ballet and its school bear the seal of the artistic triumphs as well as the symptoms of the personal difficulties of its parental figures, Alicia and Fernando Alonso. Yet, in spite—or perhaps because—of this idiosyncrasy, those very institutions have strived to reach beyond the fray of Alicia and Fernando's bitter 1974 divorce to attain the highest of rankings. Fernando's story also takes place in the crucible of the 1959 Cuban Revolution, not a backdrop in the traditional sense, but more a framework that actively advanced the fortunes of the Cuban National Ballet Company, such that it has today become the cultural institution most identified with Cuba.

How do I present Fernando Alonso's story to a world that has scant information about revolutionary Cuba? The answer is: I unroll it in the context of deep respect for the centuries-long struggle of Cuba to free itself from Spanish colonial rule and U.S. domination; I offer it with profound and unstinting admiration for the work of Alicia, Alberto, Laura, and Fernando Alonso, each a jewel in the crown of the Cuban National Ballet and its legacy. I share it without sidestepping the human foibles and mishaps that resulted in a few bumps in the road, nor the dramatic political events that left their imprint. I give the book's authority and voice over to the interviews so that the story may reveal itself in the language and reminiscences of Fernando Alonso and the dancers who were his students, colleagues, and most intimate of collaborators.

•

A steady, no-nonsense gaze met mine. I asked the sturdy, bespectacled woman who stood behind a desk in an archway a few yards from the gated entrance to the National Ballet whether I might make an appointment to meet Mme Alicia Alonso. She looked back wordlessly. I placed a small white shopping bag on the reception desk. It contained my book, *First Position: A Century of Ballet Artists*. "This is for Mme Alonso," I said, as I opened the book to a chapter headed "Alicia Alonso." Then I retrieved another parcel from the bag, "And please give her this," handing over a copy of my friend Frank Boehm's film *Alicia*, a work in progress, which he and several dancers from Chicago had begun shooting some twenty years earlier. I asked the woman her name. "Fara," she said. She waved her hand in the direction of a dancer I had noticed in Frank's film. Now, twenty years older, he was walking quickly to escape a swirl of white dust as he lumbered under the burden of the two bags of cement he was carrying to the courtyard beyond. Fara then smiled slightly and explained that the dust from the renovation under way made the office uncomfortable for Alicia. She had the flu and was staying away most days. Fara promised to give Alicia my message, along with the items I had left, and to contact me at my hotel. When? Soon.

Two days later, on my way to an appointment across Villalon Park, I noticed Fara Rodríguez standing at the front gate of the ballet building. We greeted each other, and I reminded her of her promise to contact me. She smiled slowly and nodded. Alicia was still away from the office, but there was no need for concern. An answer would come—soon.

Later that evening I attended a performance of *Giselle*. The Cuban National Ballet's version is its signature work. Its title role had brought Alicia Alonso the initial acclaim that launched her career when she stepped in for an ailing Alicia Markova in a New York Ballet Theatre performance more than seven decades earlier. As I mounted the stairs to the Antonio Mella

Theater's second tier, Fara, in a bright blue print dress, stepped out of the crowd. "She will see you in her office tomorrow at noon," she said with an encouraging smile that nearly ended with a wink.

The following day, I downed the *solo* shot of Cuban coffee that Fara had offered me and then entered the inner office of the artistic director of the Cuban National Ballet. Alicia Alonso stood perpendicular to her desk with her right hand extended. She is blind, and so could not see me. The proffered hand signaled that the visitor should move toward her to make her presence known, to spare Alicia from calling out a greeting into an invisible void. I had known that she was blind, but I wasn't prepared for a protocol that at once acknowledged and dismissed that blindness, a disability to which she has never given quarter unless forced.

Alicia thanked me enthusiastically for my book and the video, and we spoke of friends of hers whose lives and careers I had traced in the book, and of Frank Boehm's film, and Frank himself. We chatted about Cuban dancers whom we both knew, and when I related a story about a defector's characterization of life in the company, Alicia instantly converted the tale into a clever off-color joke. We laughed as if we were a couple of school chums, each shriek a delicious reproach to the defector's caricature of Cuba. The shared humor made it less uncomfortable to reveal the purpose of my visit to my new friend.

"Alicia, I am here to write a book about Fernando."

Few people mention Fernando's name in Alicia's presence, but I had no alternative. I would need her professional cooperation, even if she felt she could not endorse my project personally. I looked in her direction to gauge her reaction. She lowered her head and directed the eyes she shielded with sunglasses toward her folded hands. "Fernando? I see," she said in a voice that was suddenly quiet, if a little deeper and more tremulous, and then there was nothing more. Apparently, no one had told her the purpose of my visit. I realized that I would have to wait a long time before raising any questions about Fernando with her, but how long? I would be in Cuba for just one more week.

That evening I saw the second cast dance *Giselle*. Again, as I entered the theater, Fara stopped me to say that Alicia had invited me to join her in the mezzanine lobby at intermission. As I made my way there, Alicia arrived on the arm of her current husband, Pedro Simón, a professor of philosophy and dance critic, who is the company's co-executive director. Alicia made introductions, and the three of us spoke about the evening's performance. During a break in the conversation, a man sat down alongside me and introduced himself as a critic for a U.S. Spanish-language dance journal. Indicating a young man who chatted with Alicia and then seemed to spring away and back again, the critic whispered, "That's Fidel's youngest son," joking that "he has his father's energy!" I nodded, but I was not in Cuba to engage in celebrity gossip. Over time, I came to find the young man's interest in ballet more compelling than his provenance. During my visits to the island I would see him at other ballet functions, and was impressed that so young and well-known a male ballet devotee would show up alone, with no sheltering entourage running interference for him.

The scent of fresh-cut flowers greeted me when I opened the door to my room at the Hotel Presidente that evening. Switching on the light, I saw an enormous bouquet of two dozen red, white, peach, pink, and yellow roses in a vase on the desk next to my bed. Tucked into the bouquet was Alicia's card, bearing a black slash meant to represent an "A." I was overcome by simultaneous feelings of gratitude and embarrassment at having been received and welcomed so regally by a ballet legend I had admired for as long as I could remember. The bouquet's perfume triggered the memory of a scene from my Bronx childhood. My devoted but frugal mother, having been instructed by my ballet teacher to provide me with a bouquet for the curtain call of my first recital, took scissors in hand and scaled the chain-link fence that separated our apartment house from the one behind it. A scrawny rose bush sat between the two buildings. She snipped several yellow tea roses from the lone bush, clambered back over the fence, and tied the pilfered flowers up in a half-inch-wide powder blue velvet ribbon, decommissioned from the contents of her sewing box. The other girls in *The Skaters Waltz* received store-bought bouquets, but as we dropped into réverence during our curtain call, that nosegay of yellow roses tied in velvet ribbon imparted the sense memory of the guilty pleasure my mother took in risking life, limb, and reputation for a go at petty thievery to honor her six-year-old's scant achievement. That long-forgotten, now reawakened moment resonated perfectly with what I appreciated about Cuban inventiveness: I happened to know that Alicia's mother had once cut and sewn a Dying Swan costume for her daughter from a swath of white nylon appropriated from the wide hem of a pair of hotel curtains. I reflected on the sequence and significance of the day's events and wondered when the right moment would arrive to ask Alicia to comment on Fernando's contribution to ballet training in Cuba.

Sixteen months passed before I felt satisfied that I had done sufficient work with Fernando and his students, colleagues, and collaborators to write to Alicia to request that she answer questions about a man whose change of heart had broken hers. From the research I had done for my first book, I knew that there would have been no world-class ballet company in Cuba without Alicia's outstanding achievements and the support of the Cuban people and their revolutionary government. My primary interest in Fernando issued from his life's work as a pedagogue. If excellent teachers prepare dance students, and pull their best work from them, those same students inspire their teachers to refine their methods and approaches in an unending effort to discover their own best pedagogy. The distinction that places a teacher in a special category is that he or she educates not one dancer, but thousands, and teaches not one future teacher, but teachers of teachers for years to come. That is why a school of ballet, be it Danish, Russian, Italian, or French, is often identified with one singular teacher's name. A current of enthusiasm ripples through the generations of dancers and teachers who offered heartfelt praise and gratitude for Fernando's contribution of a scientific system that trained and prepared them for the ballet stage. One of them had urged me to write a book about him. Fernando's younger brother, Alberto, had also made an immense contribution to the development of ballet in Cuba, with an innovative body of choreography that has been appreciated and reprised abroad. I had no plan to write a book on Fernando that would diminish or detract from Alicia's or Alberto's contributions, yet I continued to encounter a small number of individuals who insisted upon interpreting my project as an attempt to elevate Fernando's role above that of Alicia or Alberto, if not the Cuban Revolution itself. I had no interest in taking sides in Alicia and Fernando's divorce, nor in second-guessing the resulting proposal that Fernando move from Havana to Camagüey when it became clear that the couple's artistic and personal differences were impeding the day-to-day work of the company and academy. Obviously, that decision removed Fernando Alonso irrevocably from the central leadership of the company, and such a change would not have been an option in Alicia's case. Still, it carried with it the advantage of making it possible for him to not only play a pivotal role in strengthening Camagüey's ballet company and school but also refreshing the ranks of the Cuban National Ballet with newly formed dancers from Camagüey.

Soon after I sent my note to Alicia, I received a reply from Pedro Simón, saying that Alicia would answer my questions if I were to submit them quickly, before the company left on an extended tour of Europe.

I sent Alicia the following questions:

- When he arrived in New York in the midst of the crushing effects of a worldwide economic depression, where many New Yorkers were out of work and looking for jobs, Fernando was able to find a day job right away, and also work as a dancer. How was it that he could accomplish so much in such a short time?
- What impressed you most about him?
- What distinguished him from other teachers?
- Having very early recognized your potential to become a great ballerina, in what concrete ways did he make a contribution to the success of your career?
- What was the best counsel you received from him?
- What are and have been, in your opinion, his most outstanding achievements?
- What were the most difficult obstacles that you [both] encountered?
- What was the funniest experience with him and what was the most moving?
- Recount a story about him that best reflects his distinctive personality and character.
- What lessons do you continue to carry with you from the many hours you spent with him in the studio?
- It is unusual for a teacher to awaken great technique, as well as artistry and theatricality in his students. How was this teacher able to achieve all of these things?

I received the following reply:

To Toba Singer

Dear friend:

Please excuse me for not answering each one of the questions you sent me, asked in order to write your book on Fernando Alonso. Nevertheless, I will allow myself to make some considerations on the theme, with the hope of being able to help you in your research work.

In the first place, I admit that when referring to these issues, I feel, myself, in an uncomfortable position. To talk about the work carried out in the field of ballet, in Cuba, or from Cuba to the world, compels me to speak out of my own participation in these events; and in a certain way, to self-assess my own work. As to Fernando Alonso's significance in the ballet, I am aware that any opinion that does not imply praise, can give rise inevitably, to suspicions, in the sense that this assessment might involve any resentment or personal subjectivity. This is due to the circumstance that Fernando Alonso was my husband for almost four decades, until our definitive separation in 1974.

I would be the last person in this world to scant Fernando Alonso the professional honor that he deserves. Besides his having been my husband for many years, and being my daughter's father, he was at my side in periods of crucial importance in my life; together, we founded the Cuban National Ballet, we shared professional work in the difficult stages before the Cuban Revolution, and we fought to establish a tradition in the art of dance in our country, contributing decisively to the emergence and development of what today is known worldwide as the "Cuban School of Ballet."

Nevertheless, for the sake of historical truth, and to contribute to the achievement of a scientific approach in the study of the "Cuban School of Ballet," I should point out some specifics.

A "school of ballet" of a national character, the Cuban one, is not created by the will and talent of a single person. It is, in the first place, a consequence of the innate genius of the Cuban people for dancing, of their natural instinct to express themselves through movement, of their culture and ethnic characteristics. Certainly, after all of it having being assimilated, interpreted, organized and enhanced by the talent of artists and professors.

When we arrived in New York, in the late thirties of the last century, we had an irregular preparation in basic ballet technique, acquired from Nikolai Yavorsky, a former Ukrainian military [officer] settled in Cuba who had learned rudiments of the academic technique in France. Although you surely know the story, I remind you that our first contacts were with great teachers of the "Old Russian School" (Alexandra Fedorova, Anatole Vilzak, Anatole Oboukhov, Leon Fokine, Pierre Vladimirov and Mikhail Mordkin) and with a very important representative of the "Old Italian School" (Enrico Zanfretta, who had seemingly learned it from Cecchetti, and had danced in La Scala di Milan). And also, with professors of the then-booming "English School" and of the "Danish School." I remember that in that period, in my personal case, there was no professor in New York with whom I didn't take some class, as long as I found out that he was a good teacher; and later I used to share my experiences with Fernando. That variety of professors and "schools" was very important for us, and for the future profile of what the "Cuban School of Ballet" would be years later. We lived, also, the beginning of ballet development in the United States (first with the American Ballet Caravan and, since its foundation, with the American Ballet Theatre). We were present during the emergence of the great movement of modern American ballet, with George Balanchine, Antony Tudor, Eugene Loring, Agnes de Mille and other choreographers. How did Fernando Alonso live and assimilate that whole process? It is I who has to say this, because it is the truth. All that experience was marked and determined by his living together with a dancer of technical, stylistic and expressive qualities, recognized from then on by all the specialists as an unusual ballerina. How much I regret that I am the one who offers these considerations!, but they are essential truths to value appropriately Fernando Alonso's formation as a teacher. I was not a product of "the teachings, of the methods and of Fernando Alonso's talent" (as some people erroneously believe). Very much on the contrary, his formation as a teacher was marked and determined by my characteristics as a dancer.

It is also necessary to remember (and this is known by all the people that were close to me in different stages) that besides the multiple teachers with whom I trained, I always had the habit of working alone for hours in a room, analyzing my technique, choosing, inventing solutions for the challenges that my dance and my vision troubles presented.

This does not deny at all that we supported each other in our work, and that, later in the Cuban National Ballet, for years I made my routine training in classes delivered by Fernando Alonso, when I was already a trained and mature dancer, technically and stylistically. Another myth has been about Fernando Alonso's supposed help, as a ballet teacher, looking for technical solutions in my dance, due to the problem of my growing loss of vision around the decade of the seventies. I looked for them by myself. He helped me, yes, but by assuring scenic aid in the form of signals, lights, etc.

It has frequently been told how, from the beginnings of my professional career in the United States, critics pointed out special features in my dance that they fancied as expression of my "Latin culture." That got us a lot of attention, and we even worried about it at the beginning, and we, Fernando and I, set about the task of analyzing my characteristics.

Once in Cuba, the first attempt to create a methodology took place in 1941, together, with the intention of helping Alberto Alonso, when he was appointed Director of the School of Ballet of the Pro-Arte Musical Society of Havana. Based on the methods we acquired from Zanfretta, and from the great teachers we had had, little by little we chose and created a syllabus and a certain methodology, very close to the one that I used personally in the attainment of my technical goals and my professional training. Pedagogic concerns did not appeal to Alberto Alonso, a very important person in the development of Cuban choreography, nor did he care for teaching. Fernando and I worked very hard to help him in that aspect. Then came the work that we carried out together to organize the National School of Ballet "Alicia Alonso" in Havana, in 1951. Besides establishing a methodology, an important aspect that we studied very thoroughly, there was the search for special resources, or rather for highlighting certain emphases in the execution of daily training. This was aimed at improving the physical line, balancing the proportions as much as possible, or to exalt virtues, according to the most frequent natural characteristics in the physique of Latin students, starting, certainly, from those peculiarities that were evident in Cuban students. What I am stating does not deny in any sense the vocation, dedication and Fernando Alonso's meticulousness as a teacher. He was always methodical, orderly and studious. And he liked to apply the knowledge that he acquired from other sciences to the art of ballet. I refer to anatomy, physics, kinesiology, etc. When Fernando Alonso stopped dancing, which happened very early, he dedicated all his time and attention to teaching; but always with my proximity and participation.

The perception of Arnold Haskell, a great critic and friend, according to which he established a trilogy in the Cuban ballet (Alicia Alonso, the great dancer; Fernando Alonso, the great teacher; and Alberto Alonso, the great choreographer), has been vastly misleading, and has caused a lot of misinterpretations. I am obliged to clarify that I was a choreographer in the company from its beginnings, mainly in the revival of the great classics, a decisive aspect in the establishment of the idiosyncrasy and artistic line of the Cuban National Ballet. I participated decisively in the creation of the methodological, stylistic and aesthetic profiles of the "Cuban School of Ballet," without ceasing to be the first figure, as a dancer of the Cuban National Ballet for 50 years.

However, it is necessary to clarify that none of these achievements would have been possible without the exceptional force of dance in

Cuban culture, without the talent of our people for this expression. And certainly, without the great creators in different aspects of the "school," their professors (among whom Fernando Alonso stands out, undoubtedly, but also, José Parés, among others), and choreographers such as Alberto Alonso (for a number of years); and all the teachers, choreographers and dancers who came later, as well as with all those who lead the company to this day.

Alicia Alonso

Havana, August 12, 2009

As Alicia Alonso points out in her letter, construction of the Cuban National Ballet was the project of many individuals. As its prima ballerina and, later, ballerina assoluta, Alicia was at the center of that effort. She assumed the role of dancer, organizer, artistic director, and creator of the current expression of the Cuban style. Her letter explains Fernando's role in systematizing the training of dancers to make them proficient in the company style. She notes that the Cuban style has its origins in the classical schools but was inflected with a Latin sensibility, authored by her with help of Fernando's careful observation of her dancing and artistry. A reader of her letter could infer that though Fernando participated in this process, he was just one of many such people, and indeed, there were many: José Parés, Ramona de Sáa, Loipa Araujo, Aurora Bosch, and Azari Plisetsky, to name just a few who contributed ardently to the establishment of the school and its curriculum, the two aspects of Fernando's work that are the focus of this book. Based on Alicia's letter, one might legitimately ask why it would be important to tell Fernando's story. This question was raised in a short debate in the pages of a Cuban ballet journal, *Cuba en el ballet*, edited by Pedro Simón (which I requested to view, but failed to gain access to). Indeed, Fernando would be the first person to agree that the effort was a collective one, with Alicia at its center, and applaud the role she played. At the same time, the painstaking construction of Cuban dance pedagogy under Fernando's direction is the central pillar supporting the development of limpid technique and virtuosic artistry, especially in the powerful male dancers who have taken first place in the most prestigious ballet competitions in the world. From the interviews presented here it is clear that Fernando Alonso is a great teacher, one of international repute. For this reason alone his story should be more widely known, especially among future generations of dancers and teachers. The telling of that story in no way slights the accomplishments of Alicia, Alberto, and the many others who built and sustained the school and the Cuban National Ballet as part of a collective and profoundly felt endeavor over the decades. A recent history of the Cuban National Ballet by the Miami-based journalist and Cuban émigré Octavio Roca advances the hagiographic argument that Alicia Alonso could have prevailed in building a world-class company *without* the Cuban Revolution having taken place, and that the Cuban National Ballet has achieved its successes *in spite of* that revolution. It is his belief that Alicia Alonso stands above and outside the process that dancers in Cuba, and a number who have left Cuba, regard as indispensable to the success of the company and school. Roca's thesis relies on the ignorance of those outside Cuba of the actual events that took place there, and their impact, during which Batista not only shut down the company and school, but in response, university students took up the defense of ballet as the center of a cultural campaign linked to the revolutionary upsurge among urban workers and agricultural workers in the countryside. Alicia's letter and the interview material in these pages make it clear that without the events leading to the revolution, the revolution itself, the laws passed by the new government, and the funding it provided to prioritize the advancement of ballet on the island, Fernando and Alicia's extraordinary talents and vision notwithstanding, their enterprise would have remained just a dream.

This is the story of Fernando Alonso, told in his own voice through his reminiscences and through the voices of his colleagues, except where I have added historical notes and documentary items, such as reviews and commentary by dance historians. In it, readers will discover what can take place when three young, talented, and inventive dancers retrieve riches from the world beyond their beleaguered but beloved homeland, where a revolution that favors their vision opens a road, and dancers from all walks of life are developed, trained, and acculturated, so that their delightful gifts, natural and acquired, may become the artistic patrimony of the entire world.

Acknowledgments

Prodigious amounts of time and effort were invested in this project by dancers, scholars, and friends, who helped with translation, transcription, editing suggestions, hospitality in their homes, and giving Fernando Alonso's story a permanent place in their lives. I would like to thank the following individuals and organizations for the diligent work and kind assistance they provided: Mauricio Abreu, Dr. Ismael Albelo, Nanny Cabot Osborne Almquist, Mindy Aloff, Alicia Alonso, Fernando Alonso, Laura Alonso, Frank Andersen, Nieves Romero Anglada, Leticia Aparicio, Dr. Gary Apter, Loipa Araújo, Rose Arcón, Ana Flavia Armengol, Manuel Gustavo Armengol, Rochelle Baum, Abby Blatt, Frank Boehm, Valentina Boeta Madera, Yannick Boquin, Heriberto Cabezas, Dr. Miguel Cabrera, Dr. Peter Callander, Lupe Calzadilla, Diana Cantú, Justin Coe, Nancy Cole, Michael Crabb, Kathryn Crowder, Yolanda Correa Crúz, Laura Cumin, Gabriel Davalos, Alejandro DeMetrius, Dr. Kevin Denny, Dr. Jon Dickinson, Pat Dimmick, Damián Donestévez González, Debbie Esquivel, Sam Evich, Lorena Feijóo, Rita Felciano, Ana Teresa Fernández, Rose Marie Frojd, Lynn Garafola, Covadonga García Mar, Christina Gianelli, Joyce Glick, Leonel González, Carmen Goodman, James Gotesky, Jim Gotesky, Robert Guild, Oliver Halkowich, Ivan Hernández, Karen Hildebrand, Melissa Hough, David Howard, Suki John, Anne Kenison, Marc Lichtman, Dr. Marc Lieberman, Luisa Lizaso, Mariel MacNaughton, Michael Mahoney, Emma Manning, Moisés Martín, Bill Martínez, Meredith Morris-Babb, Steve Mongiello, Alma Cecilia Pérez Navarro, José Ramón Neyra, Lauren Nicole, Miguel Pendás, Oscar Pérez, Wendy Perron, Ahmed Piñeiro Fernández, Vanessa Pons, Jeff Powers, Myrna Quiñones, Amity Reeves, Fara Teresa Rodríguez, Rick Romagosa, Carlo Romairone, Margaret Marchisio Luca Romairone, Salvador Orlando Miranda Ruíz, Carolina Sánchez, Maiensy Sánchez, Maiuly Sánchez, Deborah Hess Schramek, Peter Seidman, Alejandro Sené, Noé Serrano, Hari Sierra, Dr. Pedro Simón, Dr. Vladimir Smith, Dr. Richard Stagliano, Mavis

Staines, Ben Vereen, Aida Villoch, Nancy Wozny, Susan Zárate, Dr. Matilde Zimmermann, Staffs of the Cuban National Ballet, Cuban National Ballet School, Cuban National Museum and Library of the Dance, Joy of Travel, New York City Public Library for the Performing Arts, Jerome Robbins Division for the Performing Arts, San Francisco Public Library, School of the National Ballet of Canada, Hotel Presidente, and Centro ProArt.

I

Antes (Before)

1

Always Ask Why

What was your family's history in Cuba?

I was born Fernando Juan Evangelista Eugenio de Jesús Alonso Rayneri at 5:20 in the afternoon of December 27, 1914, at our family home in the Vedado neighborhood of Havana.

Beyond Cuba, my family's roots extend to Italy, Austria, and the Canary Islands. My paternal grandfather, Matías, was an exporter of tropical fruit. He died when I was one year old. My grandmother Clementina, who was his wife, died before I was born. My maternal grandmother, Mercedes Piedra, was born in Havana. She married Eugenio Rayneri Sorrentino, who came from an Italian family. Even though he was Italian, he had some Austrian forebears who were artists. One of my great-grandfathers of Austrian descent immigrated to Italy, where he became an orchestra director. Eugenio was a professor of architecture at the University of Havana. He was very interested in astronomy, and was also a volunteer fireman. My grandmother Mercedes worked very hard to encourage the development of culture and cultural institutions in Havana, and I think that by marrying her, Eugenio was expressing a preference for a life immersed in art and science. In fact, he was the designer of the national capitol building, the entrance to the Colón Cemetery, and several other architectural works of note throughout the city. Both of his sons, Eugenio (director of capitol enclave of the city of Havana) and Virgilio, studied architecture and engineering at the University of Notre Dame in South Bend, Indiana. His only daughter, Laura Rayneri Piedra, my mother, was a gifted pianist who had studied with the renowned teacher Hubert de Blanck, receiving a gold medal and diploma for her interpretations of Chopin's Concerto no. 1 in E Minor, opus 11. She was invited to give concerts at Notre Dame and the Chicago World's Fair, and she received other invitations to audition for professional concert engagements, but her father didn't like the idea of a young lady of society going off into the world, so she was obliged to remain in Havana.

Before having married our father, Matías Alonso Reverón (a certified public accountant and highly regarded employee of the U.S. Cuban Trading Company), my mother had divorced a man who was a member of the Arechabala family. The Arechabalas had made a fortune in sugar refining in the city of Cárdenas in the nineteenth century. My mother did not tell us about her past until we were much older, so it took us awhile to put together the details of the life she led before we came along. By the time we arrived, she was already a central figure in the advancement of culture and cultural institutions in Havana. She was treasurer and, later on, president of the city's Sociedad Pro-Arte Musical.

Did her father's curtailing of her career fuel her determination to play an active role in Havana's cultural life?

I think so. She may have compensated for the loss of a career by introducing as much art as possible into her surroundings. She contributed generously to the performing arts. The atmosphere in our home was centered on music. My brother and I heard her practicing the piano in our house at no. 70 Calzada, where she had her own conservatory. We would raise hell if she didn't play for us before we went to bed! From the time we were babies, she played the works of both Cuban and European composers, mostly Chopin, and we developed a preference for him that remained with us all of our lives.

What are your earliest recollections?

I remember when I was two years old knocking on my mother's bedroom door and her calling out "Fernandito, come in! Meet your new brother!" This was how I was introduced to my only sibling, Alberto Julio César Matías Pititi Alonso. It was the beginning of a very close and affectionate relationship.

My most vivid memories are of my grandfather Eugenio Rayneri. He was a rationalist who taught me that a scientific explanation existed for everything that happened. He rejected religious explanations. He used to tell me, "Always ask 'Why,'" and look for the scientific answer. I also remember how much in love I was with one of the servants when I was only four years old. Her name was Carmen, and I called her "Carmen, la chiquita" [the little one] because we had another maid named Carmen whom I called "la grande" [the big one]. When Carmen, la Chiquita, squeezed a blemish on her face, it led to a bad infection, and she died within hours. I was inconsolable when they told me.

A year later, when I was five years old, my grandfather Eugenio died. I found it very hard, almost impossible, to accept the loss of my grandfather's companionship, affection, and the many hours we spent together observing things that he helped explain to me. I felt a kind of aimlessness. There is no doubt that he spoiled us, but I gained so much from having him around that I entered a very dark world after he died, because I had lost him and it was very hard for me; he had given me a wonderful sense of observation and understanding of the reasons for doing things, a love of scientific inquiry. I didn't know what to do with myself without him!

How did your parents respond to your grief?

My mother could see how unhappy I was, and felt very sure that she knew what was best for me. She sent me off to the priests at Colegio Hermanos La Salle for a religious education. This only deepened my despair.

The priests confused me even more. They seemed to go against all the scientific principles that had been explained to me so patiently and ardently by my grandfather. He had always told me, "Don't believe in miracles: Always ask how things happen!" And so I could not understand the basis for the mysteries and miracles that the priests spoke of, and for which they offered no scientific hypothesis. It was a new world, where nothing could be questioned. I could not believe or understand it. The result was that I became very unsure of what was going to happen in my life. Being at school was not always unpleasant. My mother had insisted that I receive an artistic education, and so I was chosen to participate in the yearly choral activities because I had perfect pitch. I enjoyed being in that beautiful chapel. But participating meant spending extra time at school, and I missed the atmosphere in my home, so whenever I could, I would find a way to escape from the priests to go home.

Did you and your brother get along well?

We were very, very close, but we had very different personalities and temperaments. Alberto was more practical and aggressive; I was more romantic. Adolescence came easier to my brother. For me, it was like traveling through a time tunnel where it was impossible to predict the direction that I would take at the tunnel's end. I was at a loss to find something I really liked.

The curiosity about science that my grandfather sought to cultivate during my first few years was reawakened by the challenges of adolescence. One time, it got me into a lot of trouble.

A cousin of ours was visiting our house. She decided to take a bath when nobody was home except for Alberto and me. We had a bathroom with small windows around the upper wall. Alberto thought up the idea of setting a ladder against the wall, which one of us could hold while the other climbed to the top to watch our cousin bathe. I took the first shift holding the ladder while my brother climbed up to the top of it. Just as Alberto was beginning to spy on our cousin, we heard the front door open, meaning that my father had returned home. Alberto jumped off the ladder, and it clattered to the floor. We could hear my cousin screaming in the bathroom! Alberto ran off and hid. In the meantime, my father caught me with the ladder, and I got a terrible scolding. Of course he realized that the ladder couldn't have been set up without both of us, but I didn't say a word about my brother having been part of it, and received the only beating my father ever gave either of us up to that point. I think he may have caught up with my brother at a later time, but not because of anything I said to implicate him!

Was your father the more practical of your parents?

My father wanted me to become a certified public accountant, which is what he was. He was very good at it, and was held in high regard by his employer, the Cuban Trading Company. Eventually, he developed a degenerative disease, but the company continued to pay him his full salary even though he could no longer come to work. I was a young man at the time, and as he declined I watched him turn from a perfect and proper gentleman into a very angry, irritable person who used abusive language to insult people, unlike any he had ever used in my presence. It seemed to me that he was undergoing a profound loss of confidence, and in part it took the form of pressuring my brother and me to do this or that. I resented this, but one of my uncles, Rogelio Parera, who was married to my father's sister, Helen Alonso, was a dermatologist. In the hopes of inspiring me to take up medicine, my uncle Rogelio invited me along on hospital rounds. The greatest benefit of going with him on those rounds was that I became a good diagnostician of the tropical skin diseases that were common Cuba in that period, and at the same time I began to realize that what I really enjoyed most was physical culture and music: I loved to do exercises and adored listening to my mother play the piano, as well as to the young ladies who studied with her.

Please say more about your mother's involvement in the arts.

Under my mother's stewardship, Pro-Arte Musical hosted talent from all over the world. Among those who performed there was the Polish pianist Ignace Jan Paderewski, and Antonia Mercé, known as "La Argentina," a Flamenco dancer whose presence onstage became, for me, *the* standard by which I judged all others. When La Argentina came onstage and stood perfectly still, not moving, she exuded tremendous energy. Everybody would stand up and begin to applaud. What a personality! I tell everyone, "If you just stand onstage without moving, you are still alive, you are projecting your own energy and in that sense, you *are* moving and the audience can feel it."

What career decisions, if any, were you making at that point in your life?

On August 20, 1928, before I was fourteen years of age, I petitioned the director of the Havana Institute of Secondary Education to be permitted to take their preparatory entrance examination. I received permission the following month. After taking some courses by correspondence, they admitted me to the Institute on September 30, and I began to attend classes at the downtown campus at Zulueta and San José. At this time the Cuban president was Gerardo Machado Morales. His regime was brutal and subservient to the United States. By the time I entered the Institute there were protests in the streets of Havana, and they were growing in size. In 1927, Machado issued the *Proclamation of the Prerogatives of Powers*, a document intended to institutionalize the government, which ended up remaining in effect until 1933. Workers, students, and groups on the left mounted a huge protest against the Prerogatives. In the meantime, Machado wanted to clean house in preparation for the 1928 Sixth Pan-American Conference in Havana, so he ordered the assassination of opposition leaders. In November 1928 the protests reached a high point, and on January 10, 1929, the Cuban student leader Antonio Mella was assassinated in Mexico City.

I had entered the Institute just at the time when the student activity reached its peak, and I took part in the protests. The dictatorship responded by militarizing the schools, returning to an old practice of forcing the students to wear military uniforms and perform daily calisthenics. Many students were rounded up, imprisoned, tortured, or they were turning up dead. My family was very upset by my activism, imagining that any day I would be one of the missing. They decided that I would no longer continue my studies in Havana. So, at the age of fifteen, following what had become a family tradition, they sent me off to continue my studies in the United States. Both Alberto and I were sent to Spring Hill College, a religious institution just on the edge of Mobile, Alabama.

Physical culture became a focus and outlet for both my brother and me. Alberto went out for football. I also played football, but continued in gymnastics. The one thing I benefited from during [the] Machado [regime] was the calisthenics we had to do. I joined the basketball team and played baseball for the Junebugs, Spring Hill's junior team.

We would hunt rabbits in the back woods with .22-caliber rifles. When we got back, Ethel, the cook at the dormitory, would take the rabbits and make a marvelous rabbit stew. Once, on one of those expeditions, I caught bronchial pneumonia!

Did you experience the same feelings of alienation as those that you had at Colegio Hermanos La Salle?

Because I had blue eyes and fair skin, I wasn't exposed to the discrimination that other Latino students experienced every day, such as being called "grease ball." Still, I felt the sting of the racism, and it instilled in me a feeling of solidarity with the other Latino students. In the face of that racism, I saw hypocrisy in the religious precepts imposed by the college administration, and the required attendance at daily mass, and kept in mind my grandfather Eugenio's advice to question anything presented to me as fact. I openly broke with the religious dogma, which we were expected to accept on faith. I didn't fully realize it, but I was undergoing a profound change as my awareness of racial, social, and class differences increased. I was beginning to see the world in a different way. After having participated in the student actions in Havana, the tables were turned, and I was required to subordinate myself to an unreasonable and arrogant authority in a demeaning and racist atmosphere. It seemed to me at the time that it was no coincidence that the scientific method that was taught to me by my grandfather was crassly rejected at Spring Hill College in favor of racism and religious dogmatism.

Perhaps because of my grandfather's early influence, I found myself looking at sports and physical culture through the lens of physics. To become good at sports and gymnastics, and to transfer energy as efficiently as possible, I thought it was necessary to understand the underlying the laws of motion. To me, victory at this had more to do with proper preparation than school spirit, though I had plenty of both.

I was very eager to learn English, and I decided that the best way to accomplish that goal was to combine my interest in the young ladies with acquiring their language. My classmates—Ricardo Chiari, Rubén Vigón, and Basilio Rueda—and I would wait until midnight and then sneak over to a girls' boarding school near ours. We would throw small rocks at the dorm windows. If a girl responded, I would ask her to teach me English. It worked very well for me.

2

Pro-Arte Musical, Yavorsky, and New York

Please paint a picture of Pro-Arte Musical as it grew and developed under your mother's stewardship.

During vacations from Spring Hill College, I returned to Havana. By then, the struggle against Machado had died down temporarily. It was during these visits that I could see the transformation that was taking place at Pro-Arte Musical, largely the result of my mother's efforts.

Pro-Arte was at 510 Calzada, at the corner of D, and about one hundred meters from our home. It was a yellow building that stood between a pair of wrought-iron lamplights and looked out upon Villalon Park. It had a marble-and-inlaid-tile lobby decor, and inside was a large auditorium and several small concert halls.

By the 1930s, for five pesos per month, you could go there to study guitar, ballet, and what were called the declamatory arts. Members could also attend concerts. It had its own theater, auditorium, and ballet school. Among the artists they brought there to perform were Enrico Caruso, Mischa Elman, Fritz Kreisler and Ernesto Lecuona, Titto Schipa, Sergei Rachmaninov, Jasha Heifetz, Andrés Segovia, Pablo Casals, and Walter Damrosch conducting the New York Symphony Orchestra, Alexander Brailovsky, Ignace Jan Paderewski, Beniamino Gigli, Rosa Ponselle, Amelita Galli-Curci, and Nathan Milstein. It was not unusual to find my mother accompanying these celebrity artists on the piano. My brother and I took violin lessons there with José Vals and Dimitri Vladescu.

My mother made a special effort on behalf of the ballet school because she anticipated that it could play a role in developing an educated audience for classical performances by Cuban dancers. During her fourteen years there she promoted Pro-Arte to a wider and wider audience by offering seats to non-members and reduced-price tickets to students. At first, ballet performances were scheduled to fill gaps between opera evenings, but during her tenure ballet programs became a staple, and the result was that the Pro-Arte stage became a destination for world-class dance companies and ballet stars. My mother became president of Pro-Arte during the 1934–35 season.

Is it true that you are a member in good standing of the Spelunkers Society?

I *love* science. Using the scientific method comes from my earliest training as a child when my grandfather encouraged me to look to the laws of nature. It was then that I began to develop the habit of taking an objective look and seeing each problem as an opportunity to approach its solution with a fresh perspective.

I once spent eleven days inside the caves at Gran Caverna Santo Tomás, not seeing the light of day there. Instead, I saw internal waterfalls and rivers. Our group discovered a different tunnel into the cave by tapping on the walls. Some tunnels had been completely closed off. The air was dank. Years later, Dr. Antonio Nuñez Jiménez wrote a book on this Gran Caverna.

Did your interest in science rub off on Alberto?

Like me, at a certain point, my brother Alberto was seeking answers to help him become expert at football. He scrutinized the training requirements, and pinpointed what would serve best to develop upper-body strength and sufficient muscular acuity to dominate the field. One day, when he was at Pro-Arte observing the young ladies taking ballet class, it occurred to him that the training Nikolai Yavorsky was giving to those young ladies was exactly what he needed to become a better football player.

Who was Nikolai Yavorsky?

Yavorsky had been an artillery officer in the Russian army. After the Russian Revolution of 1917, he left for Yugoslavia. According to the stories that circulated about him, he ended up in Paris, where he got involved with a group of Russian émigré artists and intellectuals. They worked at odd jobs in restaurants, bars, and cafés. Yavorsky eventually found himself on the fringes of the Paris modern ballet circuit, with admirers and members of Diaghilev's Ballet Russe. They were rebelling against the parochial traditions of the Russian Imperial Ballet. Yavorsky picked up some dance training in this milieu and joined Ida Rubinstein's company. She had been a former private pupil of Michel Fokine.

Though Yavorsky left Russia after the 1917 revolution, when he got to France he met other dancers who shared a rebellious spark and ended up joining a small opera company tour traveling to Havana. He became very fond of Cuba, and so when the company went on to Mexico City, and was stranded there because it ran out of money, he came back to Havana. He wandered the streets and, while looking for a job, stopped in at Pro-Arte Musical. His timing was perfect: they had just decided to hire someone to teach the young ladies correct carriage and grace.

What year was it?

Nikolai Yavorsky began work on June 30, 1931. One possibly apocryphal story about him was that he had been assistant ballet master at the Théâtre Champs Elysées in Paris, where he had also been an actor, and at Barcelona's Lyceum Theater *and* the Paris Opera.

Because of my mother's standing at Pro-Arte, Alberto was allowed to observe the dance classes there, and in 1933 he decided to enroll in them. He wanted to improve his strength and facility for football. He was handsome, and serious about his commitment to the studio. He became a pole of attraction to other boys his age. This was very good for the school because he was a leader, and brought other boys to the classes. By the time I entered the school in 1935 there were 126 students, six of them male: myself, Alberto, Eduardo "Yayo" Casado, Antonio "Antoñiquito" Martínez (the brother of Alicia Martínez and her sister Cuca, who were Yavorsky's students), Enrique Armand, and Jorge Companioni. The number of men fluctuated from month to month in the period between 1933 and 1936.

You mentioned Alicia Martínez, whom we now know as Alicia Alonso. Was it through your brother or hers that you and she became acquainted?

There were two of Yavorsky's students who showed special ability. One was Delfina Pérez Gurri and the other was Alicia Ernestina de la Caridad del Cobre Martínez y del Hoyo. Alicia's nickname was "Unga," which was short for "Hungarian," a name they gave her because of her dark-brown, fiery eyes. Those girls were something! They may have been the reason that so many fellows joined the ballet class, but with the men having joined, it meant that Yavorsky could teach new material, and include pieces in his repertoire that men could dance during the end-of-year showcases.

At a showcase in the summer of 1931, I observed something new in Unga. It was her debut as Belle in *The Sleeping Beauty*, and she also danced the

Blue Bird role in that same program. The Alicia Martínez I knew as the little sister of my boyhood friend Antonio was becoming an accomplished dancer! I used to stop by their home to visit her brother Antoñiquito in the period when she had just started ballet lessons. She used to answer the door wearing pointe shoes, practicing even as I stood waiting for her brother. "My God," I had thought at the time, "she's crazy about dancing. Someday she will be a great ballerina!" When I saw her later on in a showcase in the role of a vivacious village girl, her high extensions and generous port de bras were astounding. She impressed me even more when I saw how well she finessed a mishap involving a fan. I longed to place my hands around her waist and guide her through her steps. I couldn't believe that this was the same young girl I had seen dance the Blue Bird solo some two years earlier.

In 1932, I finished my studies at Spring Hill College and enrolled in Blanton Business College in Asheville, North Carolina. I returned to Havana for my vacation, where I had more opportunities to observe ballet classes at Pro-Arte, and during this time my appreciation of ballet and the allure of the dancers had grown. On March 20, 1935, I saw a performance of the third act of *Coppélia*, called *Visions of Coppélia*, which had been staged by a Russian guest choreographer. Amadeo Roldán conducted the orchestra. Alicia danced Swanilda, Alberto danced Franz, Josefina de Cárdenas danced Coppélia, and Ricardo Florit was Dr. Coppelius. It was after this evening that I decided to enroll in the full program at Pro-Arte and take up ballet.

Were you studying ballet full-time?

After Blanton, I took a job as a bilingual typist and stenographer at the offices of M. Golodetz and Company, a British sugar-exporting firm with a home office in Havana. I hated the work! I didn't like working with numbers, commercial paper, accounts receivable, and those monotonous banking operations. I left that job for another at the Panamericana State Ministry. It was at this job that I began to realize what the relationship between Cuban commerce and the United States really was, and I was uncomfortable with having anything to do with those things. I was an artist, and I wanted my daily routine to be that of a dancer.

How did you and Alicia Martínez become sweethearts?

My brother Alberto was the one they chose to partner Alicia most of the time, but that meant that I became more a part of her day-to-day life. We had long discussions about many subjects. She taught me dance history and coached me through my classes with my first teacher, Alicia's sister Cuca.

Cuca was standing in for Yavorsky because he was traveling then. At the time, Cuca set an example for me in her stamina and enthusiasm. I had begun my training very late, but had the advantage of a strong background in sports and gymnastics. I loved the atmosphere in the studio, and made my debut on Pro-Arte's auditorium stage in *Los esclavos* [The slaves], choreographed by Cuca.

When Yavorsky returned I began to get a taste of what the other students had experienced, namely, Yavorsky's sour personality. He would yell "Dubína!" [Idiot!] at students who made small errors. One time he threw his armchair at the accompanist, Luis Borbolla. It shattered at Borbolla's feet, and my mother saw to it that the cost of the repairs was deducted from Yavorsky's pay. I learned from Yavorsky what a teacher must *never* bring into the studio.

Did you see anything else in the ballet school that you didn't care for?

Students from the wealthier families were treated preferentially. That bothered me. Delfina and Alicia, who did not come from those families, were allowed to take classes at Pro-Arte, but only because their talent and effort was outstanding. They received recognition mostly from their teachers, but little, if any, from the school's director. Those from families whose social status was glorified by Cuban high society were given special consideration and pampered to the greatest extent possible, even if they had no talent, which most did not. This rankled me!

But you stayed there anyway?

By the time I was twenty years old I had gone from a fellow who had become interested in ballet because of the beautiful young women I would be able to lift and hold by their waists, to a disciplined dancer whose life was now centered on becoming expert at the art form. I was undaunted by the prejudice against men dancing. I had been teased by male friends, or others I did not even know, which a couple of times resulted in coming to blows with those guys. Each experience of that kind made me even more certain that I had chosen the right path for myself. That was not the case for all of the men dancers, however, and by December 1934, Alberto, Enrique Armand, Manolo Agulló, and I were the only men still at Pro-Arte.

The students who were serious all agreed that the Pro-Arte studios were substandard and the teaching insufficient for those of us who wanted to succeed in the world of professional classical ballet. The groups were mixed, so exercises or enchaînements were given at the level of the beginner student. No progressive curriculum or methodology guided the teaching. Just as we were arriving at these conclusions, two other developments affected our estimate of the school.

In January 1936 the famous Spanish Flamenco dancer La Argentina (Antonia Mercé) arrived in Havana. Yavorsky invited her to class to observe the students. Also, on January 7, Mercé gave a two-hour performance of ten dance pieces on the auditorium stage. The outstanding ones were to Manuel de Falla's *La danza ritual del fuego*, Granados's *Goyescas y Danza no. 5* and *Cuba, rumba de Albeníz*.

A review of the performance by Mario Lescano Abella appeared in the Pro-Arte Musical magazine:

> There is an aristocracy of the Dance representing an extraordinary exclusiveness. Such great dancers are not produced frequently. Just as with Pavlova, La Argentina is exceptional . . . one is put in mind of dance as a rite, so complete is the spirituality. The other evening, that is what took place at the Auditorium . . . with a truly dazzling display of the art of the Priestess Terpsichore.[1]

La Argentina could thrill the audience by simply standing still! She exuded a commanding energy, smiling and tapping her foot, and this had a big impact on Alicia and me. Then, imagine! Later, in class, Alicia was recognized by La Argentina for her fiery eyes, because Mercé had noticed Alicia in a crowd of stage-door admirers the night before! To this day, I have seen few personalities as outstanding as La Argentina!

A short time after La Argentina came, Delfina Gurri and Alberto traveled abroad to audition for Colonel Wassily de Basil's Ballet Russe. Both were invited to join the company and accepted contract offers, Delfina remaining for only a short time, and Alberto becoming one of its finest character dancers. Then, Ballet Russe de Monte Carlo came to Cuba in March 1936 and danced at the Pro-Arte auditorium. The students had the rare opportunity to see Tamara Toumanova in *Prince Igor*, Léonide Massine in *Le tricorne*, and Irina Baronova in *Aurora's Wedding*, and then the next day we saw the "Baby Ballerinas" dance *Les sylphides* and *Les présages*. Afterward, the students were whispering among themselves that Yavorsky's teaching would not prepare them to dance in a company such as Colonel de Basil's Ballet Russe.

How did these events affect you and Alicia?

As we made comparisons between the dancers we had seen, Delfina and Alberto, and ourselves, it became clear that remaining in Cuba would only place limits on our professional careers. We were growing up in a climate of rebellion in those days, and we decided to break with the traditions that disdained stage and dance careers as undignified for young ladies, and take the steps we knew were necessary to change our fortunes as artists.

How did you find the courage to act on your instincts?

By the age of fifteen, Alicia had risen to the top of her class at Pro-Arte and, in a very short time, become Havana's box-office sensation, but her repertoire was narrow, and there were few challenges left to conquer in Yavorsky's classes, which I had joined when Yavorsky returned. As we rehearsed Yavorsky's *Claire de lune*, the first ballet in which we danced as partners, Alicia began to share her hopes with me, as well as her concerns. We discussed the weaknesses of the school. On long strolls through Havana, and in her family's sitting room, we also discussed our growing feelings for each other, and our career plans. Havana had once again become a tumultuous place. There were more and more work stoppages, strikes, and protests against the regime. The United States favored the dictatorship of Gerardo Machado Morales, which had declared martial law at the end of 1930. Machado sent in his troops to crush the protests. There in Vedado, we had been sheltered from firsthand experience with these government reprisals, but then news began to circulate about the students at the University of Havana having been beaten bloody, or government attacks on strikes and peasant uprisings—peasants who had nothing to eat. We began to question more deeply the social inequities we saw, even in our little world in Vedado. It gave us the courage to take the next logical step.

Alicia's father was a traditional Cuban male. To him, a young lady going after a career in ballet was tantamount to streetwalking, and so Alicia appealed to her mother: she told her that we wanted to leave Havana to pursue careers and more advanced dance training in New York.

At the time, Alicia was rehearsing Odette and Odile in *Swan Lake* for the May 1937 Pro-Arte gala. Emile Laurens of de Basil's Ballet Russe would dance Siegfried. I left for the United States for the third time in my life, this time to look for a job in New York. The plan was that Alicia would follow as soon as I could find work.

3

Alicia, Fernando, and Laura

Giant Steps across a Changing Landscape

What was it like to make the transition from being students in Havana to dancers in New York?

In 1937, New York was still coming out of the 1929 depression, and thousands remained unemployed. So, I was very lucky to immediately find a job as a bilingual stenographer at Powers X-Ray Products. I took ballet class at night. Then, Powers X-Ray Products sponsored a course in X-ray technology to train technicians for a tuberculosis survey in Harlem. I enrolled in the course and became an X-ray technician, a job that offered a better wage.

You had lived in the United States before, but what was it like to live in New York?

I was living right in the middle of New York's largest black and Puerto Rican neighborhood, and so I was able to see the *other* face of that celebrated city: the racial prejudice and miserable living conditions in the tenements. It was not so different from what workers in Cuba's barrios and those in the rest of Latin America faced every day of their lives.

Once I was settled and had a job, I could send for Alicia. She was chaperoned by Natalia Arostegui, the wife of New York Cuban general consul, Pablo Suárez. They were friends of my parents. They all traveled to Manhattan by boat.

We were married in 1937 and lived in a room I rented at 175th Street and Broadway in Washington Heights. It was part of a large apartment belonging to Irene Barbería, a Cuban woman of about sixty, who rented out rooms. Our room was both our living quarters and rehearsal studio.

How were you able to gain entry to New York's dance community?

The Depression had changed the New York art scene permanently. Because of the WPA [Works Projects Administration], there was a revolutionary fervor wherever you looked. Before, artists had been out of work and hungry. Now, thousands of writers, artists, architects, actors, musicians, and dancers could find work and create art, some of which was not only art but also political art. They mounted works that revealed actual conditions of everyday life.

Dancers were challenging the ballet traditions. They looked at everything in order to discover what felt authentic. Martha Graham, Doris Humphrey, Anna Sokolow, Charles Weidman, Sophie Maslow, and Pauline Koner were among them. They had seen or heard about, or were influenced by, the work of Isadora Duncan.

We arrived in New York during the Civil War in Spain. There was tremendous sympathy among the dancers and other artists for the republican combatants in Spain. They organized a "Dance Program for Spanish Democracy." One of the groups on the program was Lincoln Kirstein's Ballet Caravan. That is how we got to know the Ballet Caravan dancers Eugene Loring, Lew Christensen, Erick Hawkins, and Marie-Jeanne.

Alicia was pregnant, and I found her a doctor. The room we had rented would now have a nursery and a new personality inhabiting it—our daughter Laura! She was born on March 14, 1938.

How did you manage to find regular jobs dancing?

Mikhail Mordkin was a former *premier danseur* of the Bolshoi Ballet who had partnered Anna Pavlova at New York's Metropolitan Opera House. He settled in New York in 1924. He began his own school, and with help from Lucia Chase, restarted his own company. He hired me into his four-member corps de ballet for that company's 1937–38 tour.

The studio was upstairs at Carnegie Hall. Among the first dancers were Lucia Chase, Viola Essen, Karen Conrad, Dimitri Romanov, Leon Danielian, and myself. We toured in cities throughout North America. We performed *Autumn Leaves* to Glazunov's *The Seasons*.

Lucia Chase's husband, Thomas Ewing, came from a family of millionaires and was able to underwrite the company's expenses in the beginning, but when money ran out, all touring came to a standstill.

Alicia saw the tour as an opportunity for herself and began to rehearse the repertoire with me, including the Peasant Pas from the first act of *Giselle*. She heard that the WPA was sponsoring classes by Enrico Zanfretta, a teacher who by then was in his mid-seventies. The classes were in the basement of the Rutgers Church on West Seventy-Third Street. The Depression had made it impossible for him to continue running his school, but thanks to the Federal Dance Project he was able to continue teaching. He taught without music and according to the traditions that were handed down to him in his native Italy, and followed by Enrico Cecchetti, who believed that discipline, applying oneself, and repetition of progressive exercises were the secret to the molding of a ballet dancer. An advanced student assisted him by demonstrating the exercises. Zanfretta sat in the center and tapped out the beat. Really, Zanfretta's classes were a link in a chain that began with Fokine, and contributed to what would eventually become the Cuban style.

In the summer of 1938, I was hired to dance in the musical *Three Waltzes* at the Municipal Stadium at Jones Beach on Long Island. Alicia and Laurita would come along to rehearsals. There was a bridge leading from the stadium to the stage, and Alicia and I would practice our dance routines there. One day, Marjorie Fielding, the production's dance captain, noticed Alicia and said, "You're wonderful, a great dancer. I'd love it if you were to give my daughter Lorie lessons. Do you want to teach a small group?"[1] So, Alicia taught a class for the children of the Jones Beach Arena Theater dancers. Marjorie Fielding and her husband, who was the production's co-director, Charles Barnes, were so impressed with Alicia that they added a dance number to *Three Waltzes* for her, in which two men partnered her. This was her United States debut!

As a member of Mordkin Ballet, I was faced, for the first time, with the rigors of company life and the obligations that the individual company member was expected to meet. It was worlds away from Pro-Arte. There, casting had gone according to the whims and fancies of the wealthiest students' families. At Mordkin Ballet the criterion was discipline, whether in the assignment of roles, the scheduling of performances and rehearsals, performance quality, and a million more details that must be brought together by human cooperation and effort in order to achieve a harmonious result. The experience I gained at Mordkin Ballet in the three months I had there served me for my entire life, and that is what I transmitted to my students.

We knew that time was running out for the small company, and so we would go to any audition we heard about. Most were held at the Metropolitan Opera for spots in the Opera Ballet, or jobs in Broadway musicals. Dancing in operas and musicals wasn't our goal, but Alicia and I could see that it was better to be working than not. Later, when we began the company in Cuba, we realized that it is possible to extract lessons from just about any field. Musicals proved to be one of our most profitable work experiences!

How did you synthesize all of these experiences, which arrived in such a rapid-fire way?

I brought together what I absorbed from all the teachers, choreographers, and dancers who came my way—from the Italian, French, Russian, and Danish schools, even from musical comedy. I learned rhythm, timing, and the importance of not wasting time.

Also, little by little, Alicia became more confident in New York. It helped that I knew English, because it made her feel that everything she needed was in place. By mid-1938, Dwight D. Wyman was choosing dancers for *Great Lady*, a musical comedy that would be on Broadway. Wyman's daughter was a dancer, and mentioned our names to him, and a short time later we signed a contract to dance in the show. Among the dancers we worked with during this time were André Eglevsky, Leda Anchutina, Nora Kaye, Jerome Robbins, Maria Karnilova, Annabelle Lyon, Donald Saddler, Richard Reed, and Paul Godkin. *Great Lady* [with music by Frederick Loewe and choreography by William Dollar] ran just short of four months. Luckily, Wyman had another musical ready: *Stars in Your Eyes*, with music by Arthur Schwartz. He cast Ethel Merman in the starring role, and nearly all the dancers moved into the chorus line of the new musical. In *Stars in Your Eyes*, I had to sing and tap-dance. Tamara Toumanova was also in the show. Her mother would stand in the wings and shout, "Khoroshó, Tamariska, Khoroshó!" [Good, Tamariska, Good!]

All the time I was dancing in shows, I was taking classes at different studios. I would go to class in one studio and there would be an advertisement for a class at another, and I wanted to try them all. I studied at the School of American Ballet [founded by Lincoln Kirstein and George Balanchine in 1934]. I also studied with Alexandra Fedorova, Anatole Oboukhov, and Pierre Vladimirov. They were leading figures in the Russian Imperial Ballet, who had danced in the Diaghilev ballets.

The work in musical comedy allowed us the luxury of renting an apartment of our own on Seventy-Fifth Street between Riverside Drive and Broadway. Many dancers lived in that building [today the neighborhood is known among dancers as "The Dance Belt"]. Rosella Hightower lived in the same building. There was always a corner set aside in each apartment to do exercises, because there was not a moment to waste—and we needed to stay well conditioned, because the competition for jobs was extreme. Sometimes we would take as many as three classes a day, and dance in a show that same evening, and still, we took any opportunity to rehearse at home.

Who was taking care of Laura?

The landlady, other dancers, or young Puerto Rican and Cuban babysitters were watching her, and as she grew she needed more and more, and we couldn't keep up with it, because we had to look for jobs and dance in shows. When Laura was one and a half years old, we made a decision: we sent her to Cuba to be cared for by her grandparents. While the arrangement worked well in many ways, I always had a complex with respect to Laurita. I felt that we should have given her more warmth, more time, more affection, and built a better relationship with her then; what we were able to give at the time was not enough.

In the fall of 1939, some of the dancers began to organize into a group that would be known as Ballet Theatre. We attracted the best dancers, and others whose celebrity was registered later, and choreographers with outstanding creativity. These dancers represented the best of a generation.

4

Musicals, Mordkin, Balanchine, and the Birth of Ballet Theatre

You spoke earlier of the advantages of dancing in musical comedy. What are they?

By dancing in musical comedy, we came to appreciate the unique dynamic of the show format, the agility one needs to move through a performance from beginning to end, the certainty that one's rhythmic quality is consistent and fluid. The show loses its punch if that dynamism goes missing. In my opinion, the lessons learned by the first-rank dancers from those days—Jerome Robbins, Nora Kaye, Rosella Hightower, Eugene Loring, and others—are the underlayment of the style, energy, and character of contemporary North American dance. Everyone who wishes to dance classical ballet must learn those same lessons.

It sounds as though dancers moved with ease between the ballet and the Broadway stage in those days. If so, was that because Broadway offered steadier work than classical ballet companies did?

Ballet Caravan [founded in 1936] offered the best prospects for developing into a permanent New York ballet company. We joined it without even having to audition: Lincoln Kirstein, the company's founder, had seen us taking class with the other Caravan dancers at the School of American Ballet. Balanchine had wanted to showcase them on tour, so the company had access to the school's magnificent studios. I became good friends with Lincoln Kirstein. He came from a Jewish family from Boston, but somewhere along the way, had acquired a very British manner, and spoke what was called "The King's English." His wealth and social connections helped secure donations from well-to-do patrons. Lucia Chase played a similar role in the financial development of the Mordkin Ballet.

I joined the corps de ballet, but I was given solo roles, too. I was part of a group of eager dancers. Among them were Lew and Harold Christensen and their wives, Gisela Caccialanza and Ruby Asquith, as well as Eugene Loring, Ted Bolender, Marie-Jeanne, Fred Daniele, Annabelle Lyon, and others. I danced in *Encounter*, *Harlequin for President*, *Folk Dance*, *Pocahontas*, *Yankee Clipper*, *Show Piece*, *Filling Station*, *Charade*, *City Portrait*, *Promenade*, and I had my debut in *Billy the Kid*. *Billy the Kid* premiered on October 16, 1938, at the Chicago Opera House, and was one of the greatest triumphs in the history of U.S. ballet, *and* the first choreographic work by Loring in which a Cuban danced. The score was a quintessentially North American one, by Aaron Copland. It was twenty minutes long, and told the story of the notorious outlaw. I danced the Red Cowboy, Billy's friend. I spent a good part of the piece mounting a horse at one end of the stage or the other. We had a gun battle at the end, during which they killed me with a clean shot that sent me sprawling to the ground. I really got a kick out of that!

Lew Christensen's *Filling Station* premiered on January 6, 1938, at the Avery Memorial Theatre in Hartford, Connecticut. They billed it as a "documentary ballet in one act" about everyday reality, in this case a robbery and killing in a gas station. Lew's *Charade* [later retitled *The Debutante*] premiered at the St. James Theatre. I headed the opening-night cast. My partner was Gisela Caccialanza, and I had a chance to dance with the Christensen brothers in that one. While I was with Ballet Caravan, I continued to take classes at the School of American Ballet with Pierre Vladimirov, Anatole Vilzak, and George Balanchine. I also studied with Fokine, Alexandra Fedorova, Anatole Oboukhov.

World War II began in 1939, and because of the dislocation in Europe, many European artists, writers, and intellectuals came to the United States. Perhaps they saw the United States as young and vigorous compared with Europe. Thousands arrived. Among them were dancers, musicians, choreographers, painters, and ballet figures. They brought their traditions to New York, and a good amount of vitality and hope.

You didn't completely abandon Cuba during this period, did you?

When there was a brief break in the Ballet Caravan schedule, I flew back to Cuba to dance in *Dioné*, at Pro-Arte. It was the first wholly Cuban ballet, a collaborative effort of the composer Eduardo Sánchez de Fuentes and the choreographer George Milenov, who had joined the Pro-Arte staff as a substitute for Yavorsky. It was a ballet in two acts, about two lovers seeking contentment. Even though *Cubanismo* was its inspiration, it ended up looking more European than Cuban. Where there should have been mountains, there were shadowy forests inhabited by imaginary beings, not those from the Yoruba legends, either. Pre-Colombian Cubans were transformed into European nobles, because the Pro-Arte mothers had objected to their daughters wearing Taino costumes! The world premiere, on March 4, 1940, took place in the Pro-Arte auditorium. Only members were invited to attend. Two days later, they presented it to the general public. I danced Prince Giró; Alicia, under the name "Unga Alonso," danced the role of Princess Dioné. Newcombe Rice, a special guest from Ballet Caravan, danced Armando, Brother of the Prince and the palace Major Domo. Antonio Martínez was the Forest Sprite, and Alicia's sister Cuca was the Queen of the Humors and friend of the Princess. We also had ladies of the court, monsters, soothsayers, breezes, bees, flowers, pages, and servants. Every character in society and European mythology was present onstage—to the point of satire. We smuggled in two uniquely Cuban elements: a hurricane and a couple of bats. It was pretty mediocre, but it was the first ballet with occasional music composed by a Cuban, and the cast, save for Rice, consisted of Cuban-born dancers.

At what point did you and Alicia join Ballet Theatre?

In the summer of 1940, after a U.S. tour, Ballet Caravan went on summer break. We joined what would eventually become Ballet Theatre. We were part of the first draft of dancers, choreographers, designers, musicians, and composers and would share in the honor of bearing the authentic seal of the new U.S. dance style. The experience with Mordkin Ballet and musical comedy taught me a big lesson: dance must express the aspirations of the people whose culture it represents. Its value resides in its authenticity. No lesson could have better prepared me for Ballet Theatre, which I always refer to as "The University of Dance," where I earned my "Ph.D."

5

Repertoire, Camaraderie, and an Étoile

How was Ballet Theatre organized in its early days?

Lucia Chase and Richard Pleasant were the directors, and Alexander Smallens was Pleasant's assistant. The ballet masters and mistresses were Alexandre Gavrilov, Cia Fornaroli Toscanini, and Julieta Méndez. There were seventy corps de ballet members, several of who were choreographers. There were sixteen black dancers and seven of Latino descent. The outstanding ones in the early days were Adolph Bolm, Anton Dolin, Antony Tudor, Nora Kaye, Agnes de Mille, Karen Conrad, Michel Fokine, Viola Essen, Nana Gollner, Annabelle Lyon, Nina Stroganova, William Dollar, Hugh Laing, Eugene Loring, Dimitri Romanov, Yurek Shabelevsky, Miriam Golden, Edward Caton, Leon Danielian, Maria Karnilova, Richard Reed, Newcombe Rice, and Donald Saddler.

These dancers all came from different traditions. What style did the company adopt?

Our first performance took place at the Center Theatre on January 11, 1940. Right from the start there was a three-way faction fight between those who wanted to adopt the Russian style, those who wanted to adopt the English style, and those who wanted to create an "American" style. Eventually, Ballet Theatre arrived at its *own* style by infusing the traditions it inherited with the sap that rose out of what was an entirely new American dance experience. The result was the perfecting of classical technique that included a realist sensibility, but with distinct touches of humor, lightness, and a dynamism that was strictly North American.

Did things settle down after that?

While we as dancers were quite determined, the company's first season lasted no more than three weeks! The audiences loved us, and with so much public support we could have easily extended the run. It wasn't possible, however, because another group had booked the theater, and Alicia and I had not danced in the premiere performances because we were still under contract with Ballet Caravan. When Alicia returned from a Ballet Caravan tour, her friends Nora Kaye, Miriam Golden, and Maria Karnilova shared news of the company's successes. Thanks to those friends, we were able to join Ballet Theatre without having to audition. That summer we performed at Manhattan's outdoor Lewisohn Stadium, and among the new company members were John Kriza, Jerome Robbins, and Muriel Bentley. We became one big family during a turning point in what we were learning and absorbing. We would discuss, analyze, and share our views while on breaks between long hours in rehearsal or classes, or as we waited for stage cues. We debated *everything*: our new works, aesthetic concepts, and what standards the company should aim for in its artistic directorship.

How long did you dance with the company?

I danced with Ballet Theatre for eight years, first in the corps de ballet, then as a soloist. Besides the works I mentioned earlier, I danced in *Swan Lake, La fille mal gardée, Undertow, Theme and Variations, Barn Dance, Pillar of Fire, Fall River Legend*, and *The Great American Goof.*

I toured with the company throughout the United States and in Canada and England. Eventually, Alicia and I rented an apartment on Forty-Seventh Street and Broadway. Our workday began at 10 A.M. with rehearsal. We took company class at 1 P.M.; Alicia took adagio or pointe class at 3 P.M., and/or character class. Antony Tudor or Anton Dolin usually taught company class. Tudor's class was a demanding, English-style one. He insisted on a straight back, with the body inclined slightly forward. Most of his barre exercises were *à terre* [at floor level], with many *relevé* [standing on demi-pointe] balances. Dolin's were freer and showier, with more dancing and exercises *en l'air* [above floor level]. Tudor gave pointe class and Dolin gave adagio. Eugene Loring taught character class.

Can you describe the atmosphere in the company in those early days?

There was a special camaraderie that developed among the dancers and with the musicians. We were even close, physically. During the war there was a housing shortage in New York, so one dancer would rent just one or two rooms and the others would sneak in as extras. We called this "ghosting." One day, a dancer ran into the room and shouted, "They've got Kleenex at the corner drugstore!" Everyone except me ran out to buy up this item, because it was scarce!

Off they went to the drugstore, and I fell asleep on the bed, and slept like a rock. After a couple of hours, I felt terrible pain in my back! They had all returned and gone to sleep right on top of me!

There was a time when all of us were living in the same building as Rosella Hightower—all the kids found this place, very cheap, all dancers. It was Rosella's birthday *and* she had a free day, and was drinking and drinking, and so she got a little tipsy. In the meantime, a dancer at the theater became sick, so they came to fetch Rosella. She was *so* drunk! We gave her a cold shower and coffee. She had to dance Kitri in *Don Quixote*. It was very funny because she had to do an arabesque and then turn *en dehors* [outward] and do a *saut de basque* [turning jump] onto John Kriza's shoulder. When she turned back she saw *two* John Krizas and was hoping that she would choose the real one!

I want you to know that the camaraderie and warm feelings from those friendships remain with me to this day. I am a Cuban patriot, and will be my whole life, but I place great value on the body of knowledge I gained and genuine affection I received from dancers everywhere throughout the world. Among the ones I hold in the highest regard are those I met and worked with in the United States: Rosella Hightower, Marjorie Tallchief, and Donald Saddler.

How widely was the company known in the early 1940s?

In the summer of 1940 we reprised Antony Tudor's *Lilac Garden*. It became one of the company's standards. On July 15, I danced as a partner in one of four soloist couples in *Friends and Relations*, a favorite of Tudor's. Ten days later I danced a Hunter in *Swan Lake*. We premiered Tudor's *Goya Pastorale* during that run. A later version, *Las goyescas,* with music by Enrique Granados, was performed the following January at City Center. Nora Kaye and Alicia danced the starring roles as *Las majas*, Lucia Chase danced the Marquesa, and Hugh Laing was the desirable young man. I danced a pas de quatre with three other young men.

We traveled to Chicago's Civic Opera. I appeared in the operas *Aida* and *The Madonna's Jewels* and the ballets *The Great American Goof, Capriccioso,* and *Carnaval*, which Fokine himself had danced. Whenever possible, I attended any rehearsals the great master was running, especially during *Les sylphides*. I absorbed lessons and experience that would help me later on when I danced the leading role. At the end of the season, on February 20, 1941, I danced a Hunter in *Peter and the Wolf.*

The years at Ballet Theatre turned me into a confident and accomplished dancer. I had achieved stature, both financially and artistically. Many opportunities to learn came open during that short time: in my training, travels from theater to theater, and in the course of working with many artists and rising stars. Living in the United States made this possible. Nonetheless, the dreams Alicia and I shared from the time of our youth remained with us. At twenty-five years old, I continued to feel a fierce longing. A will and determination had rooted itself in me to build a Cuban company and school. Though many years had passed since my first days at Pro-Arte Musical, the memory of the old place had not dimmed: the studios, the theater, my very first classes, showcases, and classmates. I had not forgotten that I had traveled to New York for the purpose of becoming a professional dancer with a purpose beyond my own career.

Summer vacations offered me the opportunity to fully revive my identification as a Cuban. Back in New York, I would savor my recollections of our visits home. They were like pilgrimages. Pro-Arte was my Mecca. The connections at the old school were the result of close collaboration, but by 1948 they had mostly gone by the wayside. We were not motivated by some personal financial gain that we knew we would never see. We were united in our commitment. Our only intention was to bring new ideas to Cuba and link the Cuban school with the burgeoning developments we had been a part of in New York. These were crystallized in the Ballet Theatre dancers, choreographers, and musicians, and these were the specific links that held the greatest promise for connecting Cuba with a new era in the world of professional ballet.

6

Challenges and Pilgrimages

You've spoken about your professional life at Ballet Theatre. What were your personal circumstances during this period?

In 1941, Ballet Theatre wanted to expand its tours to all of the forty-eight states. Each year, there were more and more extensive tours that targeted larger and larger audiences. The expansion campaign came at a time when new problems presented themselves in our personal and professional lives. Alicia had begun to experience vision problems, and she found that she was bumping into things. The retina in her right eye had detached during a performance, and while she was recovering from surgery to reattach it her left retina detached, and then her right retina detached again. The famous ophthalmologist, Dr. Ramón Castroviejo, recommended that she take a break from dancing. This posed a career decision for me. Would I continue my own career in New York, or help Alicia in the complex and difficult process of recovering her sight? Never was there any doubt in my mind that I would help Alicia recover. It was what we both wanted, and we returned to Havana, as the doctor recommended, so that Alicia could rest her eyes. We remained there two years, until September 1943. Though Alicia had to discontinue her professional work during this period, I was able to continue to mount productions in Havana. The original Ballet Russe appeared there on July 25 and 26, 1943. They presented a mixed program at the Pro-Arte auditorium. I danced in the first performance as a guest artist in *Cents baisers*, a ballet based on a Hans Christian Andersen fairy tale, with music by Frédéric d'Erlanger, costumes and sets by Jean Hugo, and choreography by Bronislava Nijinska. Alexandra Denisova danced the Princess, and Harcourt Algeranoff was the King. I danced the Gardener. I was invited to dance in the next day's performance of Nijinska's *Aurora's Wedding*. Léon Bakst designed the sets, and Léon Bakst, Alexandre Benois, and Natalia Goncharova designed the costumes. I partnered one of the six Ladies in Waiting in the

"Florestan and Her Sisters" segment. The cast included Alexandra Denisova, Yurek Lazowsky, and Tatiana Leskova. When the dancers in the de Basil Ballet Russe were on strike, Roman Jasinsky and Anna Leontieva danced with us in Cuba. After that, I did not perform for an entire year, but it was time put to good use. I was hired as secretary to the president of Pro-Arte Musical, and so I came into contact with some of the most noteworthy artists of the time: Vladimir Horowitz, Nathan Milstein, Yehudi Menuhin, Ignace Jan Paderewski, and Artur Rubinstein, among others. On June 25, Alicia returned to the stage, side by side with Denisova, in Fokine's *Les sylphides*.

Alberto, Alicia, and I joined together with a group of artists who called themselves "La Silva" [a poetry form joining miscellaneous elements]. La Silva described its work as "Total Theater." Our director was the Spanish intellectual Francisco Martínez Allende. La Silva's goal was to organize brief but rich performances that utilized dance, mime, poetry, spoken word, and music. Besides dancers and musicians, there were actors, playwrights, and writers, such as Alejo Carpentier, Maritza Rosales, Anna Leontieva, Muñeca Sánchez, and others. The project had a short life! There was only one show on October 27, 1942, at the Pro-Arte auditorium. I participated not only as a dancer but also for the first time as a choreographer. Four pieces made their world premiere: *El juicio de Salomón*, *La condesita*, *Pelleas and Melisande*, and *La tinaja*. I choreographed a ballet to music from Claude Debussy's opera *Pelleas and Melisande*. I created a pas de deux for Alicia and myself, with voice-over verses from a poem by Pablo Neruda.

In a roundup by *El mundo*, reviewer José Manuel Valdés Rodríguez praised the program for its strengths and criticized it for its weaknesses. He found the pas de deux to be "clean, sure and harmonious, graceful, picturesque and tinged with shared humor and an easy spirit" but was unhappy with the poor audio quality of the music, as well as lighting defects in *La tinaja* and *El juicio de Salomón*.[1]

I was highly self-critical, and so it was many years before I choreographed again. Even though it didn't last long, La Silva had demonstrated the need to find avenues and resources for promoting the arts, especially theater arts. It allowed us to see the creative potential that existed on the island, the deep desire of resident artists to show their work and demonstrate how close they were to realizing their artistic goals. All they needed was the opportunity!

On November 6, 1942, Pro-Arte presented a student concert under the direction of Alexandra Denisova. It included *Aurora's Wedding* and *Petrouchka*. José Ardévol conducted the orchestra, Luís Márquez designed the sets, and Ernestina del Hoyo [Alicia's mother] and Ernesto Fernández designed the costumes. I partnered Denisova in *Aurora's Wedding*.

Of this performance, the same José Manuel Valdés Rodríguez wrote: "*Aurora's Wedding*, under the direction of Alexandra Denisova, was a real success. Presented with authentic and irreproachably tasteful sets and costumes, *Aurora's Wedding* had as its central figures, Alexandra Denisova and Fernando Alonso, classical dancers of the highest caliber, supported by a group of very fortunate students."[2]

Before returning to New York, I danced in the May 15–23, 1943, First Ballet Festival of the Pro-Arte Musical Society, a big step forward for dance in Cuba. From 1931 on, Pro-Arte had mounted culminating performances each summer, and similar functions at other times. Because they had by this time benefited from having a broader repertoire, Pro-Arte could commit itself to raising the quality of student performances to the highest level. Inviting us and other international guests helped to establish the society as a venue for international figures in the dance world.

Alicia and I danced pieces from earlier repertoire and added *The Concert* and *Prince Igor* to the programs. Alberto choreographed *La hija del general* to music by Johann Strauss, about a young woman who falls in love with her father's aide-de-camp. It was the first of five pieces by Alberto in which I danced. *Forma* was another piece by Alberto in that program. It was to music by José Ardévol. Andrés designed the costumes, and the sets were by Emilio Junco and Eddie Montoulieu. It was a one-act ballet that used the Coral de la Habana [Havana chorale] directed by María Muñoz de Quevedo. The composer conducted the orchestra.

A program note refers to the piece as "one of the most significant dance works among those of Cuban authorship," and Alejo Carpentier rated it as "one of the most important originating in Cuba since the turn of the century, as much for its conception as its execution."[3] The musicologist Antonio Quevedo later wrote that the "work embodied Carpentier's praise . . . its importance transcended its national boundaries."[4]

What was the libretto?

Forma is an exploration of the human experience. Every man has distinct experiences that have accumulated over time, little by little. If man doesn't make some sense out of these events, he and his personality, his very humanity, will be frustrated. On the other hand, when man achieves a dignified rationale for his distinctive life experiences, his personality takes shape and achieves a *form* and figure that are his alone.

Alexandra Denisova danced the role of Her; Eduardo Parera danced the role of The Man, conceived along the lines of Rodin's *The Thinker*. Alicia danced The Other and I danced His Other (I).

Antonio Quevedo wrote in *El annuario cultural de Cuba*: "His Other (I) danced by Fernando Alonso, is of primary importance and continues the scene play throughout the ballet; only a dancer of great talent, such as Alonso could deliver the intellectual complexity lent to this character."[5]

On May 21, I danced the romantic poet again in *Les sylphides*, with Alicia, Alexandra Denisova, and Cuca Martínez. The festival represented a breakthrough for Pro-Arte. Up to then, the programs were much more narrow in scope. With each succeeding festival, we introduced works previously unknown or unseen in Cuba, performed by artists of renown from the United States or elsewhere, along with new choreography and music. The art of ballet took on a new aspect on the island. No longer would it founder; it had a frame of reference that served as a concrete foundation, permanently extending the island's dance horizon.

7

Autumn in New York, and a Dawning in Havana

Is it safe to assume that the two of you returned to New York as soon as Alicia was able to dance?

We returned to New York after the first Pro-Arte Festival. Alicia had recovered from the immediate problems with her vision, and we left Havana in mid-September for New York. We joined the Metropolitan Opera cast of *Capriccio espagnol*, directed by Léonide Massine. It was my first time dancing a work by the great master. During the Met's fall season I danced in *Helen of Troy*, *The Sorochinsky Fair*, *Bluebeard*, *Aleko*, *Romeo and Juliet*, and the role of Peter in *Peter and the Wolf*. In the final weeks of the 1943–44 Ballet Theatre season I danced in *Gala Performance* and *Barn Dance*.

The success of the ballet school's first festival was on my mind during that time in New York, and we started planning a second one for June 1944. Because of our connections in New York, two Ballet Theatre dancers, Maria Karnilova and John Kriza, agreed to dance in the festival under very generous terms on their part: the school would pay for their travel, lodging, and meals, but they would pay for the rest. This was an arrangement that was repeated a number of times over the years.

The first program included a one-act version of *Swan Lake*, *The Message*, by Alberto, and *La hija del general*, reworked by Alberto. Karnilova danced the daughter, and Alicia danced her maid. Alberto danced the General, and I was a Hussar officer. The corps danced peasants, Amazons, and Hussars.

In the *Havana Post*, Clotilde Pujol commented that Fernando "was an elegant Hussar officer in this delicious ballet."[1]

In the second program we presented *Les sylphides*, *Icarus*, and *Rascacielos*, by Alberto Alonso. I danced the lead in *Les sylphides* with Alexandra Denisova, Alicia Alonso, and Maria Karnilova. Denisova staged *Icarus*, based on Serge Lifar's original work. Harold Gramatges composed the music for percussion and piano. Denisova composed the rhythm part of the score. Alicia and Mario Meytin danced Icarus and Daedalus; John Kriza and I danced the Greek boys; and Cuca Martínez, Leonor Albarrán, Finita Suárez, and María Rosa Rovira danced the Greek girls.

We returned to New York for the 1944–45 season. Among the shows we would perform was George Balanchine's *Waltz Academy*, which premiered on October 5, 1944. It had a pas de six, a pas de quatre, two pas de trois, a pas de deux, and a finale. Nora Kaye, John Taras, John Kriza, and Barbara Fallis danced it. I danced in the pas de quatre with Janet Reed, Harold Lang, and Albia Kavan. Three days later I danced one of the cadets in *Graduation Ball*. The season ended with Ballet Theatre's premiere of Antony Tudor's *Undertow* on April 10, 1945, at the Met. It was a one-act ballet with a prologue and epilogue, about the inner life of a young man overcome with guilt feelings about a murder. Hugh Laing danced the Transgressor, John Kriza was Pollux, Lucia Chase was Polyhymnia, Cynthia Riseley was Volupia, Alicia was Ate, and Nana Gollner was Medusa. Kenneth Davis, Roy Tobias, Michael Kidd, and I danced The Satyrisci.

At the third Pro-Arte Festival the following summer, Alicia, Alberto, and I undertook our most ambitious project up to that point. For the first time in Cuba we mounted *Giselle*, one of the golden works in classical ballet repertory. We invited international guest artists to dance the leading roles. In addition to the corps de ballet, there would be five guest dancers from Ballet Theatre, which had lent us the sets. Alicia and I curated the production and ran the rehearsals.

José Manuel Valdés Rodríguez predicted, "On June 5, a memorable performance [will take place] that will be remembered and valued as an event marking this date in Cuban ballet history."[2]

I danced Albrecht for the first time in my career. The cast was: Rosella Hightower, Queen of the Wilis; Simon Semenoff, Hilarion; Alpheus Konn, the Duke of Cortland; Beau Mallison, Bathilde; and Irina Lavrova, Berthe. Alicia danced Giselle. It was only one and a half years after she had been put in for Alicia Markova in the New York performance that launched her as a ballet legend of the twentieth century.

We repeated the performance for the public three days later, as Pro-Arte's homage to Alicia. Both were very successful, with standing ovations on a par with those that Artur Rubinstein received when he had appeared at the same theater.

During the following season [1945–46] in New York, I was able to dance the four best roles of my performing career. I danced in Antony Tudor's *Pillar of Fire*. Instead of princes and princesses, it presented a modern outlook, expressive steps that required expert technique. It was about a woman's frustration with the characters she interacted with. I danced in it for the first time on October 10, 1945, at the Met, in the Lovers-in-Innocence segment. Ten days earlier I had danced in Jerome Robbins's *Interplay*. Then I danced Benno, the Prince's friend, in *Swan Lake*, and Mercutio in *Romeo and Juliet*. Alicia danced the title role and was partnered by Igor Youskevitch and John Kriza.

And after such a successful season, did you continue dancing in New York over the summer?

No, I returned to Cuba that summer for Pro-Arte's fourth festival, one of three great events there. The other two were a brief appearance by Ballet Russe and Nina Verchinina and Conchita Piquer's U.S. ensemble show. From May 25 to June 1, Pro-Arte students would again dance in casts headed by Ballet Theatre artists: Alicia and I, André Eglevsky, Barbara Fallis, Marjorie Tallchief, Stanley Herbert, Kenneth Davis, Roy Tobias, and others. Alberto was general director. The festival opened on May 25 with *Swan Lake*, *Apollo*, and *Petrouchka*. Two days later we danced *Les sylphides* and *Sombras*.

José Manuel Valdés Rodríguez perspicaciously pointed to embryonic traits that would, two decades later, limn the identity of a fully articulated Cuban school of ballet:

> The four American artists [the Alonsos, Fallis, and Tallchief] who danced *Les Sylphides* . . . evinced the purest of Fokine style with a special accent, a unique flavor that is properly associated with an aged wine decanted into new bottles. There is something indefinable and yet clearly present that we have for some time perceived in the dancing of these ballet classics by the American dancers. It is as if the severity of the classical line acquires a certain languid grace and innuendo, as if in the five basic ballet positions, rigidly contained within their own dynamic interplay, there suddenly appears an impetus that is somewhat upsetting by virtue of its spontaneity and being excessively personal; as if in the courtly conven-

tion present in classical dance, so affected by the manner of the courts of the absolute monarchs, and of the reactionary and constraint-filled Holy Alliance, a gesture was leveled, an expression that was unconventional and rebellious, which clearly issued from the masses of people, vibrating impatiently and benefiting from a new, more lively and flexible geometry of human relations.[3]

Were there any new works shown that summer?

Sombras by my brother Alberto had its world premiere. It is an intensely dramatic piece to music by Jean Sibelius that emphasizes the contradiction and its complement—the binomial relationship between spiritual and carnal love. The cast was: The Girl, Alicia Alonso; The Boy, Fernando Alonso; The Intruder, Marjorie Tallchief; The Woman, Barbara Fallis; The Man, Kenneth Davis; and Childhood, Yolanda Rivero. New dancers took the roles of boys, girls, men, and women.

Pro-Arte held a gala on March 28. *Apollo* and *Prince Igor* were the featured works. Then I danced, for the first time, with Alicia and André Eglevsky in *Concerto*, which Alberto had set in 1943 for Pro-Arte. It was a formal work in a style called "symphonic choreography," to music by Bach and Vivaldi. The gala was a huge success. There were no doubts that Pro-Arte could produce an authentically Cuban ballet school. It also demonstrated public support, interest, and familiarity with the art of dance. The May–June festival presented *La hija del general*, *Concerto*, and *Antes del alba*. Igor Youskevitch's first-time presence in Cuba added prestige to the event.

Wasn't *Antes del alba* considered controversial?

It unleashed an uprising! Chela, a young widow who is seriously ill, is drawn toward her neighbor's patio by a racket she can hear from her room. She notices a young couple among the neighbors. This leads her to reminisce about the lover she lost to a fatal accident. She returns home only to find herself overtaken by ghostly visions. Caught up in her fantasies, she sets herself on fire and ends her life. Alberto set it to music by Hilario González. It went far beyond the boundaries of what a certain faction in Pro-Arte's administration could accept. The work brought out an aspect of Cuban reality that Cuban high society had worked diligently to avoid coming to terms with.

How did you manage to present it?

Pro-Arte refused to show the work because it considered the stage appropriate only for the presentation of ballets about princes and princesses. . . . To them we were glorifying Cuban society's lowest life-forms.

My mother, who was Pro-Arte's president at the time, did not oppose reworking the piece in order to show it, but the majority of the Pro-Arte leadership did. They finally agreed to compromise only if Alicia herself, whose fame was already established, not only in Cuba but in the United States, would agree to dance the starring role. The final cast was: Chela, Alicia Alonso; Inés, Dolly Wohner; Cachita, Elena de Cueto; Rafael, Alberto Alonso; Raúl, Fernando Alonso; José María, Raúl Díaz.

José Manuel Valdés Rodríguez wrote: "In general terms, the conception and execution of *Antes del alba* offered a glimpse of dread, as if there were a wish not to probe deeper into the story, so as to not provoke an uncontainable reaction rooted in certain social and artistic conventions."[4]

So, did *Antes del alba* represent a revolutionary addition to Cuba's dance repertoire?

Yes, in the history of Cuban art, *Antes del alba* is the first ballet with an eminently social theme. In his search for authenticity, Alberto created a pathway for the incorporation of elements of popular dance into classical ballet. This was groundbreaking in those years, and left a legacy of the first rank.

Antes del alba was the last work by Alberto that I danced. We had hoped that the appearances by dancers from the United States would be followed by a visit from Ballet Theatre itself. We had waited so long in Havana for this, but the cost was prohibitive. During the May–June festival we presented a broad sampling of joint repertoire, with casts headed by Igor Youskevitch, Nora Kaye, Hugh Laing, Alicia Alonso, John Kriza, Lucia Chase, Dimitri Romanov, and Harold Lang. Others onstage were Melissa Hayden, Barbara Fallis, Cynthia Riseley, Paula Lloyd, Eric Braun, and I danced, as well. Alicia danced the title role in *Giselle*, with Youskevitch, for the first time in Cuba, and we showed works not seen before in Cuba, such as *Tally-Ho*, *Interplay*, *The Three Virgins and a Devil*, and *Fancy Free*, and I danced in *Lilac Garden*, and in *Swan Lake*, as Benno, while Alicia danced Odette-Odile, and Youskevitch, Siegfried. On August 5, anticipating that the Cuban government would honor Alicia, Pro-Arte presented a tribute to her. The program included *Concerto*, *La hija del general*, and *Les sylphides*, with me as her dance partner.

Of this event, José Manuel Valdés Rodríguez wrote: "[The second movement of *Concerto*] is a terse pas de deux executed with exemplary fluidity and harmony by Alicia Alonso and Fernando Alonso. . . . In *Les sylphides*, Fernando Alonso returned to demonstrate the highest caliber of partnering, tested earlier in *Concerto*, and in which he took pride in the finesse and delicately lyrical line that are his most salient accomplishments."[5]

8

Ballet Theatre, a University of Dance, and More . . .

What happened during your tenth year in New York?

In the autumn of 1947 we returned to New York for what would be my last season with Ballet Theatre. The lineup included *Romeo and Juliet*, *Swan Lake*, and the world premiere of George Balanchine's *Theme and Variations*, which took place on November 26 at City Center. Balanchine had wanted to evoke the golden era of Russian classical ballet, and he commissioned elegant set designs that turned the stage into a grand ballroom, adorned with red drapes and candelabras. He choreographed the piece to the fourth movement of Tchaikovsky's *The Suite in A Minor*. Woodman Thompson designed the sets and costumes. Balanchine set the work on Alicia and Igor Youskevitch as the lead couple. I danced with Melissa Hayden in one of the four soloist couple variations. Others in the cast were Anne Cheselka, Paula Lloyd, Cynthia Riseley, Eric Braun, Fernando Nault, and Zachary Solov, as well as the corps de ballet.

In the final weeks of the season I danced in Agnes de Mille's *The Three Virgins and a Devil*. The virgins were The Fanatic One, The Lustful One, and The Greedy One, and they met the Devil on their way to church. As much as they tried to resist him, they succumbed to temptation. I really enjoyed dancing that Devil!

In eight years with Ballet Theatre, your repertoire expanded to include many pieces that are still danced today. What are some of the others?

I also danced *La fille mal gardée* and *Rodeo*. I received permission to take the *Fille mal gardée* score back to Cuba so that we could present the final act there. Alicia and I sat on a bench in New York's Central Park, and Alicia handed me the pages as I photographed each one with my camera. The rest was easy. In Cuba, my mother copied it onto paper lined with music staves, but we found that we were missing the part of Alain (the foppish butterfly catcher). So I whistled the music as my mother transcribed the melody for piano.

I also danced in *Rodeo*, *Filling Station*, and *Barn Dance*. Agnes de Mille's *Fall River Legend* opened on April 22, 1948, at the Metropolitan Opera House. The Lizzie Borden libretto is a one-act work with eight scenes and a prologue, and I consider it one of de Mille's best ballets. It investigates the relationship between Borden and her parents, and her motivation for murdering them. It was my New York farewell performance.

How did it feel to leave a company that had offered you so much?

Ballet Theatre had proven to be an exceptional training ground, and not only for dance, but that is where I got much of my political education. I'd get together with the company musicians to play chess, and we would end up discussing politics. Eventually, I got to know the orchestra conductors and directors, Max Goberman and Benjamin Steinberg. Their political views and dissatisfaction struck a chord with me as an echo of my own experiences with social injustice. They shared books and pamphlets on socialist ideas with me. Together with other company members and myself, they would discuss the political issues of the day. So, when the company ran into financial trouble and decided to make budget cuts, I spoke up and insisted that the management adhere to union rules so that the dancers wouldn't be the ones to shoulder the burden of those cuts. Lucia Chase went so far as to suggest that I raised these issues because of my communist political outlook rather than the company's threats to renege on the union contract.

In 1948, I began giving public talks in Cuba on political subjects. It was ironic that later on I would have difficulty entering the United States because the U.S. government had labeled me "a foreign communist." My political views were actually made in the U.S.A.

What else did you carry back from your time in New York?

From an artistic point of view, there were eight years of day-to-day work with the dancers, set designers, musicians, choreographers, and writers. It all amounted to an education of inestimable value. There was an ongoing exchange of ideas and experiences, and direct contact with so many different approaches. All of this contributed material that was not available from any academic institution, only life itself! To see the work of Alicia Markova,

Anton Dolin, Tamara Toumanova, Nora Kaye, Igor Youskevitch, and Alicia Alonso, and share the stage with them, and dozens of other excellent dancers, was to drink from a hallowed source. To follow direction from Michel Fokine, George Balanchine, Antony Tudor, Léonide Massine, Eugene Loring, and Jerome Robbins, and have their enthusiasm become mine, to receive classes in person from them, and master-level advice, was to redeem something unique.

Antony Tudor taught us so much about dancing. He carefully analyzed his psychological ballets with us, we studied them; he explained and gave classes in acting. Even when we traveled by train on tour, he never wasted an opportunity to teach us. We identified with one another as a group, and so, for example, he'd say to us: "You are walking down the street; you arrive at the corner and bump into someone you don't want to see. How do you react?" In this way, our range of experience was broadened. We profited from all those riches and carried them into our dancing.

It was the same with Eugene Loring and Jerome Robbins. I was able to observe Robbins at work every day, as he created new steps in front of the mirror. Just seeing his dedication and vehemence convinced me that each new Robbins work would be a success.

Anton Dolin was a wit. He knew how to rehearse the dancers in their lines so that each dancer was perfectly spaced from the next. He'd sit in some random space in the set, and if things weren't going as he expected, for example in *Giselle*, he'd yell at the girls: "Cows, you look like cows!" But everyone loved him, because he was very nice and spontaneous.

Well, not everyone. One time I was visiting Miriam Golden's apartment, I used the bathroom there. When I lifted the toilet's lid, I saw a picture of Dolin's face pasted on the inside of it. When I came out, I asked her why she had done that, and she told me that she had had an altercation with Dolin that she had provoked by chewing gum during his class!

Over the course of those eight years, I added twenty-six works to my repertoire. Seven were world premieres. I was very lucky to have been in New York during a time when some of the best works of the day were brought to life. As a member of the corps de ballet and a soloist, I danced principal roles. By taking class, receiving personal attention, and dancing in hundreds of performances, I benefited from the best of the Russian, French, Italian, and British schools, and at the same time was shaped by the new American style. I couldn't have attended a better school, nor studied with higher-level teachers, nor taken more effective classes, nor received better overall training.

When you think back on the company today, what virtues and weaknesses stand out?

The company undertook very risky artistic challenges from the moment it began in 1940. So, by the close of the 1947–48 season, it found itself in a major financial crisis. From nothing, it had launched the development of new dance talent, choreography, music, and theatrical firsts. How many fine works have enriched ballet repertoire because of this company? Consider its vast contribution to North American dance culture and the impact of its oeuvre beyond U.S. borders. Yet neither philanthropists nor any branch of government would help Ballet Theatre recover from its financial crisis, and so the company announced it would take a break, "until further notice."

The dancers went in many directions to find work. I returned to Cuba in the spring of 1948. I was thirty-three years old, and a very different fellow from the young man who left for New York when he was barely out of his teens and about to become a husband and father! I had acquired a broad slice of human experience. I was armed with a different worldview, enriched by an artistic vein of incalculable worth, and above all, I had made up my mind that I would now act upon my lifelong yearning to build a professional ballet company in Cuba, whatever the cost.

9

Ballet Alicia Alonso

Did Pro-Arte remain your base of operations in Cuba?

At that point, my mother, Laura Rayneri, was the president of Pro-Arte. On May 25, 1948, she announced her retirement from the presidency. The society was taking increasingly belligerent steps to tighten control over its assets. So, Alicia, Alberto, and I searched out and found new sources for funding. That process began to sow the idea of a ballet school and company more deeply, and at the same time, root out certain amateurish traits that had hung on from the Pro-Arte school's earliest days. My mother was a liberal and a progressive, and our aspirations were in keeping with her values, but that was not how others in the leadership of Pro-Arte saw our enterprise. We met with resistance from those who held more conservative, or outright reactionary points of view. The first indication of this occurred when my mother proposed that voting rights be extended to member-subscribers with seats in the first and second balconies, in other words, those who were not wealthy. The majority flatly rejected her proposal (and similar ones), and for the first time since the society's founding the opposition ran its own presidential candidate. My mother and the group's director decided to present their resignations openly, because, as they put it, there was not "in the present elections, the democratic spirit that must prevail in these civic proceedings."

Did that turn the three of you into citizens without portfolios?

Well, the school ballet festival still went forward as scheduled on June 24 and 25. It was the sixth and last such event in which I played an organizational role. I brought together an excellent group of dancers, some from Ballet Theatre and others from the original Ballet Russe of Colonel de Basil. For the first show, *Stars of Ballet*, we invited John Kriza, Barbara Fallis, Paula Lloyd, and Michael Maule. Benjamin Steinberg conducted the orchestra.

The first full program included *Concerto*, in which Alicia and I danced with Fallis, Lloyd, and Dulce Wohner, and *Swan Lake*, with Alicia as Odette/Odile, Kriza as Siegfried, myself as Benno, and Marvin Krauter as Von Rothbart. Alicia and Kriza danced *Giselle* in the June 25 performance. I debuted in *Diversiones* with Fallis. This was the last such festival hosted by Pro-Arte Musical. My ties to the school had undergone substantial weakening: I had started out in 1935 as a student for a year, then a guest artist for eight years, and co-sponsor of six festivals. From these performances, thirteen works were kept in my repertoire. I felt a great loyalty to Pro-Arte. My career as a dancer, impresario, and teacher had given an enormous boost to the advancement and continuity of the society, and the festivals that took place between 1935 and 1948 left an indelible mark on the future of Cuban ballet.

What was the next step?

In October 1948, Ballet Alicia Alonso was founded. It was the first professional ballet company in Cuba's history. Over the course of the previous sixteen years, four factors had come into play that had an impact on the future of the company. First, there was the growth over nearly two decades of the initial group, begun in 1931; second, an artistic and technical leadership was formed, trained, and seasoned, and a sizable classical and contemporary repertory was acquired; and third, and most importantly, an audience surged forward to greet this phenomenon, which, even though it was small at first, constituted a platform for future development. The work by Pro-Arte sustained itself on firm pillars that began with Nikolai Yavorsky, who passed along his knowledge to Alberto Alonso. It was then expanded and enriched by such teachers as George Milenov and Alexandra Denisova.

Another propitious factor for the advancement of the company was the permanent idea, rooted in our deepest convictions, that it was necessary to promote the organized and professional development of ballet in Cuba. We acted on the belief that we were obligated to live for a decade in the United States, far from the national reality of Cuba, so that we, and Cuban ballet, might benefit from experiencing the successes and victories achieved by New York's new ballet cadre. Past that moment, we felt no temptation to remain in New York for the sake of personal financial stability, nor did the financial uncertainties in Cuba discourage us. Instead, we transformed such obstacles into moral incentives.

We carried with us the experience and awareness gained during our time with Mordkin, in Broadway musicals, Ballet Caravan, Ballet Theatre, and the mastery we achieved through everyday work in a company of the finest dancers, choreographers, and musicians, so many of whom were great artists. The final element was chance: the economic crisis that confronted Ballet Theatre was the determining factor in uprooting us again and forcing the question of returning to Cuba to the forefront. That is how the moment we had been waiting for finally arrived!

How did you finance the new company?

Our savings became the initial capital to finance the project. Between the three of us we had no more than two thousand pesos. It was not only insufficient, it was laughable. So Pro-Arte lent us studio space, sets, and equipment. We paid the dancers, even international guests, "mañana," which arrived later than sooner in many cases. The same applied to fees for publicity, props, costumes, and other services.

We were altruistic, romantic, and generous. Because for us to take the crazy risk of starting a ballet company in a country like Cuba, where the majority of people's idea of how to enrich your enterprise was to become part of the government, one would have had to be insane. We believed that we would be able to mount tours on a par with those of Ballet Theatre, that we would enjoy many successes and thereby take in enough profit to keep going.

I must say that we had an array of talent and enthusiasm that more than compensated for the lack of funds. Forty dancers joined, the majority of them from Ballet Theatre, with Alicia and Igor Youskevitch as the company's stars. We also had Barbara Fallis, Melissa Hayden, Helen Komarova, Paula Lloyd, Royes Fernández, Cynthia Riseley, and Michael Maule. Max Goberman and Benjamin Steinberg led the orchestra; Alberto was the artistic director. We decided to capitalize on the fame Alicia had gained in the United States, and named the company "Ballet Alicia Alonso." I became the general director, while continuing to dance. Enthusiasm was the prevailing factor. It was difficult to cover the housing expenses for guest dancers, but the non-Cubans were very patient, and everyone maintained their artistic fervor.

There were three performances on October 28, 30, and 31 at Pro-Arte. The first was *Pas de quatre* with Hayden, Riseley, Lloyd, and Fallis, and *Afternoon of a Faun* with Youskevitch and Komarova. I made my company debut in the program closer, the second act of *Swan Lake*, dancing with Alicia, Youskevitch, and Maule. On October 30, I danced Peter in *Peter and the Wolf*, with Hayden as The Bird and Alberto as The Wolf. That evening's closer was *Giselle*, danced by Alicia and Youskevitch. Our inaugural season concluded on October 31 with *Les sylphides, Pas de quatre, The Black Swan Pas de Deux and Variations*, and *Peter and the Wolf.*

Our opening season was a resounding success, both artistically and financially. Expenses were covered and debts paid, but nothing remained for future seasons. Not one peso of state support was forthcoming, and yet we had to keep going. The sacrifice was substantial, especially for those with families to support. Some of those men were forced to take additional jobs dancing in cabarets. The company wages were only forty pesos per month.

According to Pedro Simón in *La magia de la danza en Cuba*, the company offered "a broad artistic profile, departing from the romantic and classical tradition, at the same time encouraging the production of contemporary works. The first years presented on the same stage, works such as *Swan Lake*, *Giselle*, and *Coppélia*, innovative works from the Ballet Russe tradition, and as a fundamental part of the repertoire, the nationally based works of Alberto Alonso and other choreographers."[1]

The initial repertoire, besides those in the inaugural performances, included *Prince Igor, Concerto, Apollo, La valse, Petrouchka, Aurora's Wedding*, and *Coppélia*, all of which premiered in 1948.

From the moment we launched Ballet Alicia Alonso, the entire direction of my life changed. I made a decision to dedicate myself to the needs of the new company. The alternatives were in front of me: to return to New York and continue my career there, or to promote and develop ballet in Cuba. I had no doubts whatsoever. I chose to settle in my homeland. As general director of the company, I took responsibility for all organizational, financial, and administrative affairs, without letting go of my dance career. I also danced a good part of my personal repertoire, and added two new works to it, *Coppélia* and the *Prince Igor Polovtsian Dances.*

10

El Maestro de Maestros, the Father of Cuban Ballet

Did the new company tour?

On November 13, under my direction, the company embarked on its first international tour. We had a contract to perform in Venezuela and Puerto Rico. The Venezuela shows were so successful that the tour there could have been extended had there not been a political coup d'état under way to unseat the country's president, Rómulo Betancourt. They declared a state of siege, and the company was kept immobilized for several days with no possibility of continuing on to Puerto Rico, until an airplane from the Río Piedras campus of the University of Puerto Rico was sent to Carácas. It flew the dancers to San Juan. The show was a triumph, but when we returned to Havana there were new problems. Before we left, Pro-Arte had let us have sets, costumes, music, and equipment. Then, when they realized that the company could be gone for as long as a year in Central and South America, they wanted to formalize these arrangements via a contract, including some modest charges for the loaned items. This led to friction between the company and the Pro-Arte directors. We settled the matter amicably by giving a benefit performance to pay off the debts to our benefactors-turned-creditors.

Besides that, we saw the new season as an opportunity to pay the outstanding debts to foreign dancers. It opened at the Auditorium Theater and lasted from December 11 to December 28. Some of the guest dancers wanted to remain in Cuba; others preferred to return home until the company's second international tour. During that season I danced in *Prince Igor* on December 11 and in *Coppélia* on December 28, where I again shared the stage with Alicia, Alberto, and Igor Youskevitch.

At the start of 1949 the company signed a contract to dance in Central and South America. Then, Sol Hurok traveled from New York to Havana to discuss a company tour of Europe and the United States. This was a major opportunity: Hurok was the most famous dance impresario in the world, but the problem we confronted was sustaining the dancers until the tour. We placed an ad in the December 16 edition of the Havana newspaper *El mundo*. We were determined to gain access to the media in order to put forward specific cultural proposals.

The ad read: "the only way to keep going is to attract the public to performances, obtain donations or government support. Without this, it's impossible to keep going. We utilize the medium of the press to call upon the public to not permit a Cuban artistic and cultural delegation such as this one to disappear without having completed its mission."[1] In response, the University Student Federation of Havana pledged to play a very important role.

Angela Grau, one of its members, explains how the organization mounted a campaign of public support that proved indispensable:

> The first thing we did to help them was focus on the Ministry of Education. That is, we built a national press and radio campaign that included all the institutions, to expose the fact that the Ministry of Education was unconcerned about culture and that this was shameful. We put out a memorandum to all the ministries. Finally, we were able to get the Ministry of Education to meet with us, and they decided to underwrite three Ballet Alicia Alonso performances. Among those with whom we were able to negotiate was La Polar [a brewery], which had a huge publicity budget. We proposed that they donate publicity for one performance and they told us that we would have to put some bears on the stage. We told them that we'd put bears on the stage, beer bottles, whatever they wanted.[2]

Did the student federation hold any events in its own name?

The federation decided to sponsor a performance at popular prices for the general public. The alliance that the students put together turned out to be something on the order of a cultural militia. The company took in five thousand pesos per performance. In every way possible, the connection with the student organization kept the company going for the better part of two years! Those who undertook this effort included Alfredo Guevara, Manuel Corrales, Baudilo Castellanos, Leonel Soto, Mario García Incháustegui, and others. The work of the students drew the attention of many well-known intellectuals. This resulted in an organization called "The Sponsors of Ballet Alicia Alonso." According to custom, the presiding offices of the organization were conferred upon the president of the Republic and two of his ministers. The day-to-day direction was in the hands of José Manuel Valdés Rodríguez, who was favored by political progressives, journalists, writers, and artists. Outstanding among them were Manuel Bisbé, Conrado Massaguer, Luís Amado Blanco, and Edgardo Martín.

What was the government's attitude toward the students' efforts?

Compared to what the student federation was willing to do for us, the attitude of certain society women and politicians stood in sharp contrast. Despite having millions, they threw us mere scraps. Even though this was infuriating, we could not afford to cut ourselves off from them.

The Ministry of Education sponsored performances on January 7, 11, and 15, 1949. The first was for the Havana Diplomatic Corps, the second for academics and scholars, and the final one was for the public, offered free of charge. On January 8, La Polar brewery sponsored a performance that was accompanied by a big publicity campaign. The last performance on January 26 was a massive salute to the student federation and the University of Havana. Out of gratitude for the student effort, we reduced student ticket prices to the minimum.

All the programs were well attended, and gave Ballet Alicia Alonso the opportunity to introduce its own style. From that moment on, the link with the masses and subsequent education of students on the subject of ballet became an integral part of the company's political life. Earlier in my career, in the summer of 1940, there had been large-scale performances at Lewisohn Stadium, but even such enormous public events had had a commercial tone to them: the larger the audience, the greater the profits! Now the goal that we were pursuing was cultural development. Ultimately, the life of the company depended on attracting and educating a broad audience devoted to ballet. Being able to rely on these young student activists to promote culture made it possible for me to disengage from the narrow strictures imposed on the company by Pro-Arte's conservative social base.

How did the company decide to take advantage of this new turn of events?

Well, we were saved in the short term, but we had no assurances for the future. So Ballet Alicia Alonso embarked on its second international tour on January 27, 1949. The tour from the north to the south of Latin America continued for nearly a year. The company visited eleven countries! Our repertoire included the traditional classics such as *Giselle, Swan Lake,* and *Coppélia*, and reworked pieces such as *Petrouchka, Les sylphides, Peter and the Wolf, Pas de quatre, La valse,* and *Spectre de la rose*. We also brought Cuban ballets, such as *Sombras* and *Concerto*.

Our first stop was in Mexico, at the Palacio de Bellas Artes. The company gave sixteen performances. Some problems arose there that we would repeatedly encounter during the tour. We were inexperienced and did not insist on being furnished with copies of the contracts we had signed. Some of these presenters went back on their word and did not pay for the shows. Once again, the student federation stepped in and came to our rescue. It used its connections with parallel organizations in Mexico to call for actions in solidarity with the artists. These won us our pay, and we were able to complete our tour across the Americas.

Are you saying that you learned more about business administration on tour than you did in college?

Oh, there's more! The second stop was Guatemala, and then El Salvador, where there were more setbacks. When the sponsors would not pay, all the members of the company met to discuss the situation. Without any hesitation, we decided to continue on to Costa Rica, where we found that conditions were more favorable. In Panama the company scored triumphs beginning with the first show, and the season ended up with a financial bonanza. We would have liked to extend the Panama stay because we were still in debt, but it would have gone into Easter week, and so it was not possible. We received news that the Cuban Ministry of Education was going to send us twenty-five hundred dollars. When the money didn't arrive, I contacted them and explained what we were facing.

They said that they were sending us two planes to fly back on, but that didn't solve the problem, and it showed that they were giving up on the company's tour. One hundred thousand pesos is not much for a government when the previous one stole forty-five million from the Ministry of Education, alone. With one hundred thousand pesos we could have had the best company in the world. Didn't they realize what kind of work we were doing? Didn't they know how people spoke of our country and its culture after having seen the performances we were presenting? We had sacrificed everything to travel south, and now that we had our foot in the door of major cities and the chance to accomplish something, were we going to splinter apart?[3]

We arrived in Colombia in the middle of Holy Week, and before we knew it there were more calamities. After dancing in Cali, we traveled to Medellin without a cent. We stayed at the Nutibaras, one of the most luxurious hotels in town. I convinced the owner to pay for the shows, which were quite well received. We were just as lucky in Bogotá, and then in Quito.

Once we got to Ecuador we finally received the money from Cuba that we had been promised, and we continued on to Peru. After that, doors opened to perform in Chile, Argentina, and Uruguay.

Chile was a disaster, financially. Various dancers left, disheartened by the setbacks. Among them was the company ballet master, Leon Fokine. One morning, when it was time for class to begin, the dancers found no teacher in the studio! One of them asked whether I would teach just this once. So I did—and not only on that day, but all the ones that followed.

Only thanks to the Flota Aérea Mercante Argentina were we able to travel to Argentina, the country where we experienced some of our greatest successes. It meant that we had to eliminate Chile from the itinerary, however. At the time, Juan Perón was in power. He fell under the spell of Cuban ballet and was enchanted by Alicia.

When we arrived in Buenos Aires we came up against a difficult situation: we had no means of returning to Cuba. Owing to measures undertaken by a gentleman of Jewish extraction, Isaac Libenson, it was possible to solve the problem. He was able to get Perón to cover the costs of the performance at Quinto de los Ólivos. They set up the stage. Stagehands from Teatro Colón took charge of the sets. The space they had chosen for the show had an open skylight and was a kind of amphitheater. Just beyond the stage there was a railroad crossing. We decided to give it a try. The freight cars fit right in with the set. When they started rolling, the set changed. The lights were hung in the surrounding trees. Perón was in attendance. Upon his arrival, everyone present, especially the students, rose to their feet and began chanting his name.

Due to interest on Perón's part, and Libenson's intervention, they made us an offer of one million dollars annually—if the company were to reside in Argentina. The Argentine government would also put a ship at the company's permanent disposal! This might have been a tempting offer if we had been looking to enrich ourselves, but to live an antiseptic existence, alienated from the native land in which our artistic culture was rooted, was not what we wanted. After we turned down his invitation, Perón proposed a farewell toast to the ship *Evita*, on which we were to sail. It bore a Flota Mercante Argentina insignia, and that is how we returned to Havana.

Did Perón's support change your fortunes in Havana?

We arrived back in Havana in December, and the company began to receive recognition from the most diverse sectors imaginable. They applauded our successes and celebrated that the name of Cuba had ascended a stairway to the stars. The Ministry of Education served cocktails and promised help. But the future was just as uncertain as the past had been. Given the tour's financial failings, it wasn't really possible to pay off prior obligations to Pro-Arte. The Pro-Arte directors therefore insisted that a special performance be mounted to pay back those debts. In fact, it was this demand that led to a definitive break between Pro-Arte and Alicia, Alberto, and me.

11

Crafting a Curriculum, Sculpting a Style

How did touring change the company?

Pro-Arte relented once we paid off our debts, and allowed us to use its costumes, sets, and equipment, but it was too little too late. After eight years of having received Ballet Theatre's full cooperation in lending sets and costumes without charge, we couldn't help but make comparisons between the two organizations. We had been able to take full advantage of the New York experience and had absorbed practical and philosophical life lessons of every kind. We were more aware of the difference between conditions in Cuba and the United States, and we made use of what we had learned, and our ingenuity, to keep the company together during the tour. We had developed into a self-confident artistic leadership. We were finally able to close the Pro-Arte chapter without any second thoughts.

The year 1949 ended with excellent prospects for the future. Of the thirteen works we had premiered the previous year, three were taken on tour: *Swan Lake*, *Le spectre de la rose*, and *Sombras*. I danced Franz in *Coppélia*, with Alicia as Swanilda and Enrique Martínez as Doctor Coppelius. I engaged in a series of discussions with the Ministry of Education and a Buenos Aires businessman whose last name was Gallo. Mr. Gallo ended up signing a contract to bring the company back to Central America, and we extended that tour to Venezuela and three European capitals: Paris, London, and Madrid.

Until the agreement was signed with Gallo, we continued to fill engagements in Cuba. From January to April 1950 we appeared at the Presidential Palace, the Pro-Arte auditorium, and in Matanzas. The city of Cárdenas and the Havana National Theater provided new sets. We added four works to the repertoire: the pas de deux from *Don Quixote*, *The Nutcracker*, *Ensayo sinfónica*, and *Fiesta*. We decided to extend our domain to the provinces.

At that time, daytime performances at the National Theater were attracting large audiences.

The daily newspaper *El mundo* reported: "It has been more than a year since the ballet has been an art form unknown to the great majority of the population. Now, ever since the Ballet Alicia Alonso performances at the University Stadium and its tours around the island, an impassioned interest in it has been awakened. The performances taking place at the National always bring together an enormous and vibrant audience, whose warmest feelings are communicated."[1]

A milestone for me, personally, was the founding of the Alicia Alonso Academy of Ballet in July 1950. When the company was founded two years earlier, the majority of dancers were from outside of Cuba. As the economic situation worsened, most of them returned to the United States. We had to fill this void, and we had outgrown the level of dancer that Pro-Arte could offer. Its best dancers were already in the company. These circumstances made the opening of a school all the more urgent. We had to train dancers for the new company in a school where the prevailing pedagogy would be that of the company's directors, in keeping with our conception of the ideal style for the Cuban dancer. We had to formulate exercises that would shape the dancers perfectly and afford mastery of technique that would free up their artistry.

We created the Ballet Alicia Alonso National Academy with the goal of being able to count on a permanent source of Cuban dancers. We were trying to provide complete artistic training embracing every level.

From that moment on I had to place limits on my performing career, even more so than when I was called upon to become general director of the company. As a teacher-director and ballet master, I began to transmit to the students the most systematized method of the training that Alicia and I had acquired over the previous fifteen years.

The curriculum included ballet, pointe, adagio and variations, folk dance, character, Spanish character, repertoire, modern dance, pantomime, and makeup. Eventually, the school's Drama Department would teach theater tech, set design, and lighting. We offered musical training in piano, orchestration, theory, and music appreciation. Other specialties were art history, dance history, costume, and aesthetics. We made sure that we had a faculty of the highest caliber. Besides myself during those eleven years, our teachers were George Goncharov (1950); Léon Fokine, José Páres, André Eglevsky, Nora Kaye, and Mia Slavenska (1951); Alexandra Denisova, Mary Skeaping, Charles Dickson, and Royes Fernández (1952); Ana Ivanova (1953); Phyllis Bedells (1954); and Igor Youskevitch (1959).

Did students audition to be admitted?

Any student who could pay the monthly fee was admitted, even if he or she did not meet the physical or aptitude requirements. The income from tuition subsidized scholarships to students with talent but no money. Among the students from that period were Mirta Plá, Aurora Bosch, Josefina Méndez, and Loipa Araújo, the "Four Jewels" of Cuban ballet. Also among the very best were Marta García, María Elena Llorente, and Menia Martínez.

You mentioned that the academy lasted eleven years. What replaced it?

The academy stopped functioning in 1961. It gave way to newer organizational forms, more in keeping with the revolutionary transformation of the country that was taking place. The academy represented the most important model for the restructuring of teaching. It was a virtual nerve center in the development of a Cuban school of ballet.

It was for me a crucible for the immense mission to create a system of instruction based on the Cuban style. From the moment I began this project I could see that it was imperative to elaborate a method conforming to the needs and characteristics of our Cuban students. It was tested in practice throughout the ballet world as those we trained took up teaching positions in other locales. My experiences at Pro-Arte and in the United States were my reference points. The academy represented the linkage of that accumulated experience. I had the chance to observe classes by guest teachers. I analyzed their methods and retained what seemed valid based on how well it corresponded to the needs of our own students. Alicia and Alberto offered important counsel. Their experiences, observations, and advice contributed to the inauguration of a new teaching style, and a methodology that helped me to develop a curriculum suited to our needs.

How did you go about creating that curriculum?

We analyzed the different dance forms and styles: from the Russian school, the Soviet, Italian, and French. To us, the Vaganova arabesque seemed to foreshorten the line, and we had to open the arm a bit more. The Italian school did it completely open. To us, it seemed that it had to be somewhere in the middle, a very nice position that did not foreshorten the line. Vaganova suffered from a big handicap in the way jumps were done. It neglected the batterie and the grand jetés. The Italians, on the other hand, exaggerated the jumps because they did the glissade with batterie preparation. And it appeared to me that what was really needed was a fusion of both styles. The flirtatious savoire faire and femininity of the French ballerinas was for me a delicacy, and I thought that the Cuban girls could do it just perfectly. We had to combine these forms, the grace and style, into one integrated body. We wanted the precision of the English, and above all there was the North American school, which contained much of what arrived from the European schools. The North Americans had a dynamism that they inherited from musical comedy. We had to import this dynamism, this show rhythm, into our ballet form.

Didn't your curriculum interpolate anatomy and kinesiology?

Such concerns arose not only with regard to the character of the pedagogical research but also in relation to artistic and physio-anatomical issues. Each pose, exercise, and step was judged according to the new criteria, its suitability questioned as to how well it served the academy's purpose. I discovered that I had an aptitude for dance pedagogy, and so I began, rather unself-consciously in the beginning, to perfect this curriculum and teaching method. I ended up devoting more than three quarters of a century to it. I discovered that the daily work at the academy of shaping dancers, developing and perfecting them, was another way to create. I was now recapturing the feeling of satisfaction that I had felt on the stage—but exponentially! It gives me more pleasure than dancing did.

Left: Fernando and Alberto Alonso. Courtesy of Fernando Alonso.

Below: Fernando and Alicia Alonso in *Waltz Academy*. Photo by Alfredo Valente, Jerome Robbins Dance Division, The New York Public Library for the Performing Arts, Astor, Lenox and Tilden Foundations.

Left: Fernando and Alicia Alonso in *Sleeping Beauty*. Courtesy of Fernando Alonso.

Below: Janet Reed and Fernando Alonso in *Interplay*. Photo by Fred Fehl, Jerome Robbins Dance Division, The New York Public Library for the Performing Arts, Astor, Lenox and Tilden Foundations.

Left: Fernando Alonso in *Peter and the Wolf*. Photo by Fred Fehl, Jerome Robbins Dance Division, The New York Public Library for the Performing Arts, Astor, Lenox and Tilden Foundations.

Below: Fernando Alonso as Mercutio in *Romeo and Juliet*. Photo by Cecil Beaton, Jerome Robbins Dance Division, The New York Public Library for the Performing Arts, Astor, Lenox and Tilden Foundations.

Fernando Alonso in *Hija del general*. Courtesy of Alfredo Valente.

Laura Rayneri, Fernando's mother. Courtesy of family of Fernando Alonso.

12

Legends and Lessons

Laura and Loipa

Observing class, interviewing teachers, watching performances—from ballets to bullfights—discussing them with Fernando, and mining his recollections suggested taking another step: interviewing those who continue to teach and coach according to the precepts and practices he developed. Fernando referred me to Loipa Araújo and Laura Alonso to capture a snapshot of the pedagogy's most current application. During the Twenty-Second Havana International Festival of Ballet in October–November 2010 I had an opportunity to speak with Loipa Araújo at the Ballet Nacional headquarters on Calzada Street, where she was rehearsing company dancers for a performance the following day. Though the Ballet Nacional has a sizable roster of ballet masters, the dancers value Araújo as essential to the company's artistic continuity. I asked her to share the details of every day class with me so that I might be able to more fully grasp how the Cuban method differs from others to produce uniformity in the corps de ballet and a disciplined mastery of each step.

She smiles, as if she has heard this question before.

"The steps are the same. We have not created new ones. A *tendu* [extension of the leg at floor level] is still a tendu. A *grand plié* [deep knee bend] is still a grand plié. It is *the relationship of one to the other*, how we break them down according to which muscles they engage, and how they are ultimately performed, that distinguishes us from other schools," she explains patiently. "Fernando proceeds from a materialist point of view, a scientific foundation. Our job is to sculpt dancers out of the material they are made of, to understand what that material is, and how to transform and adapt it to the needs of the company. The science—calculating resistance and perspiration rates, what stresses develop the musculature—this is the body of knowledge he conquered to put at the service of the steps. He had the intelligence and intuition to notice the subtleties of Alicia's training when she began studying with various teachers in New York: What was it in one teacher's approach as compared with another's that contributed to making Alicia's work distinctive, even though the steps were the same? To reach the primary goal of constructing a company required students who could be shaped in such a way as to produce a uniform quality that would make the company unique." Fernando would in a subsequent commentary add that, in Alicia, he had the rare opportunity to observe the activation and realization of the potential that had manifested itself early on. He explains that some of what she had was inherited, and some learned. He saw it as his job to capture her learning process and reproduce it as efficiently as possible to develop dancers of the highest caliber for the company that the two of them would build together.

"Fernando decided to select the best contributions from the French, Italian (Cecchetti), and Imperial Ballet schools," says Araújo.

Later, Fernando adds, "I thought, let's take the pas de deux from the Italians, the adagio from the Russians, the French neatness and fleet coquettishness, Vaganova turns, Danish balances, and English port de bras."

Araújo explains that he began trying out a high *relevé* (standing on demi-pointe), guided by the idea that the *relevé* prepares the student to learn to turn. "The higher on the toes, the less contact there is with the floor, eliminating all but the most necessary frictional impediments to turning.

"Continuing to analyze the steps from a scientific standpoint, he experimented with raising the *passé* [working leg bent at knee with toe touching standing leg] higher, it also being a key component of the pirouette and similar turns. 'The higher the passé, the easier it is to keep up the momentum of the turn,' he reasoned."

Araújo tells me that class would begin not with grand plié as the first barre exercise, but tendu. The rationale was to warm up the small muscles before the larger ones. "We have them hold the tendu for four counts," Araújo says, "but just because we say 'hold' doesn't mean that this is a static exercise. They use the time to increase their turnout and shape the feet." Fernando later comments that he doesn't wish to quibble, but in instances where the music dictates holding the tendu for two counts, they turn out their hips and shape their feet in only two. Still, the point remains the same: rather than move through the barre steps routinely, the dancers are taught from the beginning to fully utilize each consciously sequenced step in every exercise to improve its shape, tenacity, and dispatch. "You must start the pirouette from fourth position on the *front* leg," Alonso insists, or you will not marshal sufficient force or torque for the turn, "and you must always finish on the 'up' accent. You initiate the turn using centrifugal force, but then you must use the arms to break that force and transition quickly to centripetal force at just the right moment, or you will go off balance." In each exercise, the continuous straightening of the knee is essential. "Give me a point, and I will move the world," Araújo says, quoting Alonso quoting Archimedes. Alonso wanted his students to see clearly and understand the connections between points and lines and the role of the dancer in the demarcation of those relationships.

"It was not only the positions and steps that caught the maestro's imagination," says Araújo. "He scrutinized temperature and perspiration rates as well. He noted that the loss of potassium could result in muscle cramps and made sure that students took salt, saccharine, and potassium pills with lemon juice to keep cramps away."

"I have heard that his class could last as long as two and a half hours. Is that true?" I ask Araújo. She laughs and says, "We always knew when class would begin, but we never knew when it would end. He was keen on perfection, and he never grew tired of pursuing it, or helping us to understand how to arrive closer to it. He spoke of two kinds of classes—classes of maintenance and classes of improvement—and expressed a definite preference for the latter. He was fond of saying that you will never reach perfection, but you must continually seek it, because the process itself will make you a far better dancer.

"So we would start by warming up the small muscles to get the most out of the pliés we would do later, bringing to them already warmed up quadriceps and knee joints. We did *jetés* [jumps with extended legs]after the *ronds de jambes* [circling legs] to prepare for *battú* [leg beats]. He had a holistic vision: we balanced in first, second, fourth, and fifth. The accent was always up."

Did the Soviet methods have any influence on how Cuban classes were taught? "After Fernando and Alicia visited the Soviet Union, they noted the way in which the Russians used the back in their *épaulement* [shoulder movement]. It was a more legato movement. They saw the crossed arms and hands in high fifth, and we began to incorporate some of that, but in general, no, the Soviet classes did not have very much influence. Fernando asked the Russians to send a teacher and a dancer [the dancer was supposed to be Rudolf Nureyev, but he defected], and so Azari Plisetsky came. He danced as Alicia's partner and taught men's class. But Azari never tried in any way to impose Soviet methods. On the contrary, he took Fernando's classes, and paid careful attention to Fernando's pedagogic approach, and introduced only the virtuosity and power of the Soviet men's training, producing a very welcome element that is highly regarded by audiences. The end result is a melding of the Cuban neatness and particularity with the Russian virtuosity." The Cuban style was so distinctive in relationship to the Soviets, Araújo points out, that when two Cubans, Menia Martínez and Lázaro Carreño, returned to Cuba from their training at the Kirov, they had to relearn the Cuban style. Fernando adds that the combination of what they took from the old Imperial style and the teachings of the Russian teacher and dancer Asaf Messerer (Plisetsky's uncle) were of great importance to shaping the Cuban style.

Araújo says that a true test for her came when she had an opportunity to work with the French *étoile* Violette Verdy. "I then saw that Fernando had given us everything: Cecchetti, Vestris, even Bournonville, and not in a mimetic way, but he passed all of it through the filter of the Cuban body. If it didn't work for our body type, he rejected it." Fernando adds that Paris Opera's Claude Bessy filmed all the Cuban classes, and upon viewing them, arrived at the same conclusion.

Laura Alonso, named after her maternal grandmother, would eventually and inevitably join the same dance world that her parents, aunt, and uncles inhabited, and play a key role in the Herculean effort to establish a Cuban company and school: first as a student, then as a soloist in the company, and finally as one of the most in-demand ballet mistresses, exponents, and *repetiteurs* of the Cuban school. Her men's classes are legendary throughout the ballet world. She is that rare woman in patriarchal society whose leadership is acknowledged by men. Today, she has established a successful ballet company in Havana called Pro-Danza. Since Laura Alonso was born in New York, she is a U.S. citizen and may travel to and from Cuba almost as if no U.S. ban on travel to Cuba existed. Of her childhood, Laura has the following to say:

> My first memory of her [Alicia Alonso] as a dancer was in Havana. She was in a ballet with a fountain. I loved that fountain! And she had long golden hair. My father was like Prince Charming. I can't imagine what I saw, but it had to be something like "Tristan and Isolde." I was very little. The next time I saw them dance—I must have been five or six—was in New York, and it was almost a traumatic experience. I arrived, and I think I was taken directly to the theater, where I saw them both die right before my eyes! If I had any clear thought it was, "Why

did they have to bring me all the way from Havana to New York, sit me down in a theater, and they both die!" Of course, it was Tudor's "Romeo and Juliet," and my father was Mercutio and my mother, Juliet. . . .

My parents didn't want me to study ballet, but I insisted after a big fight and lots of crying. I was sent to a special school for gifted children where my aunt was a teacher. Then my mother got very angry with my father when I was eleven. She was away on tour, and he put me in our Cuban ballet company. She was furious when she came back and found out what had happened. She said, "Once you have been hooked by the taste of the stage, it is like a drug, you can't quit." She was quite right. I danced onstage until I was thirty-five . . .

I remember the family would sit at a table in our house and my uncle would start discussing a way to do a new step or movement. Then his wife [Alexandra Denisova] would say, "But that's impossible," and then my father would jump up and say, "Maybe if you do it like this." At this point my mother would come in and there would be a big argument on the new movement!

We always tried out steps at home. My family worked on the music and even the lighting at home. My grandmother would stop in to make suggestions about music, since she was a musician. And my other grandmother was an expert at making costumes. We never quarreled or argued or fought about anything at home except dance steps and dance ideas and ballets. Can you imagine a huge fight over whether a leg should be straight or bent![1]

After a long cab ride to the working-class district of Marianao, I reach the massive building, which was once a Spanish Cavalry stable, that houses Centro Pro-Danza, the ballet company founded and directed by Laura Alonso. I climb its imposing marble staircase, and then Jorge Luis, Laura's assistant, escorts me to her office. I accept a cup of irresistible Cuban coffee from him. Dancers enter the office to select pointe shoes from a large box that members of the Board of Directors of American Ballet Theatre have brought to the festival.

After Laura and I spend a few minutes catching up, I reveal the purpose of my visit. I am here to ask for the specifics of her father's method. "You are asking the right person," she says, flashing a sparkling smile. "I did all the dirty work after he gave them the scientific explanations." "Manos sucias?" I ask, citing the second half of a famous Spanish saying, "Manos finas mandan; manos sucias matan" [Fine hands issue the command; soiled hands carry out the killing]. She laughs in agreement, "Yes!" It is well known that her men's classes are demanding and unforgiving.

With a nod in the direction of the two flights of marble steps I had just climbed, she says, "Everything in the curriculum should be like a staircase. Each step, each set of steps in an exercise is constructed after finishing and mastering the previous ones. We begin with tendu." (Fernando later adds that the tendu is closest to the natural step we use when walking.) "But we teach it so that the student can feel the change in tempo and spirit afforded by the music. We do tendu for the first week," Laura continues ("and also demi plié," Fernando adds later]) "because this is the basis for the *glissade* [lateral slide along floor]." Fernando says that the glissade is, practically speaking, the basis for all movement, much in the same way that the evolved human descended from the tree. "It's all there in the film, *The Ascent of Man*," he says. "Have you seen it?" I nod.

"We then move to *degagé* [quick outward extension of working leg]," Laura says, "since that is the basis for *assemblé* [jump that brings legs together]." Fernando points out that the assemblé closes in the air, not upon landing, "but before, so that both feet come straight down—the Italian way, just how Zanfretta taught it to Alicia."

Laura explains that the syllabus details classes month by month, with the first class gradually building up to the concluding one. "We have them start to partner as young as possible—the boy and girl open the curtain, dance the mazurka and the waltz—to accustom the boys to the girls so that they are not afraid of them. "Every three months, teachers meet to refresh their method, and every year there is a seminar to exchange views on how it is going.

"What distinguishes us is our practice of analyzing and deconstructing every step. I recently figured out how to teach the basics of the barrel turn using the barre." Using her desk as a barre, Laura faces it and places both hands on its edge. She does a quarter *piqué* turn [turn initiated on a pointed foot from a stretched leg] to the right *en déhors* [outward], so that she is in *écarté* [facing outward on a diagonal]. Then she extends her right leg and comes completely around to face *en dedans* [inward], and ends up with both hands holding the edge of the desk. "It really works!" she enthuses like someone who has just shared a favorite remedy.

A visitor arrives, and then our time is up because Laura is moving that day and must meet the moving van at her home. When Fernando learns that I have had productive meetings with Loipa and Laura, he invites me to his home in Miramar to listen to my notes and add comments of his own.

"You use nine different muscles in the ronds de jambs. They prepare you for *grand battement* [high kick]. You must stretch the joints in your knees until you feel that you can completely straighten them in *développé* [gradual opening of working leg from bent to straightened]. We teach them to spot with the eyes immediately, and coordinate the use of the head and eyes. The mirror is the dancer's biggest enemy—don't use it! Notice the speed of the movement. The artistic elements will vary with age, feeling, and state of mind, and they are different for the male and female partners. The task at hand is to match all the elements to create a beautiful pas de deux.

"The first thing I teach in partnering is that the boy must follow the speed of the girl. The leading partner in the pas de deux is the woman. The man has to make her look beautiful, lovely, sensual, and open the path for her to interpret the role. He's responsible: that is the guiding principle of the pas de deux. If something goes wrong, he will be at fault. He must understand this because it develops his sense of manliness. This is why girls love to dance with Cuban boys. They tell me, 'The more I dance with him, the more feminine I feel, the more I want to make him feel manly.' The pas de deux is not a unisex enterprise."

There is a final gala that we must attend later in the evening, but Fernando wants to add something about music. "When we went to New York, we had the pleasure of taking class to accompaniment by wonderful concert pianists. Their music made you want to dance. Since my own mother was a pianist, and artists such as Ernesto Lecuona and my mother played together, I was fortunate to have been surrounded all my life by good musicians. We had three pianos in our house, two grand pianos and a spinet. When the 1926 hurricane arrived, the first things we covered were the pianos. I listened to music all the time and lived within the romantic world of my mother's music. I fell in love with her students because I loved listening to the girls play for her.

"Most important to remember: As you teach, you learn."

13

A Revolutionary Proposal

What kind of oversight was available to the company and school?

By 1950, all kinds of issues were competing for attention. The Ministry of Education had authorized the Fine Arts Board to pay an annual subsidy of thirty-three thousand pesos to the ballet. It was not enough to cover our operating expenses, and especially insulting in face of the company's cachet, but at least it staved off financial disasters of the kind that had plagued the company earlier, which we had had to spend valuable time resolving. The annual subsidy made it possible to become a viable operation for six years, until 1956, at which time the Batista dictatorship abruptly suspended its support.

We traveled to Mexico City during our third international tour. By the end of two years, we had managed to stabilize Ballet Alicia Alonso. The company danced regularly at the Auditorium Theater. The academy was progressing well, and with patience and perspective we were sowing the seeds that would bear fruit in a few years' time. Each new performance met with a warmer and warmer reception. Audiences grew in size, as well as in their level of education and enthusiasm.

The company's fourth international tour traveled to the cities of Santurce, Arecibo, San Germán, Ponce, and San Juan in Puerto Rico; to Miami, Florida; and to Valencia, Barquisimeto, and Caracas in Venezuela. We brought along four new works: *Fiesta negra*, *Lydia*, *Capriccio espagnol*, and *Paganini*. The growing repertoire reflected our artistic lineage, tracing it from its beginnings.

We showed classical ballet in all of its forms and presented a montage of Cuban works. Our goal was to contribute to the development of a national style and a school suffused with a belief in ballet's universality, but with its own characteristics, interpreted by a Cuban company. At this stage in its development the company enjoyed the luxury of dancing in a style derived from Afro-Cuban, peasant, or indigenous forms. It danced with more certainty with each new show. We honored our national composers, choreographers, and stage designers. All of this contributed to a unique stamp that would inevitably distinguish our body of work.

At this time we turned our attention to placing Sol Hurok's proposal back on the table: to carry out a company tour to countries in the Western Hemisphere and Europe. And then again as in 1949, the proposal was frustrated by the Cuban government's denial of the twenty-five thousand pesos that were necessary to make the tour possible. We maintained an optimistic attitude, and I issued the following statement: "Ballet Alicia Alonso has faith in the future of our country and in the Cuban people's natural talent and eagerness to overcome, and because of that, I firmly believe that, just as in France, Russia and England, where ballet was successfully grafted, in just a few years it will have taken root as something quite natural—Cuba can become one of the world's brightest ballet hubs."[1]

In June 1952, with the Hurok contract once again off limits, we undertook our fifth international tour, this time to Caracas and Bogotá. Our repertoire continued to broaden. During that year we premiered *Toque*, *Habana 1830*, *La fille mal gardée*, *Mefisto*, *El pilletee*, *Un concierto en blanco y negro*, and the first-act pas de deux from *Swan Lake*. Ramiro Guerra's *Toque* in four parts—invocación, ritual, danza de antepasado, and danza del origen—premiered on February 9, danced by Carlota Pereyra, Beatriz Lismore, and Victor Álvarez.

The Cuban intellectual Fernando Ortiz wrote:

> When the lights went down in the Havana Auditorium, between the dancing and the music, [the company] chanced to reach a goal that will have conferred upon Cuba a cross-cultural aesthetic from which it has been separated by bodies of water and bygone eras and the most advanced techniques, tastes and art forms of the present day, yet entering solidly among the swiftly moving clouds in which the future dawns. The art of yesterday, today and nearly of tomorrow, art "from below" and "from above"; art with a Cuban soul . . . "just Cuban," but in her complete and glorious national integrity, translated into the language of universal vibrancy. Why hasn't Cuba allowed herself to achieve what is considered art in other countries? She could have flowering beauty if she doesn't deny her deepest roots, nor rich flavor, and knows how to breathe air into her leafy foliage in the most elevated currents of contemporary culture.[2]

How did extruding Cuba's authentic culture feed the company's creative life?

The aesthetic process underlying the "art with a Cuban soul" started in Ballet Alicia Alonso with *Fiesta negra*, which premiered in 1951. Afterward, *Toque* appeared with the same intentions. In search of what was truly Cuban, *Versos y bailes*, *Estampas cubanas*, and *Sóngaro cosongo* premiered in 1953.

Did the work you were doing resonate with others outside of Cuba who were striving to revive an authentic Latin American cultural identity?

Politically speaking, defense of the Latin American identity established itself as one of the key points in the proceedings of the Continental Culture Congress. It took place in Santiago de Chile in March and April 1953, organized by the poet Pablo Neruda. Gabriela Mistral, Baldemero Sanín Cano, Oscar Niemeyer, Cándido Portinari, Diego Rivera, and other leading intellectuals of the period attended the Congress. I wasn't able to attend, but I sent a proposal to the plenary, which was read by Nicolás Guillén, who was Cuba's National Poet [see appendix G]. The proposal focused on dance in contemporary society and the arrogance with which the state assumes a protective role. The monarchies and their respective patrons had initiated this practice in colonial times. I pointed to the indifference that existed in the majority of countries. In spite of dance's increasing popularity in the twentieth century, ballet continually faced financial obstacles.

The proposal underscored the necessarily indissoluble interrelationship between classical ballet training in its purest form and the national ballet company of each country. It suggested that the canons of classical training could favorably influence the development of popular dance forms and, as such, over time, transmit their vigor, force, rhythm, gestures, and conceptualizations. Based on that thesis, it proposed a project to the Congress: to create a Latin American dance company and school with the goal of integrating "Nuestra America" [Our America] on its own terrain. It cited Ballet Alicia Alonso as an example, which, in just a little more than four years, had been able to mount productions of the highest quality.

Soon after the Chilean Congress, I was "invited" to the United States Embassy in Havana. Once I had arrived, it was made clear to me by the North Americans there that my presence wasn't especially welcome. The U.S. Embassy withdrew my work visa to travel in the United States, a measure that created obstacles for me for decades.

What happened to the proposal itself?

Not only did the idea of a national Latin American company not come to fruition, neither did major state support from nationally recognized groups, as true for Cuba as the other Latin American countries, and so our company continued to receive only the tiny subsidy it had been allotted; any additional application or request for funds was discouraged. This became evident once again when the impresario Anatole Heller contacted me with a proposal to hire the company to tour Europe the following year. Heller had hired Ballet Theatre for two tours of Europe, a good indication that we would be assured serious, organized, and successful tours under his sponsorship. The letter proposing the company tour stated that it would have to "serve the interests of its country, having an unquestionably cultural mission that would fulfill and in principle have to be accepted by your government."

How did the Cuban government respond?

The Cuban government once again turned a deaf ear to requests for aid. But the company's oeuvre, the enthusiasm of its members and our work, did not suffer on account of these rejections. On the contrary, each adversity fired up our eagerness to continue to reach for greater successes. During negotiations with Heller, I premiered a second choreographic work in which I assisted Mary Skeaping and Charles Dickson. After eleven years, I went back to trying my hand at this kind of commitment. This time I worked on a full version of *The Nutcracker* in two acts, based on the original by Lev Ivanov. The premiere was in October at the Auditorium Theater, with costumes and sets by Andrés García and Armando Fernán. Alicia Alonso and Royes Fernández danced the leads.

We ended the 1953 season with company performances in the Auditorium Theater from October to December. Besides reviving familiar works, we introduced *Delirium*, the thirty-fourth ballet to enter our repertoire.

With all of the struggles to establish the company, how were you able to find time for a personal life?

Breeding birds was one of my personal interests during that period. I had some mockingbirds in my home; I took an interest in the problem related to Mendel's theory of cross-fertilization and the key elements in this process. I crossbred canaries of varying colors and got a red one. I had three mockingbirds that I had named Attila, Alejandro, and Genghis Khan. In an especially zealous period, around February, some of those mockingbirds began singing at 2 A.M., and the entire neighborhood knew who they were!

That was tremendous! I made a few recordings of me whistling and then played them for the mockingbirds to listen to. That's how they learned the Cuban National Anthem and the popular songs "Donde estás, que no tel veo," "Toque de Diana," and others. When someone entered the house, the birds would whistle just as Cuban men do at beautiful women.

And what about speleology, and cave explorations?

During the 1940s, I made the acquaintance of Dr. Antonio Núñez Jímenez, who would eventually become the president of the Spelunkers Society, as well as a leading figure in the struggle against Batista. When Nuñez Jímenez began to work for the ballet, I discovered that he had an interest in exploring caves and caverns. His enthusiasm for spelunking was contagious, and I decided to join the society. I accompanied Núñez, Angela Grau, Favio González, the poet Rolando Escardó, and a Dr. Valcárcel and his wife in explorations and excavations in the provinces of Havana and Pinar del Río. We explored Las Faldas del Castillo del Principe, la Cueva de los Predones, la Sierra del Rosario, la Cueva del Indio, la Gran Caverna de Santo Tomás, and others. I even joined an expedition sponsored by the University of Frankfurt on the Main in the Sierra de los Organos. I celebrated my fortieth birthday in the Gran Caverna de Santo Tomás with the peasants of that region. I remained in the cavern for eleven days without seeing the light of day. We were able to chart twenty-one kilometers of cavern galleries. One of them was named after me! After 1959, I gave up pursuing my interest in birds and cave explorations so that I could fully devote my time to my vocation of ballet master and teacher.

14

Batista's Blackmail Bid

At what point would you say that Ballet Alicia Alonso had entered the "big leagues"?

On January 24, 1954, I became the general director of Ballet Alicia Alonso. The company appeared for the first time at the Auditorium Theater with a full-length *Swan Lake* in four acts. Cuba became the fourth nation in the world, after the Soviet Union, England, and Denmark, to claim a company that could mount the work in its entirety. Neither Italy nor France nor the United States had staged a four-act *Swan Lake*.

How did you approach mounting such an enormous production?

The staging was Mary Skeaping's, based on the London Sadler's Wells 1934 Nicolas Sergeyev production, which itself had been based on the original work by Marius Petipa and Lev Ivanov. We placed Luis Márquez and Alicia's mother, Ernestina del Hoyo, in charge of the design elements, which we wanted to remain as faithful as possible to John Skeaping's in the English version. Enrique González Mántici conducted the orchestra. Alicia danced Odette/Odile, Royes Fernández danced Siegfried, Charles Dickson was Von Rothbart, and I danced Benno, Siegried's friend. Other cast members were Laura Alonso, Carlota Pereyra, Menia Martínez, José Parés, Joaquín Banegas, Mirta Plá, and Ramona de Sáa.

Dance critics and the public saw it as a complete success, and the show attracted full-house audiences. The opening coincided with a deepening of the political polarization in Cuba. Batista represented the reactionary wing, having surrendered the country's resources to U.S.-controlled business interests. Since the majority of Cubans were opposed to his policies, he faced increasing opposition in the form of mass protests, led by Fidel Castro, and the July 26th Movement.

Were there artists among the protesters?

The Second Biennial Hispano-American Art Exhibition opened on May 18, 1954. The Batista government sponsored it. This angered many artists in Cuba, and it was repudiated in a big campaign in which a large number of intellectuals participated. The University Student Federation was among the organizations to raise an outcry. The students organized the First University Art Festival on May 20 as a counter-exhibition. It continued through August, just as the official exhibition did. Ballet Alicia Alonso participated by presenting its full-length *Swan Lake* at the University Stadium, sponsored by the federation's Cultural Department, and underwritten by La Polar brewery. We decided that it would be the ballet company's farewell to the Cuban public. At the end of the summer the company would embark on its sixth international tour, this time to Buenos Aires, Santiago de Chile, and Montevideo.

I had remained in Cuba without interruption since we founded the company in 1948. In 1953, during the McCarthy period in the United States, they denied me entry to the country. They said that my communist political ideas posed a threat to U.S. security. But in 1954 they made an exception and allowed me to go to Los Angeles, California, to participate in a broadcast of the TV program *This Is Your Life*. This was a show where a "random audience member" is selected by the master of ceremonies, brought to the stage, and surprised by the appearance of key figures in his or her life. Alicia was to be the random audience member.

They brought a group of us there who were linked to Alicia's life and hid us, so that she would not see us until the last minute. She had no idea that the program was going to be about her.

Did the tours provide adequate funds to keep the company in the black?

By 1955, Ballet Alicia Alonso was a viable national company, despite the absence of official backing. After more than six years of performing, this national company had shared a distinctive body of work with the public in six international tours across the Western Hemisphere. We had an ample repertoire, a successfully functioning academy, and performances in Havana for the public each year, as well as in the outlying provinces. The company's prestige extended across oceans. Recognized impresarios had proposed company tours to Europe and the United States, which would have gone forward were it not for the obstacles thrown up by the Batista government. We came to the conclusion that the moment had arrived to change the company's name. Up to that point, Alicia's name had served to amass goodwill and promote collective work, but circumstances now favored a name more in keeping with the plans we had always had in mind: to give to our country a company that truly represented our national culture. In 1955 we adopted the name Ballet de Cuba. The company danced under its new name on July 2, at the Second University Arts Festival. We closed the year with a series of shows from September to December, at the Auditorium Theater. We added three new ballets—*Sinfonía clásica*, *Ensueño*, and *Narciso y Eco*—to the repertoire. The seventh international tour took the dancers to Atlantic City. But there were not enough funds to carry the company through the 1956 season. Cuba was undergoing a period of extreme repression by Batista. When popular resistance reached its peak, Fidel Castro announced from Mexico that this year "we free ourselves or become martyrs."

Did the dancers take a stand?

On the cultural front, the branch of the National Institute under the direction of Guillermo de Zéndegui was ordered to set official policy.

Zéndegui proposed that we collaborate with the regime. If we agreed to cooperate, all the necessary facilities would become available; but to refuse would place us back in that nightmare of uncertainty. In other words, it was blackmail. We did not vacillate for one second. We voted unanimously to reject the government's proposal, and in a letter we made it clear to them that we were prepared to face the consequences of not "playing ball" with Batista. Most important was what came out of it; the events that followed resulted in a huge victory for revolutionary-minded Cubans.

What came out of it?

Well, Batista had made an offer that he was certain the ballet company could not refuse. When we rejected it, the government suspended its entire subsidy to Ballet de Cuba. At the same time, it initiated a defamation campaign against the company and its prima ballerina, Alicia Alonso, taking measures that ended up backfiring on those very officials who initiated the slander campaign. The Ballet de Cuba and its directors were accused of "exclusivity" and building an enterprise that was "at odds with the national interest."

Did the company respond?

The dancers made their response plain in an open letter that Alicia addressed to Zéndegui and signed in the company's name. She sought the advice of Mirta Aguirre and Carlos Rafael Rodríguez, two leaders of the

Cuban protest movement who helped with the drafting of the letter. The letter spelled out the monetary *dis*interest that characterized Ballet de Cuba's mission. It referred to the artistic effort that had extended over nearly eight years, and it completely rejected the so-called inducements offered by the Batista regime.

Here is an excerpt from Alicia Alonso's letter: "We have faith in the Cuban people and are certain that in defending their legitimate right to culture we can count on their commitment not to permit this artistic movement to be disarmed."[1]

Was there a response to the letter?

A confrontation between the ballet and the dictatorship took place at a performance on September 15. Leaders of the University Student Federation and the Committee in Defense of the Ballet de Cuba who organized it saw it as a tribute to the company's achievements. It was held at the University Stadium. The corps de ballet's performance was broadcast on two Cuban TV channels, and patrons in several of the most well known cabarets in Havana saw it. To everyone's surprise, a leader of the revolution, Fructuoso Rodríguez, appeared onstage. He offered words of solidarity with the company. When you take into account that the young fellow was at that time living a clandestine life, underground, this was an impressive act of courage, kindness, and support!

We presented *Les sylphides*. I danced, along with Carlota Pereyra, Ada Zanetti, and Beatriz Lismore, and Alicia danced *The Dying Swan*. This event marked my farewell to the stage. I was in my forties, and had spent nineteen years dancing. Two basic factors made me decide to retire: my age, which was fairly advanced for a dancer, and my calling to teach: it was a vocation that absorbed all of my time and effort, and I knew even then that I would value it above all else for the rest of my life.

Those final performances were actually a protest tour on stages across the country, the very last one being in the city of Matanzas on November 15, 1956. After eight very productive years, and because of an arbitrary decision by a brutal dictatorship, Cuba's first professional ballet company crumbled. But we had left behind a stellar legacy in advancing the national culture. During those eight years we built a repertoire of thirty-eight ballets. Among them were full versions of classics such as *Swan Lake*, *Coppélia*, *La fille mal gardée, Giselle, Les sylphides,* and *The Nutcracker,* as well as important works in the idiom of the first half of the twentieth century, such as *Afternoon of a Faun, Le spectre de la rose,* and *Peter and the Wolf.* The company had produced seventeen ballets by such Cuban choreographers as Alberto Alonso, Ramiro Guerra, and Enrique Martín.

Important figures who danced with the company included Alicia Alonso, Igor Youskevitch, Barbara Fallis, Royes Fernández, Melissa Hayden, Michael Maule, Nicolás Magallanes, Carlota Pereyra, Lupe Serrano, Vicente Nebreda, and Charles Dickson. Regular cast members included Mia Slavenska, André Eglevsky, Nora Kaye, and John Kriza, as guests, and the following dancers appeared in special performances: Jean Babilée, Alexandra Danilova, Nathalie Phillipart, and Roman Jasinsky. International choreographers who worked with the company included Léon Fokine, José Parés, and Mary Skeaping; as well as such orchestra directors as Max Goberman, Benjamin Steinberg, Enrique González Mántici, Alberto Bolet, and Manuel Duchesne Cuzán.

With seven international tours under our belt we had presented these works in thirteen Latin American countries and the United States, as well as in the first public performances sponsored by a national company. We had brought presentations to the provinces and had trained stagehands and technicians in specialized crafts. We had built the academy and assumed responsibility for initiating invaluable discussions, contributions, and proposals for a national culture in which dance could thrive. By 1956, I was beginning to think that all of this had been for naught. I retired from the stage, the company was dissolved, and there seemed to be no future prospects for the academy's students and graduating class.

15

The Soviet Union
Invites the Alonsos

Did any remnant of your work survive?

Only the academy survived, and I remained its director. We accepted young ladies with little to offer by way of talent, so that the institution could sustain itself financially. In studios L and 11 in the Vedado neighborhood, we offered small performances behind closed doors. There was a sliding entrance fee—from twenty centavos to one peso. One hundred or maybe two hundred people would attend. So there were still a few creative opportunities for dancers and choreographers to take advantage of.

In 1957, I had choreographed my third and final piece, *Divagaciones*. I created it for an academy showcase. It made use of a recurring theme in ballet class as a way to expose a series of dance-related concepts. There is a film of it in the Cuban Institute of Cinemagraphic Art and Industry archives, and some of our most outstanding students appear in it.

At the end of the year, Alicia received an invitation to dance in Russia—then the Soviet Union—the first classical ballerina in the Americas to have been invited there. Beryl Grey from England and Liane Daydé from France were also invited. Alicia called me from New York to tell me that the invitation was extended to me as well, and both of us traveled to what we at that time viewed as the mecca of ballet. Alicia danced there from December 1957 to January 1958.

Her success was immediate, with her Giselle praised to the heavens by the Soviets. There were standing ovations in Riga, Leningrad, and Moscow. The tour was such a triumph that they wanted to know *how* the Cuban training method produced such a polished style! So I was invited to teach a master class in Leningrad, now St. Petersburg. I taught the class under the scrutiny not only of the directors and teachers but a gathering of students as well—everyone from beginners to principal dancers! Each arrived with a notebook in hand. Rudolf Nureyev cut company class to take my class along with Menia Martínez, whom he knew and was close to, because they had studied together at the Kirov.

How did it feel to receive that kind of recognition after suffering such a defeat at home?

There was something overwhelming about it, because in that moment in Leningrad there was everything of value, everything that shined! When I appeared before all those people I felt as if I were on top of the world!

In the Soviet Union we came in direct contact for the first time with the grand Russian tradition, brought to the widest possible audience during the Soviet era. It was such an enriching experience to tour the academy facilities! I could see what it meant for dancers to receive such extraordinary state support, and how much value the Soviet public placed on this. More than anything, we were able to see that not only were there talented individuals in the Soviet Union, but huge, mature, perfectly organized companies in which distinguished stars were born. In such companies, the corps de ballet and leading dancers appeared as one harmonious entity onstage when seen from the perspective of the audience.

What distinguished the dancers?

I noticed that they danced with a fluidity and grace, whereas we tended to fall into a kind of rigidity. Because of this, beginning with this visit, I began to make a few changes; above all, to use this as a point of reference for creating beautiful port de bras.

I felt an immediate need to both assimilate what I had learned and dispense those lessons just as quickly, so that we could enrich the Cuban syllabus.

Were there any consequences when you returned to Cuba after having visited the Soviet Union during the McCarthy "Red Scare" period in the United States?

During the return trip via Lisbon, a Cuban flight attendant approached me and, chatting in a familiar way said, "I guessed that you were on a return flight to Cuba because since [the departure of] your previous flight, my uncle, who is in the Intelligence Service, has been waiting for your party in the Rancho Boyeros Airport." So it came as no surprise to us when Cuban government agents who had been stationed there, took me to the offices of the Bureau of Repression of Communist Activities, where a Lieutenant

Castaño detained me for several hours, and that was how another "offense" was added to the list of those that had generated police interest in me. By that time, the political situation had reached a critical point.

What was taking place?

The Batista regime's days were numbered. The clandestine struggle in the mountains and engagements in the cities had weakened its position. Support for the revolutionary movement was massive. Dr. Julio Martínez Páez, the public figure most associated with the ballet in Cuba, had joined the armed rebel detachments. But not even in the midst of such urgent activities did he forget his love of dance. The leadership of the revolutionary movement, with a view toward the nation's future after the victory, set aside time to study cultural projects. Dr. Martínez Páez asked me to draft a proposal for the reorganization of the company, which I did. The triumph of the revolutionary forces over the dictatorship was near. Finally, with takeover of the Presidential Palace in January 1959, Batista's regime came to an end. It was only a matter of a few months before conditions would come about that would make it possible to realize our lifelong dream for a truly authentic and viable ballet company on the island.

Después (After)

16

Cuban Revolution Triumphs— and Invests in Ballet!

On January 1, 1959, bolstered by a well-organized student movement, Cuban workers and farmers decisively defeated the Fulgencio Batista dictatorship, which in its seven-year campaign to crush them and their organizations had suspended the most elementary of democratic, civil, and human rights. A revolutionary government came to power. It mobilized every available resource to rebuild Cuba into an independent, literate, self-acting nation. In short order it would expropriate the wealth Cubans produced for U.S.-owned sugar and tobacco interests and invest it in the social wage of the beleaguered working-class majority. This required a profound transformation, a massive, deep-going restructuring challenging every layer of society to shed old ways and invent a new habitat for what the Argentine-born Cuban revolutionary Ernesto "Che" Guevara termed "the construction of Socialist Man."

Former members of the dissolved Cuban National Ballet were not inclined to stand idly by as volunteer literacy brigades took to the countryside to teach peasants how to read, and block by block, Cubans elected Committees in Defense of the Revolution, and proposed and voted for sugarcane quotas, with newly organized cane-cutting brigades drawing members from every strata of the population to maximize the harvest of the island's cash crop.

In a public declaration offered via the press, the dancers warmly welcomed the revolutionary forces and also reminded the newly formed government that the ballet company had been among those on the front lines fighting Batista's tyranny. They paid tribute to Dr. Julio Martínez Páez, who had been a medical student during the Machado regime. On September 22, 1930, during a demonstration, Martínez Páez was detained. Later, he was ar-

rested on the same night as the student activist Félix Alpízar was murdered. His medical studies were interrupted because the Machado regime had impressed him into service as an intern at the General Calixto García Hospital. After the fall of Machado, he resumed his studies and graduated. He met the young lawyer Fidel Castro and the revolutionary activist Camilo Cienfuegos. In 1957, Martínez Páez joined the July 26th Movement. After an exile in Mexico following several arrests, he was summoned by Castro to join the Sierra Maestra guerrilla forces to direct the rebel army's medical detachment. There, he fought alongside the others and rose to the rank of commander in the battle of La Plata.

•

What brought Dr. Julio Martínez Páez into the orbit of ballet?

After the victory, Martínez Páez specialized in orthopedic surgery. Later, in his eighties, he began the study of English and Marxist philosophy and pursued interests in nature, painting, music, and the ballet. By recognizing his contribution, the dancers wanted to show their confidence in the changes taking place.

In a published statement, the company offered, "with all its enthusiasm and capacity, a platform from which to reach for that great destiny which would make it possible for art and culture to arrive in the furthest corners of our nation, embarking on a promissory era that would augur for the development of the national culture, concurring with our [national hero] José Martí that 'the only way to be free is to be enlightened.'"

How did *you* view the new government?

The new government promised to satisfy the aspirations that for many years had fired the imaginations of those with forward-looking ideas. It was essential to embrace such a government. That's how I viewed it, having been general director of the dissolved Ballet de Cuba, and I encouraged the oldest members of the company to support the revolutionary measures. On February 3, as a symbolic gesture, we mounted a gala at the Teatro Blanquita. Alicia danced with our special guest Igor Youskevitch to celebrate the reappearance of the Ballet de Cuba after a three-and-a-half-year forced recess.

We repeated the program on February 15, this time as a *tribute* to the rebel army and the new revolutionary government.

Then something occurred that completely altered the future development of Cuban ballet. I was in our apartment on L Street, between Eleventh and Thirteenth, at about midnight. Alicia wasn't in Cuba. I heard the doorbell ring, Laura answered it, and it was Captain Antonio Nuñez Jiménez. He told me, "I've come with a friend," and I answered, "Come on upstairs." So they came up the stairs, and when they got to my room I saw that his friend was Fidel.

I had been in bed reading. Fidel sat right down on the bed. Nuñez sat in a chair to the side of the bed. We began a conversation about the North American imperialists, and then about the political culture of the revolution and a thousand other subjects. Fidel was gesticulating, and at one point his hand bumped into his glasses and they fell onto the bed.

We spoke until 2:30 or 3:00 A.M., I don't remember exactly. Fidel took a quick look at one of his watches and exclaimed, "Nuñez, look, we're keeping this fellow up; let's go—it's already so late!"

When we began walking downstairs, Fidel turned toward me and said: "Listen, here it is that I came to talk about the ballet and we haven't discussed the ballet at all!" I quickly answered, "We still have time!" So he asked me, "How much money do you need to reorganize the ballet?" I said to him, "One hundred thousand pesos a year," thinking that I had named an impossible figure. He then replied: "We'll give you two hundred thousand, but you have to guarantee that it will be a good company."

It was in this simple, straightforward manner that Fidel Castro entrusted the restructuring of the national ballet company to me, of course with Alicia and my brother Alberto as essential members of the team. The new government's confidence in us put an end to the financial worries. From now on, the dancers could dedicate themselves fully to making it a good company. It also signaled the immense value Castro placed on our work. It grew into an inestimable quotient of moral support. This is how I became the only Cuban artist to be commissioned personally by Fidel, and supported with substantial material resources—to undertake a task whose goal was to advance ballet! It was a great responsibility, and for me it served in no small way to renew my enthusiasm for continuing our work.

It must have been tremendously reassuring to have been approached in this way by Fidel Castro, but did the government offer official recognition?

On May 20, 1960, the president of the Republic and minister of education signed into law the Revolutionary Government Act no. 812, guaranteeing the future of the company, which Fidel Castro signed. [See appendix H for text of Law 812.] It recognized the existence of a dance tradition in Cuba and stated, "The Ballet de Cuba will be employed in all official activities requiring ballet in its various styles, and it will lead . . . to the biggest and most exemplary diffusion of this artistic genre throughout the republic."[1]

With passage of 812, Ballet de Cuba assumed official responsibility for shouldering the standard of that tradition. We had been playing that role unofficially for many years, but 812 guaranteed the company's inclusion in the revolutionary government's cultural program under the oversight of the general director of the Ministry of Culture and Education.

What were the provisions?

Now, under law, all Cuban children were mandated to receive an equal education, such that those in the countryside would have the same opportunities as those in the cities. At the age of nine years old or the fourth grade, children with apparent dance talent could now attend a vocational school near their home if they passed their first dance test. Their second exam would take place when they were twelve, after completion of the sixth grade. At that point, the students were selected by audition.

What were the criteria for selection?

The criteria were body structure, health, physical facility, and dance technique level. To pass meant to go on to the National School of the Arts, initially at Cubanacán, where the student joined six hundred to seven hundred arts students, of which about eighty were ballet students. The company was no longer private property, but instead became the property of the Cuban people.

Did the government pass the law and then leave the rest to you?

We continued talking, and as a result of a subsequent discussion with Castro, where he emphasized how important it was that the company be composed of dancers from all of the Americas, *including the United States*, we circulated a call to join the Ballet de Cuba across all the Americas, and artists responded. In the summer of 1959 we convened an international jury to select dancers. Serving on it were the North American dance critic Ann Barzel, dancers Alexandra Danilova and Igor Youskevitch, and the teacher, Anna Leontieva. We selected forty dancers. Among them were Mirta Plá,

Joaquín Banegas, José Parés, Laura Alonso, Loipa Araújo, Aurora Bosch, Josefina Méndez, Margarita de Sáa, Ramona de Sáa, Ceferino Barrios, Eduardo Recalt, and Adolfo Roval. Many came from classes that I had taught. Alicia and Youskevitch were the principal dancers. I functioned as general director and president of the Artistic Commission. The company Board of Directors consisted of Alicia as honorary president, Dr. Julio Martínez Páez as president, and Dr. Antonio Nuñez Jímenez, Alberto, and myself as the three vice-presidents. Other board members were Haydée Santamaría [recognized internationally as an outstanding combatant in the Revolutionary Army], Angela Grau, José Ardévol, Delia Echeverría, Alfredo Guevara, Enrique González Mántici, Manuel Corrales, Manuel Duchesne Cuzán, and Blanca Martínez del Hoyo.

How did you broaden the composition of the school and company?

The ballet academy began advertising contests in local newspapers to attract new scholarship students, including Afro-Cubans. It toured orphanages and discovered talent among children there. Over time the number of Afro-Cuban company dancers increased, with many more men than women.

When did the company resume a regular season?

Ballet de Cuba opened on September 17, at the Auditorium Theater, with *Giselle*. On October 1 we left for a tour of South America. We went in the role of cultural ambassador, carrying a message of brotherhood and solidarity to those who drew inspiration from the Cuban Revolution.

For the first time in Latin America there was a printed handbill for a tour, and it was also the first time that a touring company presented full-length ballets: *Swan Lake* in four acts, *Coppélia* in three acts, and *Giselle* in two acts, with no cuts. We toured Venezuela, Brazil, Uruguay, Argentina, Chile, Peru, and Ecuador and received press notices.

Montevideo's *La mañana* wrote: "One finds Fernando Alonso as one of the key elements in the Cuban choreographic group. Under his direction, the Ballet de Cuba has undertaken an effort towards popular acculturation of an unquestionably transcendent nature, crossing the Island in several different tours, and mounting open air presentations in stadiums, public squares, as well as in its seasons in Havana, for which one must credit him in great measure with the Ballet de Cuba's finally having reached the highest pinnacle."[2]

Now that you had government support, did all finally go well on tour?

From the beginning of this tour, we sensed reactionary pressures operating internationally. They seemed to be bent on crushing the revolutionary process under way in Cuba. At this point, a five-year period began during which the crudest of efforts were undertaken from abroad to enforce the U.S. blockade of Cuban ballet as part of a larger strategy directed at "destabilizing" the revolution. Of course, this only resulted in even more determination on the part of the island to strengthen its position.

Why do you think ballet was a target?

The reasons were not artistic in nature. Pointe shoes are not conventional assault weapons. For the United States, any successes registered by our little island were seen as a provocation—even those of our highly successful ballet company.

Did touring continue in spite of this?

The seven-country Latin American tour would be the last of its kind on that continent during that period. When it came time for a second tour in 1960, they exerted political pressure on governments under their influence *not* to engage us. Only Mexico would receive us.

On October 19, 1960, U.S. president Dwight D. Eisenhower imposed a trade embargo against Cuba, with travel restrictions added by President John F. Kennedy. The result was a wholesale trade and travel blockade of Cuba, with an ensuing "secondary boycott" aimed at intimidating third-party U.S. allies engaged in commercial transactions with Cuba. Except for President James Carter, each succeeding U.S. president has either added restrictions or conditions to the blockade or chosen to enforce existing ones more stringently.

Did the blockade reprise obstacles that the company faced in the early years?

From the end of 1960 until 1965, Ballet de Cuba toured twice, but only in Eastern Europe. The fifth tour, at the end of 1966, was very special. By the summer of 1964 the First International Ballet Festival had taken place in Varna, Bulgaria. The progress of Cuban ballet had been very obvious there, with the West beginning to see what we had been doing in Cuba, even a few years prior to the revolution. So, the National Ballet of Cuba was invited to Paris to participate in the Fourth International Festival of Dance. Apart from Mexico, the trip would be the first embargo-era visit by the company to a country outside of Eastern Europe.

How did the critics receive you?

There were, of course, tributes to Alicia's exceptional artistry, as well as recognition of the mastery the Cuban dancers had achieved as a company.

In Bucharest's newspaper *The Contemporary*, Toma Maiorescu pointed to the pedagogical work as the basis for the company's cutting-edge successes. The seven-month tour generated interest and support for the Cuban Revolution among Eastern Europeans, where spirit of the kind shown by the Cuban company had been systematically discouraged by the *bureaucratized officialdom there*. He wrote that there was "close contact with workers, adoring audiences, professional artists, etc., of the various countries that were visited, allowing the Ballet to collectively gain experiences in the role of artists who are part of a new society."[3]

Did the touring shift your focus away from performing for Cuban audiences?

No, not at all! We began to share what we had learned on tour even more directly with the Cuban people. We went to factories, schools, hospitals, places where workers congregated, communication centers, town squares, church plazas, and military bases. Our goal was to bring the art form closer to the majority of the people. We went where there were no real theaters, and performed on flatbed trucks. We urged the workers in these remote areas to view ballet as their art form, as a great artistic mobilization for the people to enjoy. Attendance grew in direct proportion to these efforts.[4]

Where does the secret to the success of the Cuban company lie?

It can be found in the presence of a ballet school with a unified pedagogical system, scientifically constituted, which bears the seal of the fully and profoundly classical style.

Between 1968 and 1974 the Cuban National Ballet carried out six international tours, substantially weakening the ballet embargo. Critics offered their high praise for the ballet master and general director of the company. Mexico's *Excelsior* reported, "The Cuban National Ballet is in this art form, one of

the most seasoned, most articulated companies in the aesthetic and professional sense, thanks to Fernando Alonso's intelligent direction and the great
ballerina Alicia Alonso."[5]

**Do you believe that the ballet company has crossed borders that
other Cuban institutions have not?**

Five months after the company debut, we hosted an International Ballet Festival in Havana. In part this signified how much importance the revolutionary leadership assigned to the art of ballet. It turned Cuba into a recognized
international destination for dancers.

Also, Cuban dancers won a large number of prizes in the decade of 1964–
74. The prizes registered the impact of the systematic and coherent nature of
our pedagogical work, and our technical and artistic rigor. [See appendix D
for a list of prizes.] Each student presentation was a test in the international
arena of the efficacy of our pedagogic method. Each prize confirmed acceptance and support for our training.

17

Constructing Ballet Schools, Extending the Revolution

Was the company able to expand its repertoire during this time?

After reorganizing ourselves to take full advantage of our improved situation, we focused on encouraging creation of new Cuban works, in form as much as in content. We incorporated pieces with Latin American themes at the same time as we broadened the repertoire of classical works and contemporary pieces. While I was general director from 1959 to 1974 we brought nearly eighty new works to the stage. [See appendix E for list of selected works.] Without a doubt, *Carmen* was the company's greatest achievement in the contemporary genre during that period. My brother Alberto Alonso set it on the Soviet ballerina Maya Plisetskaya. When Alicia Alonso took over the role it became one of her best, equal only to Giselle. It is considered by many to be the best version of this ballet, and has been staged by companies all over the world.

What unexpected opportunities opened up?

From my perspective, it was impossible for me to distinguish my artistic activity from the life of my country and the transformations that were taking place, the anxieties and the successes. For me there had always been a political approach, even prior to 1959. Now it was reaffirmed and validated. I saw it coming to fruition. For example, now, delegates attending a convention in Havana, whether trade union or cultural, could take in a performance. We introduced visiting dignitaries to the culture of the new Cuba by inviting them to the ballet. The ballet hosted commemorations of national holidays.

We were able to undertake a more thorough reorganization of ballet instruction. We decided to dissolve Academía Alicia Alonso, which I had been directing since 1950, and the Cuban state assumed full responsibility for dance instruction. The pedagogy I had developed over the years became the foundation for the curriculum.

Our funding problems were now a thing of the past. Among the first measures taken was the extension of ample credit at the Havana Municipal Department of Fine Arts. We were able to take old study plans, redesign them, and begin to use them in 1961, and the Municipal Conservatory began to function as the new ballet school in a nearly ideal location for dance education. This culminated in the creation of the National School of the Arts in Havana. The home we selected for it was the former country club of the elite who had fled Cuba, and we gave it the name "Cubanacán," Cuba's indigenous name. The plans for its design were mounted in an exhibit that won the prize at the 1964 Eighth International Congress of Architecture. The design included expansive domes that sheltered the schools, with studios for music, visual arts, and performing arts, where we taught ballet, modern, and folkloric dance. The U.S. blockade made it hard to obtain construction materials, but in spite of that, remodeling the country club was one of the revolution's earliest and greatest achievements. Because we were unable to get rebar [structural concrete reinforcing rods], the architects Vittorio Garatti and Ricardo Porro decided to retain the seventeenth-century vaulted ceilings built by Catalonian monks.[1]

To conserve electric power they devised a natural air-conditioning system. The seraglio lattices and colonial-period Andalusian shutters kept hurricane damage to a minimum. We completed the remodeling by 1965, and by 1971 there were seven thousand students. They ranged in age from nine to seventeen. They lived in the Miramar neighborhood that surrounded the school. Before the revolution, only the wealthiest families lived there. I was director of the National School of Ballet and Dance Program until 1968, and then I was its adviser until 1969. By stages, Cuban dancers were educated and readied for their careers. In the first years of the revolution we accepted boys and girls from ages nine to thirteen. In the beginning there was no grade system yet in place. With a few modifications the school followed a system I designed in the 1950s for the Alicia Alonso Academy. We enlisted the help of some Soviet advisers. Ramona de Sáa, who became the director during the early part of the 1970s, extended the course of study from five to eight years, so that the students could remain there until they reached eighteen, the age at which professional dancers usually begin their stage careers.

Were more children able to study dance?

Selection for more advanced study was by audition. Criteria were body structure, health, physical facility, and technique level. Those who passed attended the middle-level school and eventually auditioned for what is today known as the National School of the Arts. At the same time, a parallel process began with the addition of schools throughout Havana. Vocational schools offering our curriculum gradually emerged in various provinces as well, not all of them yet able at that time to offer all of the artistic specialties—for example, only Camagüey and Havana offered middle-level schools. [See appendix F for a list of the elementary schools.] Over the course of that period we made it possible for *all* Cuban children to develop their artistic talents as fully as possible.

18

International Recognition Abroad, at Home, on Film, and in Print

In October 1961 the World Peace Council sent an invitation to Alicia and Fernando to participate in festivities celebrating the eightieth birthday of Pablo Picasso. The events took place in various locations along the French Riviera, and ranged from bullfights to a factory visit in Vallauris (where the famous artist from Malagá had worked on his ceramics) to an enormous gala lasting more than four hours with a banquet and exhibition of the master's works. Celebrities congratulated the famous painter, among them musicians such as Isaac Stern, Leonid Kogan, Svetoslav Richter, and Igor Markevitch; opera stars from La Scala and the Metropolitan Opera; and a dance delegation that included Alicia, Fernando, Rodolfo Rodríguez, and Yvette Chauviré.

•

What was it like to meet Picasso?

Alicia and I met Picasso in Cannes. He spoke of Cuba in an admiring and affectionate way. He even sang Cuban songs to us. Later, during a luncheon, Picasso mentioned to us his own connections with Diaghilev. Then, he presented us with his famous dove of peace. He had drawn it for us and written a dedication next to it on one of the event programs.

Can you tell me a little more about company tours within Cuba during that period?

On October 9, 1962, we began a national tour under the most unusual of circumstances. It began in Güines, a suburb of Havana. The company traveled from there to Matanzas, Cárdenas, and Cienfuegos. When the day for the engagement in Camagüey arrived, on October 23, 1962, we learned that Cuba was on the brink of war. Cuba had been caught in the middle of a conflict between the United States and the Soviet Union. The Cuban people took extremely seriously a situation that could have resulted in our annihilation. Yet, even though a state of war had been declared, we continued the rhythm of our everyday lives.

Are you saying that the company continued with its tour?

After the performances in Camagüey we danced in Santiago de Cuba, and then I took the company to the front lines to perform for the Border Battalion guarding the Cuban territory occupied by the United States Naval Base on Guantánamo.

Can you describe the 1963 filming of *Giselle*?

Six years after I retired from the stage, I returned to dance again in a film version of *Giselle*. Over a period of several months we worked with the Cuban Institute of Art and Industrial Cinematographers (ICAIC), taking great care to prepare for the filming of this ballet classic. We researched each detail of the ballet: the historical epoch, geographic setting, dress, customs, and dance style of the period, and even created psychological profiles of the characters. We hoped to strike a balance between the special qualities the film medium could bring out and the characteristics peculiar to the dance stage, and achieving that result ended up being one of the film's greatest merits. Alicia, Alberto, and I worked with the film director Enrique Pineda Barnet, and the film was considered the standard in Cuba for offering retrospective documentation of the work of the Cuban National Ballet.

ICAIC's proposal was to preserve Alicia's legendary dance interpretations for posterity. Alicia was partnered by Azari Plisetsky in the role of Albrecht, and I partnered her as Hilarion. Others in the cast were José Parés, Mirta Plá, Josefina Méndez, Laura Alonso, Aurora Bosch, Silvia Marichal, Eduardo Recalt, and Ceferino Barrios. Filming began on October 17, 1963, in the Amadeo Roldán Theater. The director was Enrique Pineda, Tucho Rodríguez was director of photography, Eduardo Arrocha designed the costumes, and Efrén Castillo designed the sets. Manuel Duchesne Cuzán, of the Cuban National Symphony Orchestra, conducted the music. It was filmed in black and white for a panoramic screen and was ninety minutes in length, and is valued by the BNC [Ballet Nacional de Cuba] as an artistic and historical document, a worthy legacy.

Arnold Haskell wrote that the film *Giselle* "combines in notable proportions the stage version and the particular requirements of film technique. It will stand as an exceptional and exemplary work."[1]

The following interview with Enrique Pineda Barnet by Francisco Morán marked the thirty-seventh anniversary of the release of *Giselle* and appeared in the spring 2002 online edition of *La Habana elegante*:

Q. How did you prepare yourself to undertake the filming of a ballet that had grown into a legend very much linked to the professional and artistic career of Alicia Alonso?

A. I prepared by thoroughly studying the genre and, in particular, *Giselle*. Alicia and I studied the School of Cuban Ballet, saw BNC performances, attended rehearsals, classes, interviewed dancers, choreographers, teachers, read a lot, watched ballet films. At the same time, I conducted acting and dramaturgy workshops for all participating dancers and prepared the film's entire creative team with background on ballet and *Giselle* in particular. These workshops continued until 1992.

Q. What did it mean to you to direct Alicia Alonso, and by extension, the BNC?

A. It was a challenge, and I felt the historic responsibility that was at work.

Q. Was it hard? If so, why?

A. It was hard because of its complexity, its significance, and the lack of specific experience.

Q. What is the difference between directing an actor in any given film and a dancer (even when the dancer is clearly an actor)?

A. They are two different mediums of expression, each with their own languages, specific techniques, requiring different methodologies.

Q. One of the artistic merits of *Giselle* is that it is not merely a filmed ballet, but a production that intelligently and sensitively combines the requirements of film and theatre. How did you achieve that?

A. [By] carefully respecting the differences as well as the particularities. For example, the concepts of space and time. Virtuosity, but interpretation. Drama, but subtlety.

Q. Did Alicia Alonso's conception of *Giselle* itself, influence the direction?

A. Inevitably.

Q. How? In what way?

A. In that indispensable interrelationship between creative individuals who share mutual respect and understand that the main thing is work they are undertaking together.

Q. Do you recall any of her suggestions or any comments?

A. I remember all her suggestions. I think that there is a basic confidentiality that I must respect. However, outside of the film, I remember a recommendation of Alicia's when I underwent coronary surgery in 1992. Alicia called me and said, "Enrique, 'was' is over, life goes on." That recommendation reminded me of the synthesis of all of Alicia's recommendations.

Q. Was there a meeting with the National Ballet staff who were to participate in the filming to arrive at a common dramaturgic approach?

A. Of course. At times, because of your questions, I'd like to think that you were there and this is a nice compliment!

Q. Do you recall the intervention of any dancer other than Alicia Alonso?

A. All the dancers, one by one, together and individually, were both consulted and consultants. There were very meaningful interviews and rehearsals with Josefina Méndez, Mirta Plá, Menia Martínez, Aurora Bosch, Laura Rayneri, Loipa Araújo, José Parés, with Rodolfo López, who was given the role of Albrecht, and then couldn't do it—with Azari Plisetsky, Ana Marini, Margarita and Chery [Ramona] de Sáa, Mirtica García, Alberto Méndez, Eduardo Recall [sic], Otto Bravo and certain other members of the corps de ballet. But above all, absolutely above all, with Fernando Alonso, who was indispensable and without whose collaboration nothing would have been possible. The presence and significance of Fernando Alonso in the film *Giselle* is as important and essential as that of Alicia Alonso. Both are the undisputed parents of this work. We know almost everything about Alicia, it seems that we don't know enough, or we ALL KNOW, but not enough is said. Fernando is the great teacher, the great choreographer, the great artist, the great accomplice, the great collaborator, indispensable for the film *Giselle* and for the Cuban Ballet.

The British dance critic Arnold Haskell began his relationship with the Cuban ballet during the 1964 Varna competition by observing Fernando's classes. Some time later he again attended Fernando's classes in Cuba, and offered his impressions to the public: "I have observed Fernando Alonso's classes daily. It has been a great experience. He appears to have eyes in the back of his head, so that he gives to a class of twenty dancers twenty private lessons, correcting them gently, with patience, and always explaining with the clarity of a scientist. This is the pure classical school."[2]

Had Cuban ballet pedagogy reached a turning point?

Varna confirmed what José Manuel Rodríguez had postulated years earlier: there had begun to be discussion of a new way of dancing, a different way, a style that could be authentically designated as the Cuban school. In the beginning, some called it the Alonso school, The three of us—later to include a fourth when Laura began to teach—came to know dancers, companies, and choreographers from diverse schools. These contacts enabled us to gain an appreciation—and even more—to study at close range the basis for the characteristics of each group's work. We weren't content to limit ourselves to observation. We identified which of the many characteristics could best accommodate the Cuban dance temperament, bearing in mind the test of time, and for the most part remaining faithful to the Cuban vocabulary. By choosing heterogeneity, we rejected any traces of "cultural colonialism, and opened up an avenue to all positive external influences.

Over an amazingly brief period of thirty years, between the 1940s and 1970s, elements came together which, once assembled, created the Cuban National Ballet style, registered on an international level in 1964, as much by dance critics as by juries in special competitions.

The renowned Soviet ballerina Maya Plisetskaya's analysis, recognition, and praise capture the role of Fernando Alonso as the pedagogic steward of this process: "I believe that yes [a Cuban ballet school exists]. In the first place, the Cuban dancers possess a high level of individuality, developed along lines of proper principles, with a proper pedagogy. In the second place, Cuba has a great ballet pedagogue in Fernando Alonso. And lastly, the principal ballerinas of the Cuban National Ballet can be leading figures in any company in the world."[3]

From the critic Clive Barnes: "The dance style of the Cuban National Ballet is a superb mix. I believe that it has been imposed as much by Fernando Alonso as by his wife (Alicia Alonso), and it appears to be a conscious effort to combine the virtues of many schools of dance."[4]

And from the Belgian dance figure Maurice Béjart: "Under the direction of . . . Fernando Alonso, the Cuban school of ballet has been able to take its place among the greatest ballet traditions, nonetheless conserving a pro-foundly original personality."[5]

What were Arnold Haskell's criteria for a new dance style?

The Cuban school met the test of Arnold Haskell's hypothesis. He said that there are five elements that must come together harmoniously in order for a dance form to qualify as "new": a charismatic ballerina, a multifaceted pedagogue, a creative choreographer conscious of the school's nationality, financial support and encouragement from the government, and a popular audience with artistic sensitivity. Haskell's elements are givens in Cuba. From the 1940s, Alicia Alonso acquitted herself as an outstanding figure on the international stage, becoming an inspiration for other artists and, even more, for fellow Cubans. Scarcely ten years later, I received recognition for the pedagogy we developed in the ballet studio, demonstrating our mastery of the full idiom of dance, and the psychology of our students. As this was taking place, Alberto Alonso was creating pioneering choreography, clearing a path for expression of the Cuban experience through dance.

When, after the triumph of the revolution, the central national governing authorities decided to offer all the financial support and encouragement to which the Cuban ballet was entitled, it not only anointed the company, it added the finishing touches enabling the emergence of the cultural conquest which is today the Cuban school of ballet. And so it was that we Cubans, a talented and artistic people with a rich popular and folkloric dance tradition, came to take our place alongside a select group of nations, able to exhibit a dance style exclusively our own.

19

Camagüey

The Center of Gravity Shifts

What were the factors that contributed to your divorce from Alicia Alonso?

I discovered that while I continued to admire Alicia's artistry above that of all others—as I do to this day—I found that I was no longer able to remain partner to a marriage that had become unsustainable in an amicable way. On the one hand, I was young, and in daily contact with accomplished young women yearning to dance roles for which they were suited. On the other, I could see that the strength of ego that helped to fuel Alicia's success had also made her feel possessive about the roles she was dancing. This was logical, but she was slow or reticent to entrust them to interpretation by others. Imagine making so many gains while having to contend not only with aging but loss of eyesight! She was determined to let neither condition interfere with her career, and as it turned out she danced well into her late sixties. Still, a decision to use one dancer in a role is in itself a decision to not use and develop another, and those dancers who were placed in a second cast, or not cast at all because Alicia continued to dance into her sixties, were the very youngest dancers. Logically, they wished to begin dancing those roles before reaching their forties [by which time most dancers retire or have retired]. So, while I admired Alicia as the greatest dancer on the ballet stage, in my role as a ballet master teacher and general director of the company I felt strongly that the younger dancers had to acquire the experience of interpreting the roles Alicia was continuing to dance, just as we had done when we were young. We did not see eye to eye on this, and began having sharp disagreements, and in 1975, I could no longer live with the constant arguing, and I left what had been my lifelong home and the center of my family life, and we divorced.

Had you fallen in love with someone else?

I had become involved in a romantic relationship with Aida Villoch.

Did the divorce have repercussions for the company and the school?

Because Alicia and I had been public figures, a number of people in our professional life began to take sides in the breakup, and the company camaraderie suffered as a result. So, a proposal was put forward that I go to Camagüey to direct the ballet company there, and I agreed to do that.

Did your decision to leave Havana prompt concerns on your part about the future of the national company?

Alicia seemed intent on ending my relationship with the company as general director or in any other capacity. I have always been concerned that pursuing such a course would result in her compromising herself, but also the company and school, resulting in liabilities for which I would ultimately be held responsible. If Alicia was determined to keep me away, I was just as determined to continue teaching. Options presented themselves, including an offer to teach at the Ballet de Nancy in France. I decided to accept the position as general director of the Ballet de Camagüey, which, though smaller than the BNC, has become Cuba's second most successful ballet company. Aida Villoch accompanied me there as my wife and collaborator.

What made you agree to take on what some would consider a lesser role inside Cuba, when you had an international reputation, and could have headed a school or directed a company abroad?

I considered going to Camagüey to be in the best interests of my country and its commitment to dance. We worked very hard to bring ballet to Cuba, and by going to Camagüey I could continue our work.

What happened in Camagüey?

Soon after we began our work there, Ballet de Camagüey and its school became a conduit for talent that the BNC availed itself of. The national company began to take our best dancers. One year they took eight!

Would it be fair to compare the national company and academy to children of divorce, in that they became the symptom bearers of the personal rupture between yourself and Alicia?

Well, yes, in some ways they suffered; in others, they benefited. Overall, the divorce itself failed to slow the progress of ballet in Cuba. It continued to receive enthusiastic support from the state, even during the Special Period's economic hardships. The dancers continued to receive excellent preparation. The pool of talent grew, and the audience grew in both numbers and sophistication as the years went by.

A major goal of a socialist revolution is to close the cultural and educational gap between the city and the countryside. In the words of Armando Hart Dávalos, a leader of the Cuban Revolution who became minister of culture:

> An art that aspires to be national must undertake to definitively overcome cultural centralism. On the other hand, socialism presupposes a break from the cosmopolite, and the participation of all the elements of the society in the intellectual movement. This we must raise to a higher level in the hierarchy [of revolutionary priorities] with marked emphasis on support of artists and writers from the 14 provinces and the Isle of Pines. The schools functioning in the 14 provinces will help provide the outlook required to arrive at the important solution. But such a solution must have both immediate and long-term effects.[1]

As if he were responding to the challenge posed by Hart's remarks, Azari Plisetsky spoke on the occasion of the Third National Ballet Festival of the Schools of the Arts, which took place in Camagüey, and said:

> Camagüey is [a] very firm cornerstone in the construction of Ballet in Cuba. . . . The thinking was to support the Provincial School from here in order to conquer all the misfortunes that normally occur during this kind of event, and emerge with an organization that is one hundred percent solid, and the results are better than what was foreseen based on an activity such as this: We are achieving at last the moving of the center of gravity to other provinces without any reduction in quality.[2]

Ballet de Camagüey was founded on December 1, 1967, by Vicentina de la Torre Recio. Its debut performance at the Teatro Principal featured *La fille mal gardée*, *Les sylphides*, and the pas de trois from *Swan Lake*. Six months later, the company danced *Coppélia*, *Swan Lake*, and *Don Quixote* on the García Lorca stage at Havana's Gran Teatro. Its dancers had been trained in the academy that de la Torre Recio opened in 1957. In the first decades of the twentieth century Gilda Zaldivar Freyre taught there, and the Salón de Ballet del Colegio Privado Zayas [the Zayas Private Ballet School], founded by Ondina Montoya, also offered classes.

Aurelio A. Horta Mesa, commentator on Cuban culture and author of *Camagüey: Una razón en puntas* (Camagüey: A pointed argument), says the following about de la Torre Recio:

Perhaps the most outstanding example [of cultural institutions] was to be found in the teaching of ballet in the provinces, which traced a spiral, and has made possible a fruitful exercise that, traditions aside, comes together in a body of work. In its function of capturing, or familiarizing us with reality, we know that art defines a manner of work that is eminently ideological and formed by aesthetic taste. In the instance of ballet in Camagüey, there arose a pedagogic example that, for an epoch, explains the basis of this development: Vicentina de la Torre Recio.[3]

In 1951, when she was twenty-five, de la Torre Recio decided to devote herself to the advancement of dance in her hometown. She attended summer courses at the Ballet Alicia Alonso School on scholarship. In November 1956, when the school closed its doors temporarily, she returned to Camagüey and joined the new Zayas school, opening her own Academy of Ballet on September 12, 1957.

Over the years, Ballet de Camagüey's artistic directors have included Joaquín Banegas, Jorge Rodríguez Vede, Regina Balaguer, and Fernando Alonso. Its repertoire includes the works of Azari Plisetsky, Iván Tenorio, Gustavo Herrera, Alberto Méndez, Alberto Alonso, Jorge Lefebre, Menia Mártinez, Francisco Lang, Lázaro Mártinez, and José A. Chávez. The company infuses classical tradition with an audacious contemporary repertoire, drawing on the contribution of Cuban choreographer Jorge Lefebre, who directed the Royal Ballet of Wallonie in Belgium and was an exponent of Maurice Béjart's Ballet of the twentieth century. Ballet de Camagüey has performed in the Americas and Europe, and its members have worked with prestigious international companies. While technically and aesthetically faithful to the Cuban school, the company has succeeded in etching a distinctive choreographic style, as evidenced in such pieces as *Saerpil*, *Cantata*, *Sikanekue*, *Tango episodios*, *La bella cubana*, and *Medea*.

What surprises awaited you in Camagüey?

I was familiar with the history and nature of the group I had agreed to direct, and certainly the challenges there. I knew that if I had been interested in a prestigious job, I would have not gone there, and instead accepted an appointment abroad.

I felt that it was important to do what collective opinion decided would be best. So, I consciously took this smaller company under my wing, and it was a big change from the life I had been living in Havana. From general director of one of the best-known companies in the world, I became artistic director of a provincial group, whose name in 1974 was scarcely known even on a national level. From Havana, with all its cosmopolitan advantages, I moved to a remote city in the country's interior, far from the political and cultural source that had sustained my work. My teaching reputation was well established in New York, Moscow, Paris, and Tokyo, because our students took first place year after year in international competitions, and were among the brightest stars of the ballet stage. I didn't see how restarting my life and career on another front could do any damage.

What is your assessment of the progress of Ballet de Camagüey since 1974?

Today, with about fifty dancers, the Ballet de Camagüey is a jewel in the crown of Cuban dance. Countries with far greater resources cannot claim local or regional companies with international ranking equal to that of Ballet de Camagüey. Three elements make up the secret to its success: a post-triumph decision by local authorities to provide material support, a commitment to the acculturation of Camagüeyans, and the pedagogical effort and enthusiasm with which Aida Villoch, myself, and other young figures such as Osvaldo and Pedro Beiro, Manelín and Zoraida Rodríguez, and Dania Cristia acquitted themselves in order to win support for the company, both within Cuba and abroad.

Aida Villoch answered questions about this period in a March 2006 online interview with José Manuel Cordero Hernández in *La Jiribilla*:

> For me it was a great blessing, a gift that fate [and] God reserved for me, the company allowing me a stupendous career surrounded by youth whose average age was 20 years old, in a location filled with greenery, fresh air, where I felt like a butterfly, unbridled in my dancing from dawn to dusk. Camagüey received me as one of its beloved from 1975 until 1992. . . . At only 19 years old, I assumed important responsibilities. . . . I could name various works in which I felt that I danced my

best, especially *Giselle*, having felt all the dancers so close around me while I danced the mad scene or, at the end, the death scene, which was so moving and unforgettable for me. . . . The audiences, to whom I dedicated myself in body and soul, were like a thermometer, a sounding device, [conferring] the responsibility of continuing to develop each time out, sharing something different so as not to defraud the audience, to maintain a full house, and respect for quality. . . . [Fernando Alonso] meant everything, absolutely everything, at the professional and personal level. The friend Fernando branded my career—all of it—and continues to stand as an example I admire and love so very much and who even today, when I have some doubt, is there with his wisdom, typical of the great ones, and with that modesty. I always felt blessed to be able to share so many years at his side and appreciate all that he shared in making me a great ballerina. I was with him at his side during the development of this company with the many joys and successes that bound us together, more so because of our professional relationship. Truly, I feel very proud of all that I experienced and if I were to do it all over again, it would be exactly the same, because for me it was an honor to share the great teacher of teachers Fernando Alonso, and be part of his history, as well as that of ballet in Cuba and especially of Camagüey.[4]

How would you describe the company's evolution?

Ballet de Camagüey's evolution proceeded from two distinct periods. From its founding in 1967 to 1970, the company mastered a traditional repertoire. After 1967–70, younger choreographers left their contemporary seal on its oeuvre. When we arrived we began to experiment with a transformation that expressed itself in the substantial improvement of the company's material conditions. When we came we established a permanent site, a large facility with plenty of land, where we built two enormous rooms that were probably the largest of their kind in Latin America at the time, a pointe shoe factory to meet the company's most urgent needs, and workshops in which to make costumes and sets. During the time that I was director the company increased in size, raised its artistic and technical level, and achieved its distinctive profile. Overall, the art of ballet gained prestige among the public, as well as with regional government authorities, and throughout Cuba.

Do you think this would have occurred had you not accepted the proposal to go to Camagüey?

Thanks to the commitment of the revolutionary government and the experience I had acquired over the years and brought to Ballet de Camagüey, it attained international ranking. This occurred not only within Cuba's borders, which would have been sufficient, but also, beginning in 1978, across Europe, Asia, and the Americas. Several of its principal dancers have acted as advisers to other companies or served on international juries. I was invited year after year to be present and share my knowledge at dance events around the world. For example, in 1980, I staged *La fille mal gardée* at the Plovdiv Opera Ballet Theater in Bulgaria. Aida Villoch and Osvaldo Beiro accompanied me.

Also, I was able to make important connections through having aided, advised and collaborated in the establishment of the Colombian Classical Ballet Institute, the Mexican National Dance Company, and similar institutions in Ecuador, Peru, Bolivia, Guyana, and other countries.

In 1984, Ballet de Camagüey made its debut at the 120 Festival Internacional Cervantino in Guanajuato, Mexico, alternating its performances there with shows at the Theater of Fine Arts in Mexico City. Two years later, in 1986, UNESCO invited me to join the International Council on the Dance. Also in 1986, I chaired the First Methodological Seminar on Dance in Trujillo, Peru, and served on the International Ballet Festival jury there. In mid-1987, Jorge Esquivel and I traveled to Argentina, where, under my direction, Esquivel danced with Eva Evdokimova, one of the world's most famous ballerinas. I gave master classes in conjunction with performances in Buenos Aires and Catamarca. In 1988, I traveled to Belgium, along with Pedro Martín and Guillermo Leyva, to develop a broad program for the Wallonie Royal Ballet. We staged Jorge Lefebre's *Excalibur*, a work that was later performed in Holland and France. In the last days of December of that year I went back to Wallonie Royal, this time with Aida and Pedro Martín, to help stage *Degas* and a new version of *The Rite of Spring*, both by Lefebre. We also went to Lyon, Marseilles, and Nîmes, and while in Paris we participated in the International Dance Festival 160. We took these programs to Holland and the German Democratic Republic. I also staged *Coppélia* and *Les sylphides* for Wallonie.

My brother, Alberto, joined us for a tour of Greece and Cyprus. We presented Alberto's new choreographic work, *Medea*. The public received us warmly, as did the reviewers, but we were also honored with official recognition. The president of the Republic of Cyprus received and congratulated me onstage in a ceremonial moment that they televised nationally. I was decorated with the country's coat of arms, and they invited me to participate in their Pro-Isadora Duncan International Seminar.

How would you summarize your experience in Camagüey?

Three decades after it was founded, Ballet de Camagüey had achieved a high ranking in the ballet world. The company finally wove together its hopes with reality. We were endowed with substantial material resources, unthinkable for dance companies in neocolonial countries, and we were much envied by certain companies in the so-called developed nations. Still, all manner of difficulties confronted the company, but we cultivated an atmosphere of optimism among the young ranks. I gave them constant encouragement. Neither the narrow scope of the countryside, nor the distance from Havana, nor the apathy of the media, proved to be obstacles to success. We broke through routine functioning, strengthened collective determination, fostered a contagion of enthusiasm, and the dancers took the dangers and obstacles that came their way in stride.

Regarding Fernando Alonso's efforts, Aurelio A. Horta Mesa wrote the following:

> It's necessary to underscore here the prodigious effort carried out by the National Directorate of Artistic Education . . . in the formation and perfecting of a network of schools that assume the implied obligations that one would demand from our culture [of] cadre-level professional artists . . . the force of DOING, that artistic effort [that] increases respect and esteem for the worker who is an artist and our *teacher*. Camagüey undertakes this stage with the incomparable sap, ever youthful and creative, of Fernando Alonso, teacher of teachers, who fashions jewels: a man of great works. In 1975, the directorship of the BC passed to him, and this represented for the teaching of Ballet, in the province, a spark plug, a breath of fresh air between two barres. . . . Teaching Ballet de Camagüey has as its founding principle and always authentic, the basis for generating inspiration, Vicentina—and the spur of the scientific rigor—Fernando—resulting in a generation of dancer-teachers, teacher-coaches, all artists, who dialectically brought to the fore the epoch of an inviolable stage on which the teaching of art in Cuba unfolds.[5]

Fernando Alonso and Elena Vinogradova, Kirov Ballet with Ballet Camagüey. Courtesy of Fernando Alonso.

Cubanacán, first home of the Escuela Nacional de Arte (National Ballet School). Courtesy of Marten Pérez.

Maria Elena Martínez, Yolanda Correa, Fernando Alonso, and Barbara García at Ballet Camagüey. Courtesy of Beatríz Martínez and Roberto Díaz.

Frank Andersen, former artistic director, Royal Danish Ballet, with Fernando Alonso and Pro-Danza dancers. Courtesy of Maiuly Sánchez.

Fernando Alonso examining dancer's foot. He built a pointe shoe workshop next to the studio and found a maker, but satin was scarce. Courtesy of Beatriz Martínez and Roberto Díaz.

Jorge Esquivel and Aida Villoch in *Giselle*. Courtesy of Jorge Esquivel.

Adriana Covarrubias presents Fernando Alonso with recognition award at the Festival Iberica Contemporanea in Querétaro, Mexico, July 2007. Photo by Daniel Ochoa, courtesy of Centro Pro-Art.

Fernando Alonso coaches dancer at Pro-Danza rehearsal. Courtesy of Michael Crabb.

Laura Alonso dances "Czardas" from *Coppélia*. Tana de Gámez.

Fernando Alonso coaches students at School of the National Ballet of Canada's Assemblée Internationale, Toronto. Courtesy of Yolanda Correa Cruz.

Fernando Alonso coaches Cuban Ballet School students at School of the National Ballet of Canada's Assemblée Internationale, Toronto. Photo by author.

Fernando Alonso with student in Betty Oliphant Theater of the School of the National Ballet of Canada, Toronto. Courtesy of Yolanda Correa Cruz.

Fernando Alonso; granddaughter, Ana Flavia Armengol; wife, Yolanda Correa, and her daughter, Maiuly Sánchez, Miramar, Havana, Cuba. Photo by author.

20

Révérence

At ninety-six you are still observing classes, taking rehearsals, traveling the world. Do you follow a special regimen?

I continue to follow my faithful sidekick: precision. I have practiced it from primary school; taming the body has always appealed to me. Sports activities helped me understand the principles of shaping the muscles and helped me in my dance career. For most of my life I have practiced swimming, gymnastics, and weight training. I still exercise several hours a week. I have given up only two activities—owing to accidents. Once, when I was playing football, I was blocked by one of the bigger players and because of that my lower jaw was dislocated. I went a week without eating. Another time, I was boxing with a priest at the Colegio Hermanos La Salle. It turned out that he had been a Florida State champion. But he was disgusted with me because I lowered my guard too much. So he hit me hard and knocked me out. Clearly, these were dangerous sports.

Are dance and sports compatible?

Sugar Ray Robinson, who was one of the greatest fighters in the ring, practically danced. Later, I saw him perform onstage. [Olympic track champion] Alberto Juantorena, the Cuban, was very much admired for the elegance he displayed during his career.

Both sports and dance have their styles and their stars. For me, of the two, it was ballet that ultimately prevailed. The threads tying them together are technique and mastery over the body, the instrument with which dancers express themselves. I am an admirer of Balanchine. I agree with him that the woman is the ideal instrument for the artist's expression. For that reason, I have always preferred to teach girls' classes.

Can you offer a balance sheet with respect to Balanchine?

I don't care for the ballerina who does not master technique. So, among the choreographers, I value Balanchine for the way he distorts technique in his works. I prefer his earlier works, such as *Concerto Barroco*, *Ballet Imperial*, *Theme and Variations*, and *Apollo*, to his later ones.

Are there other choreographers whose works you especially admire?

Oh, yes! I am very fond of the choreographic works of Fokine, Tudor, Agnes de Mille, Jerome Robbins, Yuri Grigorovich, and Alberto Alonso.

Who are your favorite dancers?

Without question, I place Alicia Alonso at the top of my list. There is also Yvette Chauviré, Galina Ulanova, Maya Plisetskaya, and Nora Kaye. Among men I favor Erik Bruhn, Mikhail Baryshnikov, Rudolf Nureyev, Vladimir Vasiliev, and Royes Fernández, even with his limitations. I admire the elegance of Igor Youskevitch, but he lacked technique because of a late start in studying ballet.

Does a dance work have to be in the classical ballet idiom to please you?

We have to struggle to create our own dance forms. For new times, new forms, but coherent, inspired ones. Not [just] to break with what is traditional. At times we want to be innovators but lack artistic loftiness. Mediocrity is always in the market for a home. Everyone has the right to search for his or her path, expression, defeat, but one needs to know what to look for and has to have something to offer.

How long should a performing career last?

A dancer must retire when he or she is no longer in good enough condition to appear onstage without looking old, because this is an art form that belongs to the young. Retirement age depends on each individual, their nutrition, circulatory system, outlook, and attitude toward life. And this applies to both sexes. Ballet is for me a plastic art, which, above all, requires plasticity. As in sports, the older dancers will have acquired stage experience as actors do, but when a young person dances beside them, one can see the difference. A dancer must retire between thirty-five and forty years old (much closer to thirty-five), assuming that he or she has had good training for the better part of his or her career.

What role do you play today? Do you think there is room in Cuba for another ballet company?

Even though I was one of the three founders of the first professional ballet company in Cuba and played a central role in the development of another, I don't think it would be good idea to begin a new company in Cuba at this time. I feel optimistic about the expansion of our academy. After the triumph of the revolution, having solved our most basic problems of support and funding, a new problem emerged in the national school of ballet. Up to that time, we had centralized the teaching so that it took place in one single academy, but with the new plans we launched a broad, new, fanlike arrangement of centers. While I was director I was able to oversee the pedagogic practice and safeguard our canons, but as many more teachers participated a process of definite disassociation began.

What is the current state of the schools?

At the moment, the leakage has come under control. There is a commitment to incorporate new elements that work well, as much as there is to avoid assimilating negative ones.

Over the course of my career I was able to put into place a school and a company that helped to bring forward a good number of stars and a ballerina assoluta for all time. Alicia has said, "I don't give classes, I take them. Fernando is my favorite teacher. He has helped enormously in my career. He has been my most severe critic."[1]

Why haven't you choreographed more pieces?

I don't consider myself a choreographer. I feel that I am more of a pedagogue than a dancer. It was indispensable to dance principal roles in order to later do the rest. To achieve balance in my life, I realize that it always gave me more satisfaction to create dancers, to shape artists, than the fact of having been a dancer myself. The most important and significant thing in my trajectory has been to see how new generations of artists have been developed. This continuity is truly what makes a school what it is—and allows one to discover the beauty in teaching.

After having reached the peak of your career, as a dancer on the best stages of theaters on several continents, having become cofounder of one of the most celebrated dance companies in modern times, the creator of a teaching system recognized among those in the most exacting circles for its superiority, an acclaimed teacher

responsible for the excellence of the Cuban ballet dancer, and one whose name is recognized as one of the most outstanding teachers in the second half of the twentieth century, in 1992 you decided to embark on yet another adventure by assuming the directorship of the National Fine Arts Institute in Monterrey, Mexico. Why?

The Cuban National Ballet was taking all the best dancers from Camagüey! After they took eight all at once it made me angry, so I went to Mexico!

Are you saying that you allowed your anger to carry you off course?

Yes. Instead, I should have seen this as a tribute to our work in Camagüey.

What did you do in Mexico?

I was there only for a short time. I worked with the National Ballet Company in Mexico City and directed the company in Monterrey, but I was unhappy with the situation in Mexico, where I did not have the liberty to make changes in the way that we had done in Cuba, so I returned to Cuba. Now I coach, and I participate actively in the annual Encuentro de Academías master workshops, classes, and performances. These bring together students and teachers from every school on the island, and throughout Latin America. Canada, and Europe. I also take some of the Pro-Danza rehearsals when Laura is away, and I advise competition contestants and accompany them abroad now and then.

Can you speak about some of your recent travels?

In July 2007, Centro ProArt in Querétaro, Mexico, sponsored a two-week-long International Festival of Iberian Contemporary Dance, bringing together dancers, teachers, and choreographers not only from Mexico, but Cuba, Brazil, Argentina, and Spain, who danced and taught master classes in a variety of styles from flamenco to classical ballet. The organizers invited me to be the festival's guest of honor. In a special homage they presented a slide show of photos from my career, and the festival's director, Adriana Covarrubias, presented me with a recognition award.

In October–November 2009, during its Fiftieth Anniversary Celebration, the School of the National Ballet of Canada hosted an Assemblée Internationale where fourteen ballet schools from Europe and North, Central, and South America brought a selection of students and pieces choreographed by them, to be danced by mixed casts from the participating schools. I attended it, accompanied by Ramona de Sáa, the current director of the Cuban National Ballet School, and Mirtha Hermída, who is Ramona's assistant. We brought with us student presenters, a student choreographer, Denia Luisa Suárez, and my wife, Ana Yolanda Correa Cruz. The conveners invited me to give the closing address. [See appendix C for text of speech.] It was just one month away from my ninety-fifth birthday, but when they introduced me they said that I was ninety-five, and so I had to correct them!

On the day that Fernando and Aida Villoch arrived in Camagüey, they stopped a woman on the street to ask directions. Her name was Ana Yolanda Correa Cruz [called Yolanda or "Yoli" by close friends]. Her mother had named her Yolanda after an adored character in a Mexican ballet film that featured dancers from Ballet Theatre—though Fernando was not among them, because he was at the time tending to Alicia while she was recovering from eye surgery. After working for some time as a pharmaceutical technician, Yolanda undertook a stage career, became an accomplished actress, and rehearsed in a theater located in the same building as the studios of Ballet Camagüey. It was in this way that Fernando and Yolanda became reacquainted, and following the termination of his marriage with Aida Villoch in 1985, Fernando and Yolanda began seeing each other, and married soon thereafter. At their modest home in the Miramar section of Havana, Fernando takes pleasure in sharing reminiscences, as well as the company and accomplishments of his family, whose members also include his daughter, Laura Alonso Martínez, who directs Cuba's Compañía Pro-Danza and travels the world teaching and staging ballets; his grandson, Iván Monreal Alonso, who danced with the Ballet Nacional de Cuba; his great-granddaughters, Carmen Monreal Novoa, Camila Monreal Escobar (who is studying acting in Brazil), and one-year-old Lucia Monreal; Fernando's stepdaughters, Maiuly Sánchez and Maiensy Sánchez, both classically trained musicians; Maiuly's husband, Manuel Gustavo Armengol; and Fernando's step-granddaughter, Ana Flavia Armengol, who is currently studying ballet.

During Fernando's ninetieth-birthday celebration in 2004, ninety dancers, each holding a candle, descended the ballet school's grand staircase in a tribute to their teacher. Shortly afterwards, the online magazine *Librinsula* published an interview with the maestro, in which he said: "There are three things that will never change: my love for women, admiration for the art of the dance, and my dedication and love for my country. These will never, ever change."[2]

Recuerdos (Recollections)

Introduction

As I began my research on the life and career of Fernando Alonso, I quickly discovered that there were few primary sources in print offering confirmation of the details of his life. Yet, simply mentioning his name to Cuban and non-Cuban dancers alike, or that I was writing a book about him, brought forth profuse and at times overwhelming praise for Alonso and his work. Without exception, each said the same thing: "It's about time someone wrote about him!" The Cubans immediately began to share memories, and I realized that there was an abundance of oral history to be harvested from these captivating, thoughtful, and eloquent dancers.

Several non-Cubans expressed surprise that there were "so many" dance families in Cuba—in actuality, six or seven instances where there are two generations of dancers from the same family. Sometimes that observation seemed to issue from a delight that Cuban dancers are following in their parents' footsteps. At other times it seemed to impugn the Cuban system for fostering nepotism. To my knowledge, there are some dance families in Cuba, but not as many as there are, for example, in Europe, or even the United States. Whatever the perception may be, I thought it might be illuminating to examine Fernando Alonso's contribution as seen by dancers from two different generations, as well as dancers from two generations of the same family. I was interested in what Lázaro Carreño, who trained at the Kirov as well as with Fernando, would say compared to what his nephew Yoel, who trained in Cuba more recently, during the twilight of Fernando's teaching career, might have to say. My experience as a dance journalist has been that often the most substantial interviews are those that occur in conversation between two dancers—or between a dancer and a choreographer, or a dancer and a set designer—while the interviewer "drives." So, I decided to interview a mother and daughter, Lorena Feijóo and Lupe Calzadilla, each of whom shared unique takeaways from their experiences under Fernando's tutelage, and then Lupe's daughter, Lorna Feijóo, and Lorna's husband, Nelson Madrigal, whose impressions of Fernando were more alike, because they developed in the crucible of the systemized method consolidated under the secondary leadership of the school, their teachers having been those whom Fernando trained.

The wish to reflect the entire span of Fernando's teaching career prompted me to choose dancers from opposite ends of the timeline of his professional life, beginning with such recognizable stars as Donald Saddler and Alicia Alonso, with whom he had begun his career, and at the other end, the very youngest of his students, such as Grettel Morejón and Tania Vergara. I requested an interview with Morejón after having seen her dance in *Napoli*, staged by Frank Andersen, at the Twenty-First International Festival of Ballet in Havana. To me, she embodied the synthesis of what Fernando's teaching strove to elicit: I saw a technically adroit dancer who knew her character down to each minute detail.

Outsiders sometimes question whether Cuba is lagging behind the current contemporary dance lexicon. My interest in Tania Vergara stemmed from her decision to choreograph contemporary work and build a company around her oeuvre. In a similar vein, I chose René de Cárdenas because I observed him coach a pas de deux class and was impressed with the results he was able to pull from his senior-level students. I then learned that he, too, was from a dance family, choreographs contemporary works, and enjoys a successful career as a teacher and choreographer, both within and outside Cuba. Little is known in the United States about the careers of Cuban-trained dancers whose work and reputations reach beyond the borders of Cuba—those who teach, choreograph, and produce shows on the island and abroad.

Carlos Acosta is an international ballet star who is by far the preeminent ambassador for Cuban ballet in the world today, having accomplished the daunting task of bringing the Ballet Nacional to the stage of the Royal Opera House, and the even more impressive reversal, of bringing the Royal Ballet to Cuba. I was able to interview him for four hours for my book *First Position: A Century of Ballet Artists*, during which time he shared his opinion that Fernando Alonso had made a unique contribution to teaching ballet, in part by teaching his students the laws of physics. I find very stimulating what Acosta has to say on a wide variety of subjects, and wanted, with this book, to offer him a chance to say more about Fernando's dominion of influence.

As students or teachers, Alicia's partners were also collaborators with Fernando. Two such dancers are Jorge Esquivel and Azari Plisetksy. I knew Jorge, not only because of his having been the prototype of the Cuban male dancer as Alicia's partner for more than twenty years, but because he had also taught my son, James Gotesky, when James was an upper-level student at San Francisco Ballet School. Jorge had impressed James as a teacher who, though he spoke little English at the time, was able to demand the seemingly impossible of his male students by simply tuning into their frequency. Azari Plisetsky, whose early life has been shared with the public by his sister, Maya Plisetskaya, in her autobiography, *I, Maya Plisetskaya*, brought huge benefits to Cuban ballet in his adult years, partly as a result of his collegial and friendly relationship with Fernando, the resulting development of Cubanacán, and the articulation of a powerful Cuban men's style and stage presence. Fernando is known for having taught women, but I felt it was important to give Azari an opportunity to discuss Fernando's work with male dancers.

John White left Cuba out of anger at the Cuban Revolution's expropriation of U.S. holdings and what he understood as anti-Americanism, expressed in the revolution's termination of the U.S. prerogatives associated with those holdings. He relocated just outside of Philadelphia, accompanied by one of Cuba's most gifted principal dancers, his wife, Margarita de Sáa. In spite of the break between White and the Ballet Nacional, Fernando considers him a good friend, and when I viewed the documentary film *Two Faces in the Mirror*, about the lives and careers of the twin Cuban dancers, Ramona and Margarita de Sáa, I discovered that White had tempered his stance toward Cuba after he and his family traveled there in recent years and were welcomed to reunite with the dancers they had known in the early days of the company and school, including Ramona. I wanted to learn more from him about the period immediately following the revolution and what he had gained from his experiences in the company and school during that time.

Ramona de Sáa was a name that Carlos Acosta continually returned to as I interviewed him in his dressing room at the Royal Opera House. According to Acosta, she had played an important role in convincing the directors of the Ballet Nacional that Carlos could have a successful career abroad that would in no way represent a betrayal of the Cuban Revolution, but on the contrary, demonstrate its riches. She struck me as a person with confidence and vision, and I wanted to profile her key role as Director of the Academies who continues the work of Fernando Alonso.

Aurora Bosch and Loipa Araújo are the two surviving members of the Four Jewels of the Cuban Ballet. Today, they are very much the Lilac Fairies of the current company. Like the Lilac Fairy character in *The Sleeping Beauty*, their eyes are everywhere, and their personal reminiscences are of incalculable value, whether it comes to restaging a work, coaching a dancer, or rescuing original steps. Both hold Fernando Alonso in the highest regard for his contribution to ballet pedagogy, strict adherence to the principles of classical ballet, and devotion and loyalty to the system that he, Alicia, and Alberto put into place with the unconditional support of the revolution.

At seventy-four, Laura Alonso is as much the apple of her father's eye as she was on the day she was born, and Fernando's only regret is that she has never fully been accorded the voice, or role she deserves, in the Alonso family. He is very proud of the work she does with her own company and school at Centro Pro-Danza and of her international reputation as a first-rank teacher and repetiteur. She shed light on Fernando and his work that could have come from no other quarter.

I first read about Menia Martínez in Diane Solway's *Nureyev: His Life.* In her teens, when Martínez was studying at the Kirov, she quickly became one of the three most important women in Nureyev's turbulent life, the other two being his mother, and Dame Margot Fonteyn. When Fernando introduced me to Menia during the Twenty-First International Festival of Ballet, I asked to interview her, because from every indication, she was a force of nature, and would not hold back in her descriptions or opinions about Fernando's role in the development of ballet in Cuba.

Finally, I want to return to Alicia Alonso, whose stellar dancing has inspired dancers and choreographers the world over. She *is* Cuba to those in the dance world. Since she has remained silent for nearly forty years on the subject of Fernando's apparent contribution to ballet pedagogy, I wanted to offer her a chance to share her views on that important subject.

I would like to thank those whom I interviewed for making themselves available, locating photos, taking time to translate e-mailed responses, and helping to bring Fernando Alonso's story into sharper focus with precision and eloquence.

Aurora Bosch

Aurora Bosch's first ballet teacher was Magda González Mora (Auñon), and as a scholarship recipient Bosch studied with Alicia and Fernando Alonso, eventually becoming one of the Ballet Nacional de Cuba's celebrated "Four Jewels." A prizewinner in many competitions, she was awarded the Gold Medal at Varna in 1964; the Anna Pavlova Prize and the Dance Writers and Critics Award, which was created for her in 1966 in Paris; the National Fine Arts Institute Prize in Mexico in 1971; the Gold Sagittarius International Art Prize in Italy in 1977; and the National Dance Prize in Cuba in 2003. She was a founder of Cuba's National Ballet School, artistic director of Ballet Clasico de Mexico, and guest teacher at the Ballet Nacional de España, Ballet du Rhin, the Zurich Staats Oper, the Budapest Opera, Vienna Staats Oper, and Copenhagen Opera Ballets, Pittsburgh Ballet Theatre, San Francisco Ballet School, and Central School of Ballet, London. Bosch received a doctorate in arts and sciences from the Instituto Superior de Las Artes de La Habana. I was able to interview Aurora Bosch at the Hotel Presidente in Havana on November 1, 2008, during the Twenty-First International Ballet Festival.

Who was Fernando Alonso to you?

From the very beginning, Fernando was a coach. When we were in the academy I received a scholarship. I didn't have direct contact with him then, because at that time he was the general manager of the company. My first teacher was Magda González Mora. She was a member of the company. We would peek in at the door of company class. Fernando would have the students do the steps again and again. So, I think what I got from him was the discipline in here [points to her heart] to look for perfection. In dance, it's so hard because you have to use your body and mind to look for it, and not be weak when faced with something that is not what it should be. I saw this in Alicia. She would go and go, and Fernando would work with her and insist in such a sweet way on repeating it. For him, it came from his culture, a person with a very wide knowledge of culture. His mother was a musician.

My family couldn't afford to give me music lessons, but Fernando would say in class to the pianist, Lorina, "Play such and such a Schubert étude for me." I can't always remember which one it was, but when I teach I know what music I want. He gave us anatomy class. He was himself a curious person, always trying to find out the whys and the hows of things. Each one of us touched him in a general way, as well as in a special way because of our personalities and tastes. My grandfather was a chemical engineer in a sugar plant. I was the first granddaughter, and when my grandmother read that the Alicia Alonso Academy was coming to audition children, she didn't say anything to my grandfather, and took me there, and then a month later I received a letter saying that I had been accepted into the school.

Fernando told me seven years later that my grandmother never paid a penny, and this was during Batista, so there was no support, but they chose me, Mirta Plá, and Margarita and Ramona de Sáa. Mirta actually had begun at the state academy, and finally came with us as the first scholarship student. Little by little, they built a company through the academy, because without money there was no other way. They only had students whose families had money, with or without talent, but who had no interest in ballet, and so they realized they had to keep us. We had two classes a day, as well as a class in makeup.

I must say that Fernando is a person with a very well balanced personality, who was capable of working with Alicia to develop a methodology. The only way that made any sense was for him to prepare, and try his ideas on her, and then later, with us at the academy. He kept a copybook because he used to write about jumps in one section, and in another part, adagio, and in another part, barre. I don't know how it fell into my hands, but I remember those variations. We inspired or gave him ideas. He realized that too much grand plié would give us big thighs. He had the dominion of the body in mind all the time.

Our country has a warm climate, and we would perspire a lot. There was a pharmacy nearby. He would call the pharmacist and say, "Make me up some pills that are half saccharine and half salt," and he would give us the pill. "Take it with a little water," he'd say. We'd finish the barre and take a pill. The salt was potassium. Saccharine reaches the bloodstream very quickly. He was always trying things, in the same way that he and Alicia decided to go to the United States and the first thing they did was musicals. They stayed because of Mordkin and Ballet Caravan. I realized later that all these initial things he gave us, as dancers, were also lessons in teaching, a kind of parallel education in which he was constructing both dancers and teachers, and this was possible because he had such great capabilities. In the first five years we were taught the first syllabus with classes twice a day and pointe class, and he would say, "Aurorita, a teacher never finishes class in a day; you will have the same class tomorrow, and you can look for something new then, and this is going to make you a better teacher, and make you more of a professional in your training."

During the revolution they needed teachers, and the Puerto Rican dancer José Parés was in the company and stayed many years, and was one of the special dancers who had good eyes and understood the psychology of teaching. As his group began to dance professionally they also began to teach. The same thing happened with us. At the same time we were studying dance they put each one of us in a group. We didn't have enough boys, so we went to an orphanage, and boys were recruited from there. I remember Fernando saying, "I can't be everywhere at once." So, it was Laura, Margarita, Ramona, me, and Alicia's dancer partner Joaquín Banegas. Fernando would be in my class for fifteen minutes, and then fifteen minutes in another. One day he said, "Aurorita, may I say something?" He told the class exactly what I had said to them just fifteen minutes earlier, but this time they did it! I told him, "I just told them exactly the same thing." He said, "I know, Aurorita. Don't worry. It's just that it was coming from a new voice. Each teacher has to use a variety of approaches, and check yourself at the end of each day as a dancer, and when you teach, as a teacher, to find what was good, bad, what needs fixing and what you'll do the next day to follow up." That was the only existing methodology then. Now we have methodology class.

Of course everybody has special qualities, but in Fernando I saw a friend whom I could turn to when my parents divorced. He had those human qualities that helped me through the hard times.

To be a teacher of teachers he had to be both a dancer and choreographer. Our schedule was packed. We would finish a *Swan Lake* performance at the theater at 11:30 P.M. and be in the studio the following morning at 7:30 A.M. They'd pick us up in a little bus. We'd be teaching from 7:30–9:00 A.M. and then there was company class at 9:30. It was so hard, but I'm very grateful to have had that experience.

Fernando, Alicia, and Alberto studied with Yavorsky, who came here by accident, but they reached the limits of what he could teach them. They knew that they wanted to dance, and return to build a ballet company in Cuba, because obviously, they could have gone outside and stayed. They arrived in New York just at the time that Diaghilev had died. Some dancers went with Colonel de Basil's company. The style in New York was not all Russian. There was Cecchetti, Bournonville, and French. Fokine, Tudor, and Dolin were there. They could have approached this as a kind of cocktail to toss down, but instead they took in all the information and worked with their heads. We Cubans have roots in Spain, Lebanon, China, Africa, and they had the courage and intelligence not to copy, and they had the benefit of Alberto's experience, so instead they selected from their experience and used the company as a laboratory. Within the framework of that laboratory, they could see in relief what the idiosyncrasies were that produced the Cuban line. They took what was useful from the Russians, French, English, and Italians. They put in a little of their own. Our temperament comes from our Moorish roots, our flexibility and rhythm from the Afro-Caribbean heritage. Identifying these characteristics is difficult, nor should we do that, but you can see them in class. The Russians and others are a little more controlled, not that they aren't temperamental too. For many years, Alicia was the only one to do Alberto's *Carmen*. Josefina never danced *Carmen*. Lorna was the first one to dance *Carmen* again. That happened because Alessandra Ferri wanted to dance it with the Cuban National Ballet corps de ballet, so the opportunity presented itself, and Lorna did it.

Their marital problems had a big impact. They tried to present themselves as a united couple for the sake of professionalism, but they disagreed, and decided to divorce, and it did not take place in a very good way. Fernando went to Camagüey. It was very, very hard for us because Fernando left, and though he did very good work in Camagüey, it left a hole here in Havana. After awhile, the Ballet Nacional collaborated with Ballet de Camagüey. So, especially given that problem, it shows that our school and style is very solid. Many dancers have left the company, and not all have been principals, but wherever they go, they are ambassadors, known for the Cuban style. It brings a lot of merit to their work. What happened with Alberto leaving, well, those things happen everywhere. We didn't fall behind in spite of the many obstacles placed in our way. I admire Alicia and her accomplishments tremendously, but when it comes to confidence, I have Fernando's and he has mine. He taught us that whatever comes up, take the approach that I'm going to do my best, and I want the people to enjoy it along with me.

If Fernando could be brought back into playing a role in the company today, what should it be?

I think it would be important for him to act as an adviser to the company.

What about him is unforgettable?

At the Varna competition, we learned so much because it was outside of the classroom. I remember him saying to us, "You must be aware of *all* corrections, not just those given to you." I must say that whenever someone, anywhere, compliments me on my classes, I always say, "Yes, thank you, but my personality, knowledge and way of teaching, come from what I learned from my teacher, Fernando."

Carlos Acosta

On the advice of a neighbor, Carlos Acosta's father, a truck driver, sent his son to ballet school to introduce discipline into the rebellious boy's life. Having danced with the Cuban National Ballet, English National Ballet, and Houston Ballet, Acosta is now a principal dancer with the Royal Ballet of London. When asked to name the best male dancer of the past decade, the majority of contributors to the prestigious London-based international magazine Dance Europe chose Carlos Acosta. Acosta is partial to Cuba, and returns there regularly to dance, renew old friendships, and recharge his authentic self. In 2010 he arranged for the Royal Ballet to appear on the Cuban stage for the first time in Cuba's history. I was able to interview Carlos Acosta at the Hotel Presidente in Havana on November 2, 2008, during the Twenty-First International Ballet Festival, in which he had performed the solo piece Le bourgeois.

What special contribution did Fernando Alonso make to your dance education and career?

I think the first thing is that Fernando is conceived of as the father of ballet, the architect of a whole movement that started in 1948 when he and Alicia returned to Cuba and the movement became the school that trained my teachers. Thanks to those teachers—that is where I came from. It's like a family tree, passed on from generation to generation, and even though some of those on the tree may be infirm, even though your grandfather isn't around anymore, even though he never rehearsed me as such, the traditions still run through the blood, and I can sense that I have some of that knowledge from my teachers who were Fernando's students. I think that is the most important connection for me.

What does the legacy you just described mean to you on a personal level?

Actually, my teacher, Ramona de Sáa, was one of Fernando's students, but I never worked with him; he never took me in rehearsal. He was in Camagüey or Monterrey at the time I was in the school. Even Alicia, who was here in Cuba, and director of the company, did only one rehearsal with me, *Spectre de la rose*. Josefina [Méndez] was rehearsing me, and Alicia walked in and began speaking about Fokine, making general points, and because she is still the director, and I'm still more or less a member, I have more contact with her than Fernando. So now, I visit Chery [Ramona de Sáa] whenever I am here, and so, especially now that Fernando is back, I often bump into him at the school. He now asks me to take some of his rehearsals, and is interested in seeing how I approach them; he's very flexible and very open-minded, and not critical. He is very much a compendium of knowledge. I remember one time, there was a thesis presentation by Miguel Cabrera; it was a socially constructive and informative evening. My generation is the opposite of theirs. We didn't have the benefit of having gone to the plantations on trucks in order to build an audience by dancing, and educating them by explaining what pointe shoes are, what a double tour is. My generation doesn't know much about that. I'm still learning all about that period—so important to know! At that event, in the course of the thesis, there was a tape of Fernando speaking in a philosophical way, and it impressed me so deeply. He is so knowledgeable, and feels so good about sharing what he knows, and the way he spoke was a revelation. It made me appreciate him more, because before that, he wasn't around. You knew his name through the teachers. I saw a tape of him from during the Cuban Revolution, and he had a gun. He took off the gun and holster and asked someone to hold them while he lifted a dancer in a promenade. There he was back in those days, making the revolution and still teaching these kids how to dance! I thought, "What the hell? These people were really something!"

He is the father of dance in Cuba. That's the most accurate way to describe him. He's the source of everything we have.

Do you think the Cuban style will stand the test of time, and that there is a basis for it in the ballet world of the future?

I think Alicia was the guinea pig. Actually, Ramona really wrote the definition of the Cuban school. When they began the school, they were able to sit back and study the Danish school, Vaganova, Royal Academy, French, all those schools, and choose what from each would be aesthetically beautiful to help create a Cuban identity. The Russian *passé* was crossed. That really defines it. They are aiming for a different kind of placement. You have to be a connoisseur and expert to know these details. The ability to dance big came from Vaganova. The Bolshoi has such an enormous stage that you *have* to dance big. There is a purpose to it: in order to reach the audience, to make an impact and influence the way of dancing, but on the other hand, if you bring that to an intimate audience it is going to be too much—overwhelming. We get that from Vaganova. But there was a time, like you said, where the world was divided into boundaries and camps, and people didn't travel as much. For Russia to come to the U.S. was a big deal because of the KGB and all that nonsense. And so it kept the world more isolated, and you could easily spot what was French or Vaganova. Now the world is different, and we travel more, and everyone is merging. Now, if the Russians are more stylish, it's because Svetlana Zakharova danced with Paris Opera, Diana Vishneva with ABT [American Ballet Theatre], etc. There are all these influences, and if you travel all over the world, you have to change. You see fewer Russians with the crossed *passé* and more with *retiré passé*. Much more is available to everyone. That can't help but have an impact on the Cuban style. What defines the Cuban style, in part, is creating men who are very powerful on-stage. For example, in the ballet that you saw last night with the boys, or if you see the older group of twenty, with those *big* legs, *that* is the Cuban phenomenon. I think when you see a Cuban you are going to expect that kind of powerful work. This is something we achieved that makes a difference.

Azari Plisetsky

Azari Plisetsky is a member of a family of renowned Russian performing artists, most notably his sister, the ballerina Maya Plisetskaya. Plisetsky danced with the Bolshoi for six years, but then, in 1963, after Fernando and Alicia Alonso requested that a guest dancer from the Soviet Union be sent to Cuba, Plisetsky was chosen. An experienced partner, he danced with Alicia Alonso for ten years, during the time that she was experiencing the gradual loss of her eyesight. With Fernando's encouragement, Plisetsky began teaching at Cubanacán, and ENA (the National School of the Arts), working especially with male students. He has taught for companies in Spain, at Ballet National de Marseille, and Ballet Lausanne. Of the Cubans he says, "They have dynamism," and strong folkloric traditions which inform their classical ballet.

"There is nobody to whom dancing comes as naturally." He points out in an avuncular way that because he was Lázaro Carreño's teacher, who was my son James Gotesky's ballet master, he is therefore my son's "ballet grandfather." I was able to interview Azari Plisetsky at the Hotel Presidente in Havana on November 6, 2008, following the Twenty-First International Ballet Festival, and also by e-mail on February 22, 2010.

What is the history of your career, with whom did you study ballet, where and when did you join the Cuban National Ballet, and which were your most important roles?

I finished the Bolshoi school in 1956. My teachers there were Alexander Varlamov, Nikolai Tarasov, and Asaf Messerer. I danced with the Bolshoi until 1963. In March of that same year I began my work with the Ballet Nacional de Cuba as a principal dancer and teacher. I danced practically every role in the repertoire there. I created my own choreographies: *Canto vital* (Mahler), *Avanzada* (Alexandrov), *Primer concerto* (Prokofiev), etc. My favorite role was Don José in *Carmen*, which Alberto Alonso created for Alicia and me.

What impresses you most about Fernando Alonso?

Fernando Alonso helped very much to integrate me into the repertoire, working with me on the new ballets, offering counsel of great professional value. We alternated giving class to the company; I helped him to develop the young dancers and students at Cubanacán, especially coaching the male casts. It was a magnificent experience to see his manner of teaching, his methodology and meticulous work with the details.

What distinguished him from other teachers?

Fernando Alonso is a highly cultured person. His curiosity and love of learning are unceasing, and the breadth of his interests very vast: anatomy applied to dance, spelunking and speleology, astronomy, hunting, and so many other things. We would go diving, and he would describe the underwater world to me. In our tours of the Cuban interior, he made me admire and appreciate the beauty of Cuba.

What is the best advice you received from him?

At Fernando's side I developed as a teacher. He said to me, "While teaching, one learns." His observations, remarks, and notes during class and rehearsals served as lessons to me. His patience was exemplary.

Ramona de Sáa

Ramona de Sáa, formerly a principal dancer with the Cuban National Ballet, is director of the National School of the Arts. I interviewed her on March 21, 2008, in her office on a busy day during the April 2008 Encuentro Internacional de Academías de Ballet (International Conference of Ballet Academies), where students from all the schools in Cuba, as well as schools from twenty-one other countries and their teachers, come each year to Havana to compare notes on teaching methodology, and participate in a student showcase. De Sáa directs the event.

When did you begin your dance career?

My identical twin, Margarita, and I began at the Ballet Academy Alicia Alonso in 1950. We were part of the founding class that launched the academy for children who had been studying in public schools. I was in the sixth grade when we auditioned. The panel members were Fernando, Alicia, Carlota Pereyra, and Magda González Moro. The test was very similar to the one we give today in our artistic training subsystem. That is, they observed the biotype and physical conditioning, such as the flexibility of the feet, knees, etc. I went in first, and then my sister went in. When my sister went in, Fernando and Alicia (who was the one in charge) told her, "But we already saw you . . ." She said, "No, I have a twin sister." And we were both admitted at the same time. I think we caught the panel's attention there. There's a photo someone took of these twins with well-conditioned bodies and all the rest. My sister now lives just outside Philadelphia with her husband, who is North American. There's a nice documentary called *Mirror Dance* that was made about us by two North American journalists. It was so good that it won prizes and everything! It's the story of two people in very different social contexts, who, for love of dance, have worked to develop themselves, and given all they have to the art.

It was there that we began our careers with the master teacher Fernando, who worked a lot at that stage in the Alicia Alonso Academy with the group that I mentioned, and later on, from among them, they selected those who showed the most promise. In 1954 we were already working to go on the first tour of South America with Ballet Alicia Alonso. Fernando was a very demanding teacher, very dedicated, and a person who, for our generation, apart from being the teacher we idolized, also helped us so much in our personal development. I'd say that he, as much as Alicia, prepared those of us of that generation for the life and responsibilities they would later give us, not only onstage, but also when they told us in 1962, when we were twenty-three years old, "You have to assume the management of and instruction at the National Ballet School," which had just been founded. Fernando was the director of the National Ballet of Cuba and the first director of the National School of Ballet after the triumph of the revolution. So, his was a long vision, projected from before the time of the revolutionary triumph, from his position inside the Alicia Alonso Academy. Once we had the necessary social conditions in the country, the program could produce qualified dancers in less than seven years, using a uniform teaching method and imbuing a singular style with the traits and seal of the Cuban ballet school. He and Alicia provided our country with the basis upon which we later created what was called the "Artistic Training Subsystem," which we have been perfecting this whole time. We were then able to construct from that the changes and transformations to meet the current dance requirements of our country.

Everyone credits you as the jewel of ballet training in Cuba. What distinguishes your method of working with teachers and students?

The *fifth* jewel! [Four dancers in Cuba were lauded as the "Four Jewels" of the Cuban National Ballet: Josefina Méndez, Mirta Plá, Aurora Bosch, and Loipa Araújo.] Our method contains something very particular, and it's precisely this program that we designed to impart that method and transmit it to the students. In other schools, the curriculum is a relationship of steps. In this school, in order to create habits in the execution of movement, the program is divided into units; the first unit, which continues for several months, is the one in which we introduce these movements in phases and stages of learning—the most basic forms up to the most complex—over a course of eight years, which will endure for an entire career. In other schools one studies a step as a step, but there is not that breaking-down, fractionalization, selection of movements that incorporate one learned movement into others. This one prepares the way for the next, and so forth, and when one has finally entered the national school, he or she comes with a sculpted body. The tendu is the mother of many, many movements that emerge from that step. We have codified this very well, and have also created the attack, the balance, and a dance style where you lift the legs as high as they can go without limits, and I would say that another very important ability in dance is to capture the masculine and feminine qualities. In the woman, femininity is conveyed in stylized gesture, such as approaching head movements from the fulcrum of the gaze. And yes, we put a lot of work into it, because we place a lot of emphasis on this, above all, for children in the elementary level. It becomes better interpreted in the intermediate level and best expressed among the girls whom I am showing today. How does one explain this to a girl who has no ballet frame of reference—and so OK, but she's a girl with immense potential, in terms of her body? And yes, I think that she will arrive there.

When you are faced with a student who is technically brilliant but shows no affect, how do you work with that student?

Yes, there are students who require more work to achieve a feeling of expressiveness in the face. There are others—I'm not saying that each student has this talent—a few—who have a talent not only for technique but also for artistry. We work a lot with acting as an assigned classroom subject. And yes, teachers try very hard to achieve that expressiveness in the student. There are some for whom it is easier and others for whom it doesn't happen until they enter the company and gain theatrical experience, artistic experience. Some come by it naturally, and some don't have it. One must enjoy it, take pleasure in it, so that you don't think about the technical difficulties, how hard it is on the body, also to enjoy the movement as much as you can, and the ballet teachers have to be very strict in achieving this. In the beginner level it isn't so easy. In the intermediate level you are working hard to perfect technique. The opening-night gala truly achieved this, really showed different styles, and it was where you could see the school shine!

Do you use a light or heavy touch with the students?

Maestro Alonso taught us to never use violence in class, and this is important. He even used a stress ball to avoid getting upset. Violence? No. Convincing! One must touch, but in such a way that you don't create a situation of panic in the student, because there are teachers who truly create terror in the children, and this is bad. Neither Fernando nor Alicia ever transmitted terror, because if in a ballet class that lasts an hour (in *our* system, an hour and forty minutes) we are terrorizing the student, he or she won't come to class. We are, or we characterize ourselves as, energetic. We demand discipline, but we try to create a conscious discipline in the student, and an internalized discipline, so that they understand the whys and the wherefores, and build for themselves the qualitative habits that this specialized art form requires.

If you could find one word to describe Fernando Alonso, what would it be?

I would say that the word would be "perfectionism." He is a tireless perfectionist who demonstrates that working is when you think you are giving the maximum, he always goes to that one detail, always looks for perfection, harmony, and whatever he presents of himself would be the maximum that he could give to each student or dancer. That enables you to become a demanding perfectionist too.

Has the Raúl Castro team offered the same level of commitment to ballet as the Fidel team?

Support to our artistic training system, to all the revolutionary values, continues with the current leadership team, the newly selected government administration of the nation. This is one of the achievements of the revolution. Honestly, culture, education, and health care remain goals for *other* countries. I have traveled enough in other countries to realize that medicine is a business just like art is a business in those places. We are able to have a school such as this, where children pay nothing at all, where everything is given to them, and there is a spiritual preparation for each and every one of them and their families, which at the moment they may not be able to appreciate the value of, but over time they will realize how important it is.

They don't know that through these exchanges—via the workshops—we can now share knowledge, thanks to improvements in media technology. Before, we were more isolated because there were no computers. The means of dissemination were more limited. Now, they are more conscious of what you give them, and the level they are reaching. Some of our students are at this workshop, but many also participate in international competitions. We have exchanges with other schools, and when you consider the diverse realities of technical levels, you can see what you have given them.

Yes, they perceive this, and receive it, and in truth, they are very grateful students. I graduated the group of students now entering the company, and was also Carlos's [Acosta's] teacher. All are very grateful. Yes, they know and are familiar with what the reality is. I think that Carlos is a person who misses his country very much and harbors great feelings of nostalgia.

Lázaro Carreño and Yoel Carreño

When he was eleven, two years into his ballet training at the Cuban National Ballet School, Lázaro Carreño accepted a scholarship at the Leningrad Vaganova Institute, where Mikhail Baryshnikov was one of his contemporaries. Having won first place, and gold medals at international competitions, Carreño began his teaching career in the 1970s, and among his students were Joan Boada, José Manuel Carreño (who is Lázaro's nephew and Yoel's half-brother), Luis Serrano, Carlos Acosta, and Lorena and Lorna Feijóo. His career has taken him from Havana to Zaragoza, from Madrid to Houston and Caracas, from the Ballet du Rhin to Lodz.

Yoel Carreño, Lázaro's nephew, began as a student at the Alejo Carpentier Provincial School of Ballet, and in 1998 he graduated from the National School of the Arts. He then entered the Ballet Nacional de Cuba. As a student he won the Gold Medal at the Fifth Encuentro Internacional de Academias de Ballet in Havana. He has performed with the Ballet Nacional de Cuba in Europe, the Americas, and Asia and is currently dancing with the Norwegian National Ballet. I was able to interview Lázaro Carreño and Yoel Carreño at the Ballet Nacional de Cuba building on Calzada in Havana, on November 2, 2008, during the Twenty-First International Ballet Festival, where Lázaro had just taught and where Yoel had just taken company class. Yoel was performing several pieces from the company's repertoire during the festival.

What did Fernando Alonso contribute to your development as a dancer that no one else has?

Yoel: Honestly, I worked very little with the maestro, but have been able to become close with him, and he has provided me with a source of wisdom and knowledge, an understanding of dance, unlike any other person. He is a living legend, an encyclopedia. The way he reasons gives you a different concept. He opens alternative paths, new ways of seeing what you are doing, helping you to improve immensely.

Lázaro: Fernando was my first teacher at the National School. He was the founder, and as the director, he would give class. Even though at first he was teaching only girls' class, after having been in the company for a while I got a chance to work with him as a teacher and *repetiteur*. As my nephew says, he's an exquisite person who looks after each detail, technically as well as artistically. He is a very wise and cultured person, with an ample vocabulary, and he's very explicit while teaching or explaining what he wants you to know. That's very important. He has always set an example for the company as a professional, in his discipline and work habits. He represents all those things in a single individual for the Cuban National Ballet. We truly felt his absence when he left. We really needed him with us here.

I have heard the maestro give a dancer a correction and follow it up with the words "Now make a habit of it." What habits have you learned from Fernando Alonso?

Lázaro: He didn't used to say that to everyone. It was just a habit that *he* had when he was corrected. It was a habit he used when correcting the dancer, but in a general way a method for letting the dancer know what he or she did wrong. To make a habit of a correction means that every time you do something wrong, you must remember the correction and never forget it; always keep it in mind to keep repeating that step correctly so you keep improving. It's a pedagogical method to make the student understand his or her mistake and why it happened, because there are students to whom you may say something once and they never repeat the mistake, but there are others you must correct over and over for the same mistake. So to "make a habit of it" makes the dancer understand how important it is to be corrected and how important it is not to repeat the mistake, that there is a reason for everything that is taught.

Yoel: I agree completely.

What do the words "Cuban style" mean to you?

Yoel: The Cuban or Latin technique has to do with our roots. We have a very distinct characteristic that one can notice when observing our school as compared with others. Fernando wanted that to stand out, for this detail to be observable whenever we dance, so that the audience can notice that we are Cuban and Latin and that we have an alternate understanding, a different way of dancing and expressing and feeling movement. Fernando has a North American formation and background, as does Alicia. They shared a career together. They wisely shared what they learned, shared the stage with many artists: Russians, English, Americans, French, and Mexicans. But they were very intelligent. When they created the Cuban ballet school, they based the curriculum on the best principles of each of those schools. They believed they could be adapted to meet the needs of the Cuban ballet school.

They chose the best of the English, the American, and the Cecchetti schools, the best of everything. Have you noticed that Cubans are very expressive when they speak? They speak with facial gestures and their hands. We took those forms and translated them into our overall dance. Cubans are very expressive in every way. As they created the school, they did so without violating the academic patterns, because we have always shown that we can dance as well or perhaps better than the Russians. Maintaining the principles of dance, we have infused them with our personality and character. The movement, the very same movement can be done with so much character, with a different tension, but in the case of the Cubans we are more explicit in the expressiveness, giving quarter to our natural idiosyncrasy. So all these things were blended into our teaching method, and that is why the Cuban school of ballet is a little bit different from the others.

In your observation, what is missing from those dancers who have not had an opportunity to study with Fernando Alonso?

Lázaro: When Fernando was here, the artistic principles of the company were pronounced, unconditional, and obligatory. Nobody could violate them. After Alicia and Fernando split up, these principles suffered a change, such that they were no longer followed properly, and so the succeeding generation did not stick to them. Today, it requires very hard work to stage pieces such as *Swan Lake*, *Giselle*, or *The Sleeping Beauty*, because these principles no longer exist. It is more difficult for the *repetiteurs* to transmit the work and for the few dancers who still know them. These principles were established in our epoch, everyone knew them, and so we didn't have to take as much time with these works. A dancer would do it, the next would just follow, and so on.

Yoel: You saw them constantly, so there was continuity.

Lázaro: They were principles and we followed them. They were unconsciously etched in our brains, so these principles have worked well for Yoel because he has seen them up close. It was easy for him to get these principles, but those who haven't had that luxury are completely lost. When trying to dance a role, as in *Giselle* yesterday, certain things caught my attention. In the first act, with Fernando there, those things would never have happened. The first boy who danced Albrecht had no wig! With Fernando, that would never have happened! If he doesn't wear a wig, he doesn't dance. In *Giselle* that is unforgivable! It's like Yoel. He has his own principles, patterns, and concerns about the work. He is intelligent, reads a lot, and has seen many performances. When he has doubts, he asks questions, but if the *repetiteur* doesn't curate the style, form, or story, what can he tell the dancer? Only elements of the choreography, but that's all. When I'm in charge, when I'm artistic director, I begin to explain details that perhaps they've never heard. That's because I have plenty of knowledge about the character, story, style, but not everyone can do that. That's the difference between a master and a teacher. Fernando did everything in a colossal manner. We have lost this, and mainly for men, because more guidance has always existed for the women.

> **If you could turn back the clock and bring Fernando Alonso back into playing a central role again in the company today, what role would that be?**

Lázaro: Artistic director.
Yoel: Artistic director.

Tania Vergara

Tania Bolivia Vergara Pérez is artistic director of Endedans, a contemporary ballet company in Camagüey, Cuba. She is also professor of character dance at the Instituto Superior de Artes and the Academia de Artes "Vicentina de la Torre," Camagüey, and a member of the National Artists Union of Cuba. She was awarded the 2008 Ibero-American Choreography Prize. I was able to interview Tania Vergara by e-mail on November 6, 2008, after having met her at the Twenty-First International Festival of Ballet in October and November 2008, where Endedans was performing.

> **Please speak about your experience with Fernando Alonso in Camagüey.**

Right from the beginning, Fernando Alonso's image has been a substantial part of my career within ballet, his name having been invoked by professors, teachers, dancers, historians, aficionados, all the way to the people who follow the comings and goings of dance in Cuba. He becomes someone distant, unreachable, yet at the same time close at hand and tangible: end-of-year exams, demonstration classes, or some important rehearsal were formal occasions on which to notice the maestro in attendance. Sometimes very serious, sometimes not so much, as he would walk down the hallways, and perhaps ask you a question. Most astonishing from my girlhood memories was to notice how he never forgot a face, even after having overseen hundreds of students in his pedagogic work. Once I found myself in Havana with a friend in a Cuballet summer course. When we saw Fernando there surrounded by people, we just sat timidly in our seats thinking he wasn't going to recognize us. To our surprise, he turned to us and said "Hey, Camagüeyanas, aren't you going to say 'Hello'?"

After finishing my studies and beginning my tenure as a teacher at the Vocational School of Art Luis Casas Romero, our encounters assumed another tone. I was no longer alongside someone who executes and is corrected, but rather with ballet students seeking support to perfect their technique. Now, I could stand alongside all the teachers, listening to everything they had to say related to one step, each correction of a mistake, each reflection upon a movement. Their interventions were sacred to us. I even remember the teacher Beatríz Martínez, who wrote down the most trivial words, such as "open the window more" or "I need a little water." Merit wasn't won by simply having an important name, nor founding a Cuban school of ballet, nor even directing the Ballet de Camagüey, the country's "second company"; he won respect and veneration thanks to the precision of his analysis, his faithfulness in keeping up with the development of different groups of students, his infusion of vitality into the very center of the school of ballet, his scientific knowledge, and even more, because nothing relevant within the teaching system was separate from him. There were no promotions, methodology meetings, demonstrations, performances, or festivals that he did not attend; he was there with his athletic gait and sharp eyes. He was so demanding that he even participated in the young children's physical entry exam, and would point out the orthopedic problems, or curvatures of the spine that others failed to note.

How would you describe his teaching method?

His teaching method is ruled by a firm scientific conviction in the wisdom of centripetal force inside a turn, the angle necessary to turn out, the laws of equilibrium, in which muscles intervene in every step, a sense of the "y" in jumps, turns, and other movements. He knew the importance of the standing leg, the various head placements which correspond to movement. He shared a broad spectrum of physical probabilities and possibilities grounded in his knowledge of physics and kinesiology, and consolidated a Cuban methodology, which, together with Alicia, became the "Cuban Miracle." Nor does it stop there. His formative years in other dance schools, contact with important choreographers, his tact in dealings with first-rank companies, acquired as a result of his enlightened upbringing, his affinity with and sensibility to Cuban and universal art, placed him in the optimal position to master the various styles of the great classics, the histories that surrounded their origins, the whys and wherefores of each gesture, the musical accent in each such variation, the specific characteristics of this or that pas de deux, a dominion that doesn't register as a scholastic method as much as an artistic arsenal necessary to confront a piece.

I have heard many intelligent and up-to-date assessments from Fernando Alonso that nourish my dance culture like sap: his concern for the artistic sense, its loss in the overestimation of technique by younger dancers, his analysis of a disciplined and knowledgeable audience faced with something that is scandalous or frivolous, requiring only virtuosity and bringing nothing to the choreographic art form. His foot-stomping masculine presence onstage was characteristic of the Cuban school of ballet, as was his insistence on conserving the styles in the great classics, respecting the step sequences in variations, with dancers not executing just the ritual spectacular steps. But—there is a sentence, deep and wise, that I keep intertwined with my brain and also sealed in my heart: "Dance not only with the muscles of your body, also work with the muscle of the heart."

Menia Martínez

Menia Martínez studied ballet in Cuba and the Soviet Union, where she became a classmate and the beloved friend of Rudolf Nureyev. Having danced in Cuba and helped to bring ballet to Cuban television audiences, she then danced with Maurice Béjart and married the dancer/choreographer Jorge Lefebre. She lives in Brussels but returns to Cuba often. The following interview was conducted at the Ballet Nacional de Cuba studios on Calzada Street in Havana, on October 29, 2008, during the Twenty-First International Ballet Festival.

What unique contribution did Fernando Alonso make to your development as a dancer?

I found myself onstage before an audience very early. Fernando created an interesting methodology in the school because he brought in an actress to give us acting classes. He was seeing to it that we had a complete education. As I liked acting very much, it was amazing to take those classes. Fernando studied in the United States and spoke about having been interested in the human body, and he worked in a clinic where X-rays were made. So, it was he who taught us makeup, and not the actress who taught acting class; he gave us dance anatomy class and showed us slides of the human body. He explained things in terms of the exercises that we were made to do correctly, and how one could [potentially] harm the body, physically. I never had a single injury. In my generation there were four or five of us—no more—to whom he gave private classes. The anatomy class helped us a lot because all of us were teachers very early on. By seventeen years old, I was giving class. Thanks to Fernando's anatomy classes, we could teach how to assume the positions without injuring the head and legs, and yet work the entire body with exactitude. So they were as complete as if they were private classes. Since Fernando couldn't invite teachers who were specialists in each of these areas, he himself taught all of it, except acting, which was taught by the actress Violeta Casals. Casals was a woman of great importance to the Cuban Revolution. During the revolution she went up to the Sierra Maestra and was the voice that went out over Radio Rebelde to call out: "Here Cuba: We are in [their location on that day]." When I returned from the Vaganova Institute, Fidel wanted to meet with us to discuss organizing the arts instructors, and Violeta Casals became the head of a four-person team consisting of herself, Alberto Alonso, Sonia Calero, and myself. Sonia and Alberto were the folkloric representatives, Violeta was the drama representative, and I was the classical ballet representative. I came back to see the revolution for myself and was surprised to find out that Casals had worked in the Sierra Maestra with the guerilla [forces].

There are many documents on Violeta Casals; I have many photos of myself with Fidel Castro and Che. Che came to see Violeta Casals and us. She always thought that I would become an actress. This stage of the school was very good for us, the little tiny group that Loipa Araújo, Josefina Méndez, and Mirta Plá joined after Aurora and I did.

My life changed when I went to the Vaganova school. When I left, Lázaro [Carreño] came in. Because Lázaro began in the National School of the

Arts, he already had a foundation from there. Because I was admitted into the Vaganova school, I think I was always a little suspect [of being a KGB agent], but it actually happened accidentally. I was the youngest in a delegation of young people who attended a Polish youth festival. The delegates told me that the Bolshoi Ballet was there, and they said, "Why don't you audition?" The Cuban poet Nicolas Guillen, president and founder of the Cuban Writers Union, was traveling in Paris and said to me, "You have to audition because the situation in Cuba is very hard; the company lost its subsidy." Fernando and Alicia told me, "Try by any means to see if they will give you a scholarship." So, Nina Timofieva, the Bolshoi prima ballerina, who adjudicated at the audition, told me, "I am passing you. You have good physical conditioning, but you must take this to the Ministry of Culture in Moscow, because there are additional conditions that must be met." Since Nicolas Guillen was going to Moscow, he took the letter, and so, they gave me a scholarship to the Vaganova school. I began to cry because I thought, "If the capital is Moscow, the best school would be there." Afterwards, when I understood that they were sending me to the school associated with the Kirov, [where] the teachers were the successors of Vaganova, I realized how fortunate I was. When I returned to Cuba I took part in a process that was outstanding for creating arts teachers and national ballet schools: the development of the Cubanacán school and the El Visiones school. They asked us to teach, I taught in the National School of the Arts, as did Josefina, Mirta Plá, and Loipa. Very fine dancers from there emerged, who were contemporaries of Lázaro Carreño: Ámparo Brito, Rosario Suárez, and Ofélia González.

What course did your career follow once you returned?

Alicia Alonso was the principal dancer from Ballet Theatre. So, Fernando returned to Havana, and he molded us. Even though I went away, I came back, and was considered part of the Cuban school because, for a dancer, the first steps, the first years, are fundamental; after that there comes a kind of perfecting, but when one begins there has to be the guiding hand of a good teacher. I am lucky because I began late, at eight years old, but with a good teacher, and this determined how far I could go to become a prima ballerina.

By the time I returned there were so many things—television, arts instructors—and I was so busy that I didn't take enough interest in myself as a ballet dancer. We created a ballet TV program, and after that other ballet teachers would come: Rodolfo Robal, for example. It was very nice because every Thursday there was a ballet on TV that I both danced in and directed. We brought many Russian dancers! They weren't dancing *Le corsaire* here yet, nor *The Red Poppy*, a very old ballet, or *La bayadère*. These are ballets that I incorporated into the Cuban TV repertoire, as well as the Kirov version of *Cinderella*. We showed extracts from *La bayadère* and *Le corsaire*, then also *The Dying Swan* and *Black Swan*, and since there was a corps de ballet we could mount a few things that TV audiences here were unfamiliar with.

This program disappeared over time. There is a TV program called *Danza eterna* every Wednesday, which, in the beginning, was directed by Pedro Simón, and now by Ahmed Piñeiro [see appendix B], and all of us have appeared on this TV program, myself included, as well as Josefina Méndez, Aurora Bosch, and international guests have come here from Europe. They've done interviews, put on ballets by Isabel Valdéz, having left with all the ballets that she danced here. Nobody is without ballet because we have this ballet program. There is also the program *Bravo* that features interviews with dancers and shows the ballets in which they have danced. There's a program where Alicia speaks on dance. There are "specials" that discuss ballet, contemporary dance, classical ballet, and the art in general, but each Wednesday, *Danza eterna* shows a ballet. They did a program on Maurice Béjart, one on the anniversary of *Edipo rey*, which my husband Jorge Lefebre mounted here. When my husband was director of Ballet de Wallonie, Fernando was director of Ballet de Camagüey, and we invited him to bring many choreographic pieces. Jorge Lefebre and Fernando had a great collaboration. Fernando mounted *Coppélia* and *Les sylphides* and shared his ballet class with us. He took the Ballet Nacional to Paris, where they performed on the Champs Elysées. In those years, Fernando was general director of the BNC. I mounted four ballets for the Ballet Nacional. During the anniversary of the Ballet Nacional, I am remounting a ballet of mine, and am also going to remount ballets from the huge repertoire of Jorge Lefebre. Fernando has so much interest in this that the collaboration will not be lost. He would like Laura's company to incorporate a Lefebre ballet into its repertoire.

What, in your opinion, is the future of ballet in Cuba?

When I come here, I give classes to Pro-Danza. Everything that Fernando has helped to create has a very strong foundation, and that is very important for ballet in Cuba. It's like when they ask, "OK, and after Fidel Castro, what?" There is a complete structure and organization. There are young people who relay that continuity by chance, because new ideas always bring changes into society. The ballet is a great institution in this country. So to those who say that in the absence of Alicia this company will most likely be absolutely destroyed, I answer, "Who knows how they shall come about—I don't know, but there are going to be new relays, new ways of transmitting our traditions." It's common to hear, "OK, if this government falls, will there be another one?" I believe that the people are quite attached to what they have built here, these kinds of traditions, and at the theater, it isn't very expensive to go, it's easy: musical theater, dramatic theater, ballet, and when Laura came with her company, they kept on going also. With Danza Contemporánea there was a huge cultural outpouring in the country because the people had come to like it, and weren't about to let it go.

With the fall of the Soviet Union, the Russians created a completely different political structure, and now it's very expensive to get into the theater there, and they don't fill the house. I know this because I stay in touch with them. I danced for two years with the Bolshoi and know that theater quite well. I worked outside of Cuba for two years, left Ballet de Cuba, and went to work there in an official capacity because an invitation was extended to me. So after having traveled all of Russia with *Don Quixote* with the Bolshoi, I knew the entire work from its creation on the new dancers. Today, they write to me and tell me that where there were no entrance fees before, now there are. Now at the Bolshoi Theater there are many from the diplomatic corps coming to shows, foreigners, tourists, but not working people, because it costs way more at the door than before. In spite of the transition, and even though the system has changed, the ballet tradition remains. Yes, the audience, the people are educated, and *they* aren't going to change.

What place does Fernando Alonso occupy in Cuba today?

A foreign journalist interviewed me a short time ago and asked me, "For you, who is the most important person in dance today in Cuba?" I said to her, "Without leaving any room for doubt, Fernando Alonso." That is my personal opinion because he was the creator. Without him we would not have existed. Alicia owes much to his creativity because he guided her, created a method for working where one danced with the eyes shut. He created it especially for her, and after that, from time to time, he would ask us to do that in class, and I would laugh because I couldn't. He invented an entire work method for those with physical problems, which Alicia had with her vision. So, she owes him a lot. And we owe him a lot. And Cuba owes him a lot. And every time that I have the opportunity, I insist on this, because I believe that it is only fair, and that history owes this to Fernando. From the school that he created came those work methods, theater, specialized dance styles, makeup, what he taught us about anatomy. He put all of this together in one complete method so that we would have that wealth, and wealth it is!

I came from a family with no money, and was given a scholarship. Fernando brought me books to read, records, and a record player, so that I could listen to classical music: Rachmaninov, Tchaikovsky, Wagner, Beethoven, Bach, Brahms (who was his favorite composer). So, eventually, I left to attend the youth festival. At fourteen or fifteen I would have had to continue training for at least a year or two more until I was seventeen. But I didn't lose out, because Violeta Casals had begun to teach at the University Theater. I did a play, but wasn't able to study ballet. So I went to the Havana Conservatory and studied there. Fernando proposed, "OK, you can't come to the school anymore, so I will come to the conservatory to give you private ballet class." So, Fernando was giving me private classes. I went to the choreographic school and that ended. Then, he ended his marriage with Alicia and went to Camagüey because he married Aida Villoch. I wasn't able to complete my ballet training, but in every way I came away with great reminiscences. My family always respected Fernando because he brought me so much because I had no means of buying books, nor records, and he brought those things, and engaged in conversation with my mother and father, who was a very cultured person. After the triumph of the revolution, my father was named ambassador to Uruguay. He was an independent leftist, not a party member. I asked my older sisters, "Did Dad attend party meetings?" My older sister said, "Never." He had his own ideas, but never belonged to the party. But Fernando was among the Cuban intelligentsia of that epoch. Others were González Manchester, composers, intellectuals, and yes, *they* belonged, and in the beginning they say that Alberto Alonso donated generously to the party. My older sisters belonged. I never did, as I was at the Vaganova Institute when the triumph of the revolution came, and never had a reason to. There was a lot of revolutionary activity, very intellectual, in my family. My mother, my father, read a lot, and my father had a very interesting collection of books, some of which were the books Fernando brought to me, non-political books. He brought me *The Iliad*, books by Balzac, books on the French Revolution, art and ballet books. He spoke often of the Ballet Theatre epoch, of José La Gestauer whom I later met, Lucia Chase, the dancers, and Tamara Toumanova. There was a school colloquium organized when Alicia returned from the United States. We were able to see how the dancers from Ballet Russe danced. So, when I studied at the Leningrad school I already knew about this because there was something that we have now lost, there was group cultural education. Fernando sat in, and Alicia also; but above all, Fernando, because he was who he was, and he spoke about who Toumanova was, and Danilova, and about both Ballet Russe companies. We were transfixed, listening. He brought books that showed the golden era of Ballet Russe. Then he spoke about companies of the time. When I arrived at the Vaganova school they gave us classes in theatre and dance history, of which I already knew a lot. I brought a world history book to Brussels, on *The Iliad* and *The Odyssey*, a huge tome, a gift from Fernando. He taught me about Doric architecture, Ionic, Corinthian, the columns, and historical material, the philosophy of art. It is true that I had difficulties with my artistic development because of the problems between Fernando and Alicia, and myself as a person, but the riches I received from Fernando were enormous. He had tremendous respect, fondness, and admiration for Alicia, and they had an artistic meeting of the minds. She wasn't happy that I left to dance with Béjart, but because I was appreciated for my work outside of Cuba, when Béjart invited me to join his company, I was permitted to leave Cuba, legally. Then, I married my husband, Jorge Lefebre, and came back to mount *Edipo Rey*, which she adored. The relationship between us improved. She is always eager to see me when I return from traveling.

Are there lessons from the early days that you would like to share with the Cuban dancers?

I see things done here that are wrong, including the omission of Fernando from important historical documents about the ballet because of the break between him and Alicia, and I speak my mind about them. I ran into a Ministry of Culture dignitary who talked of "writing a book in which I am going to include a lot of material on the ballet." I told him, "Well, I hope you will tell the truth." "The truth? How so?" he asked. I said, "If it's a book that tells the truth, it must say that the Ministry of Culture hasn't mentioned the name Fernando Alonso. Yes, Menia Martínez has been mentioned in the newspaper, but it is Fernando Alonso who spoke about the history of the ballet since 1948. Who struggled for the ballet to reach out to the people?" The dignitary was angry, for sure, but in the end, Fernando's name was mentioned. . . . So, if you write, I hope that you will do a better job than our Ministry of Culture!

Aurora Bosch. Courtesy of Aurora Bosch.

Fernando Alonso, ninety-fifth birthday celebration, Camagüey. Courtesy of Roberto Díaz.

Lorena Feijóo, principal dancer, San Francisco Ballet, and her mother, teacher Lupe Calzadilla. Photo by Chris Hardy, courtesy of *San Francisco Chronicle*.

Lorena Feijóo, Lupe Calzadilla, and Lorna Feijóo, principal dancer, Boston Ballet. Courtesy of Moisés Martín.

Carlos Acosta, principal dancer, Royal Ballet of London. Courtesy of Asya Verzhbinsky.

Ramona de Sáa with Fernando Alonso, Sergiu Stefanschi, and Damián Donestévez González, Toronto. Photo by author.

Tania Vergara, artistic director, Endedans dance company. Photo by author.

Grettel Morejón, first soloist, Ballet Nacional de Cuba, in *Napoli*, staged by Frank Andersen. Photo by Nancy Reyes, courtesy of Ballet Nacional de Cuba.

Alicia Alonso and the author. Courtesy of Fara Teresa Rodríguez.

René de Cárdenas

René de Cárdenas, whose parents are both dancers, danced with Ballet Nacio-
nal de Cuba for three decades and has been a guest dancer, ballet master, and
choreographer in Bulgaria, Canada, Chile, Poland, Colombia, and Spain. He
has created approximately a dozen short pieces that entered the repertoires of
several Cuban dance companies. His best-known piece is Sonlar, performed
by his own dance company, La Compañía René de Cárdenas. International
critics have compared Sonlar with Broadway productions such as Stomp and
A Chorus Line. In 2005, his compilation of short stories, Hatania de los reme-
dios, was published in Cuba. I was able to interview Rene de Cárdenas at the
Academía de Ballet building on March 19, 2008, after he taught partnering
class to students at the Encuentro de Academías.

What specifics of technique did you learn from Fernando Alonso?

For me, the starting point is love and respect for the career of dance. I always
wanted to be by Fernando's side—that's the first thing that comes to me. The
outstanding thing about him, the star he was born under, was his mastery
of teaching. It's especially outstanding for a good dancer whose career was
short. From childhood on, I always knew him as a teacher.

More than anything else, I had the opportunity to work with Fernando
on achieving a professional career. While in the school, I used to work from
two positions of the hands where I both held and raised them at the same
time. He told me that holding the hands higher, even if they were not as visible, would create an aura of inner magic and mystery. In a rehearsal, I had
my hands way in front, and they are so *big*, so he said, "No, no, no, back!"
So, I was obliged during my career to be aware of this. Fernando has always
inspired in me respect for and dedication to my career: to dance is greater
than to love!

As a student, what were the big lessons that you learned from
Fernando Alonso?

I began to study from the age of eight years old, and as soon as I graduated I joined the Ballet Nacional de Cuba, and participated in the Varna
Competition in 1978. I won First Prize there for partnering. The good work
I did with a North American dancer set a precedent for young couples in
partnering. I danced a good thirty years with the BNC and different com-

panies here, as well as in Latin America and Europe. Then I was a teacher and a choreographer, and now I'm here [at the Encuentro de Academías], to teach pas de deux. I have a company that has done two productions. The first, *Sonlar*, is a dance and percussion show that we have mounted for the last two years in Spain, France, and Portugal. Now we are about to go to Italy with it, and are already working on the possibility of the next production, the next creation. Whenever I'm in Cuba, I always join the school faculty for pas de deux technique class, as well as when the company invites me to give company class. The maestro lays the foundation for the pas de deux and pointe technique in physics. I lean a little bit more in the direction of a practice in which I have incorporated Fernando's masterly corrections from beginning technique, based on the same principles. As we heard during the Encuentro, it is not *how it's done* so much as *how it's taught* to be done that is so important. We are never done finding a point of departure or, rather, the place from which we continue—even after fifty years—of reviewing our partnering technique. A book with his program, with his methodology, is our starting point. The maestro has taught us much about how to observe in order to see the technical details, and that has enabled me to look for the essence of every movement in every step. My parents were my teachers, and I was well trained by them in my home, and because of that I enjoyed looking for ways and means to make things understood. When I give a class I try to offer various examples, but never bad ones. The maestro Fernando Alonso taught me this. Rather than point out what's incorrect, give the correction. Perhaps at another time one can say to the student that this is the wrong way, so that he or she may see what must not be done. I always avoid saying that, and look instead for what must be done to make the step come out differently. I stand by what my teachers taught me, Fernando and before him, Uvanti and Joaquín Banegas. I pointed out to the maestro things that were being done which had been changed because at the time, the dynamic and the technical level of the Cuban school had declined a lot. There were things that could be done another way, and we had conversations to define such things in the Cuban school—the technique of entire groups had changed, departed from the norm. Yes, I want to make the teaching somewhat more dynamic in terms of the images that we use. Insofar as technical steps, I try to make changes that seem timely, that go along with today's technical level of the Cuban ballet school; the current levels are very good. Whatever conversation, whatever word Fernando might say, is an edict, something well established, and much more, because now and then he will say, "Fokine told me thus and such." So then later on, Fokine is present in the words of

Fernando and through the voice of Fernando. "Anton Dolin told me such and such." These are personalities from the universal century of the dance world. What Fernando points out is a dictum from that world. Fernando's wisdom embraces both the technical and the artistic. I never saw him dance, and yet I have the wisdom that he has transmitted to me over the years, and that is crucial.

What is exceptional about your interactions with the maestro?

This is my day-by-day practice. Each time I see Fernando, there is always, besides the pleasure he takes in his work, his willingness to answer any kind of artistic or technical question. In fact, by virtue of this, he places me in rehearsals I haven't attended! I think, "Fernando, I am in rehearsal!" because he is speaking. Everything he says, even a gesture, is responding to many things that over time have changed day by day. Nonetheless, he'll say, "No, but this originally was like this." And it's a daily way of rescuing steps. Fernando's voice brings these things together artistically.

What are the challenges posed in partnering?

As in technique class, it's to search for what makes the step work the way it does. Perhaps it's difficult to see from a distance. When I see a step that doesn't go well, which a thousand dancers have succeeded at—it doesn't matter here or not here—it is not working. So OK, why is it not working? One has to look for what might be as much something on the part of the male dancer as the female. Because there are times that the male dancer is well developed, but there's something in the step that is not going well; it might be the timing, it might be the preparation, it might be the feeling, because dance is made up of feelings. Many times we will go for the technique, paying attention to the technical, physical part, and so it's not the feeling that helps us lift, turn, and that is critical. Fernando, for example, told us that many times he would turn with his eyes closed. And in class he asked us to close our eyes when doing a balance, so that in closing them, we capture the essence of everything by ear. They gave class so that barre finished that way. Being able to memorize where things are, that's what is so incredible about Alicia: With so little vision, almost none, she was able to dance! It's an indication of Fernando's wisdom that he keeps his counsel. Fernando doesn't have to speak in order to project; his wisdom is projected. To know that he possesses so much history in his hands and in his head, so much that has been created *besides* the Cuban school, a school of ballet, and such a successful school for fifty years! He projects calmness that comes from the security he has when he speaks with such exactitude about things. It confers confidence. He focuses on something technical, sought from the already-recognized French school, Russian school, and when the decision was made to say, "Let's create a school," it had to be the last word in schools! When the facts were in, one could see that the technique and artistry had characteristics that were so different from other schools, and reestablished what had been codified hundreds of years ago. Fernando's foundation is scientifically based, as is the classical ballet pas de deux in dance technique. He always speaks about how crucial physics is in understanding the centrifugal force that is the key to turns. Knowledge of how centrifugal force works helps us in closing the arms, gradually shifting to the creation of centripetal as a counterforce to give the needed impulse to establish the momentum necessary to master the turn. Brute force must be vanquished to enable you to do the things you want to do.

I was saying this today in the workshop, how there are lifts where the girls want to help by jumping *more*, but without jumping to *discover the coordination* that results when both dancers head for the same point at the same time. *Aiming* to arrive at the same place is enough. If you accomplish this, you can do without the additional force. It's customary to find a point where both dancers, without exerting any force, are tightly coordinated, the arms in sync before any step is taken, with no need of added force. Coordination creates enough force to drive the step.

Fernando has always brought in a good harvest. So he gets great results, thanks to the work in the school, to the foundation they have received, *that* is what feeds the Ballet Nacional, as well as Ballet de Camagüey.

John White

Born in Southern California, John White came to ballet via athletics, having excelled in track and field. His received his early instruction from former Ballet Russe stars Oleg Tupine and Michel Panaieff. After performing with Alicia Alonso and Igor Youskevitch in Giselle *in Los Angeles, White continued his studies with Antony Tudor and William Dollar in New York. White was invited to join Ballet Nacional de Cuba when it was under the direction of Fernando Alonso. During his stay in Cuba, White met and married Cuban ballerina Margarita de Sáa. He was promoted to soloist and became maître de ballet, teaching company men's class and also a boys' class at the state ballet school, Cubanacán. White studied the Vaganova teaching method under the Soviet teacher Victor Zaplin, who had accepted a yearlong residency in Cuba during the time White was there. After returning to the United States, White freelanced as a teacher and ballet master for several years before joining the Pennsylvania Ballet Company in 1969. In 1974 the Whites opened the Pennsylvania Academy of Ballet in Narberth, a Philadelphia suburb. Today, White is considered an authority on the Vaganova method, having conducted teachers' seminars for over five hundred teachers over a period of nearly twenty years. He is the author of* Teaching Classical Ballet *(University Press of Florida, 2008). I was able to interview John White by telephone on December 7, 2009.*

What brought you to Cuba?

I was studying ballet in Hollywood. Michel Panieff's studio happened to be a gathering place for well-known dancers because Hollywood was producing a lot of musicals. My first teacher had recommended that I study there. It was 1957. I was not quite a "finished" dancer. In the summer of 1957, Alicia Alonso brought six of her best female students to the Greek Theater in Hollywood. Big-name stars danced there. She was there to stage *Coppélia* with the six dancers, and they did that. Alicia's partner was André Eglevsky. I continued my studies for the next year, and by the end of that year, when Alicia was invited back for *Giselle*, I was a more polished product. She brought the same group of girls. I auditioned and was chosen to perform. Her partner this time was Igor Youskevitch. She wanted me to dance the Prince's Friend. I was rehearsing a good bit with Igor. He became a mentor for me. He recommended going to New York, offering to introduce me around. I went to New York in late 1958—early '59. The first Bolshoi Ballet tour of the U.S. was in 1959. Sol Hurok hired a Russian ex-dancer I had known in California as a translator, and he was tasked by Hurok Touring to retain supernumeraries for big ballets. He didn't really know the New York scene that well and asked me if I could give him a hand, which I agreed to do. I helped put together a group of fifty extras for *Romeo and Juliet* and *Swan Lake* (with Galina Ulanova) and had backstage access. I didn't get to know the Soviet dancers, but I got to watch them at work. They impressed me tremendously. In the spring of 1959, Igor and I were taking class, and he invited me to join Alicia and him for a reprise of *Coppélia* in Havana. Alicia invited half a dozen of us to her dressing room to explain that there was a good likelihood that there would be a subsidy for a ballet company. After many questions, the majority, virtually everyone except one or two, accepted. I had already signed a contract that I couldn't get out of, so I explained that I couldn't go, or couldn't go immediately, but maybe later. Alicia said that they would see how the first three months went, and whether the government would support them. At the end-of-the-year break, the U.S. dancers came home, and there was a party, and everyone said Alicia was great and Fernando was a great teacher, and had toured Latin America, and they were waiting to see whether there was a permanent subsidy, and that Alicia felt that it was likely that there would be, and they were eventually notified that there would.

I had excluded myself, but contacted Alicia by telegram. I wrote that I would like to come back with the others in the beginning of January 1960. I didn't even wait for her response; I wrote: "I'm coming with the others STOP. Will be there in a few days STOP." Margarita was present when the cable came. Alicia told her, "Vanya—my Slavic nickname—is coming with the others." So I showed up. The season hadn't yet resumed. I introduced myself to Fernando. He didn't seem to know what to do with me, but he told me, "I don't know for sure yet if everyone is going to return. Come to class. I don't know if we have openings." Two or three days later, one of the New York guys decided not to return. After class one day, one of my friends said, "Look at the bulletin board," and there was my name!

What were your initial impressions of the classes taught by Fernando Alonso?

I was very impressed; he was a conscientious and focused teacher with a grasp of what he was trying to achieve. I could tell the difference between a good and poor teacher. He was very serious. He took whatever time he needed to achieve his goals. Classes scheduled to be an hour and a half went two and a half hours depending on whether he was achieving his goal. He was developing idiosyncratic ways of doing things. I knew that he and Alicia had studied with very good teachers, and had been in Ballet Theatre, and had had good teaching, but again, as a dancer, I wasn't really analyzing. Fernando had a very masculine-oriented approach, but could deal well with the female dancers, and they liked him very much, and could work well with him. While he had no objection to gay male dancers, he discouraged cliquishness among gay men in the company and made it clear that the studio was not a domain for that. There was no resentment of this on the part of those dancers; they respected Fernando's wishes in this regard because they respected him. More specifically, with regard to work in the studio, he would say, "What you do outside of the workplace is your own business. Here, we emphasize the differences between masculinity and femininity." There was no resentment of this either, because the gay men thought he was fair-minded and that what he was asking was appropriate because the ballet roles are clearly defined.

When he gives a correction, Fernando Alonso has a habit of tagging the correction with the words, "Make a habit of it." What habits did you develop as a result of studying with him?

I subscribe to that approach 100 percent. The student should be told what comprises the habit, and then the habit has to be created. I was tuned into making my place secure, winning his attention, and roles that would come up, and promotion. Underneath, I realized I was fortunate to be working with a superior director and teacher. He seemed to enjoy teaching, and creating dancers. He did it every day and looked forward to it. Just like any teacher or director, he had a couple of favorites. His favorite was Mirta Plá. She was the one he pretty obviously leaned toward. Margarita, Josefina, and Mirta were made principals. Mirta was usually chosen. Margarita's Queen of the Wilis was beautiful, but Mirta was chosen. Nobody complained. Margarita never resented it, and she was very grateful to him for everything, and feels she owes her career to him. The Soviet tour was supposed to have been a six-week appearance in Riga, Moscow, and Leningrad, but we received such good press that we got extended through additional invitations. We went to all the Eastern European nations except Albania and Yugoslavia. We even went to China and North Korea. When we were in the Soviet Union we had classes with Soviet teachers. I had some awareness of the training of the Russian dancers, but when I saw it in full force I realized that they were onto something, and they weren't interested in satisfying anyone's curiosity. I took advantage of every opportunity onstage, of every opportunity to talk. When the tour was over, a group got together and asked Fernando if a Soviet ballet master could come. He arranged to bring one ballet master and principal male dancer. The principal was supposed to be Nureyev, but Nureyev had just defected. So they sent Azari Plisetsky from the Bolshoi instead. Margarita and I had seen him dance in *Faust* in a small concert in a meeting hall, so we knew that if he came it would be a huge coup; Victor Zaplin, one of the Bolshoi ballet masters, began working with the company. You must have a women's and a men's class, so Fernando did that, and he was teaching the men's class. I felt that this was the chance of a lifetime, but along with that, because I was so enthusiastic in accepting technique, Zaplin and I became good friends.

Zaplin met with Fernando and explained that you have to have a school to feed the company. Their private school had been given up, and so they had to build a school on the fairways of the golf club. Most of us were not particularly happy to be volunteer teachers, but we understood the importance of creating the school. Another Russian male and two women came to help build the school. Peter Gusov—an outstanding character dancer with the Bolshoi—gave me some coaching for Head Warrior in *Prince Igor*, all the more fruitful for learning the Vaganova method. They translated their nine-year syllabus into Spanish, beginning with Grade I.

As far as the school, the Russians eventually left, but had been there for more than two years, and their influence was strongly felt by those of us who were serious and admired their method. Neither Fernando nor Alicia seemed convinced: Alicia didn't want to change her approach. She was intransigent in not wanting to give up Cecchetti or the Imperial Russian school. As Fernando became a teacher he began developing his own ideas. The Russians left, and Margarita and I were on our way to the United States by 1964. Ramona, Margarita's twin sister and a principal dancer at the time, had a serious knee injury and was happy to teach. Ramona and Fernando put together the Cuban school. There is no question that the Cuban school produces excellent dancers. Fernando and I are strong proponents of retaining the artistic quality; he feels disappointed in the emphasis on technique quantity and hopes to exert some influence, with higher, bigger not allowed, and the Russians discouraged it. Fernando is a little disheartened by it.

What did you retain from those classes that you have used in your curriculum and teaching method?

In spite of my great admiration for Fernando as a teacher and ballet master, I felt that the Vaganova approach was superior, and I never had any opportunity to see him teach younger students, but I felt that the Vaganova method answered my questions. I personally have become an expert in the United States because there are few who have been taught to teach. There are plenty of Russian dancers, but few have undergone pedagogue class; some are good at it and get good results. So I have for many years been teaching the Vaganova syllabus seminars at Bryn Mawr and I will put the Vaganova method alongside the Cuban method. Luckily, we were able to put together a group of people to go to St. Petersburg to get into the school and visit, and prepare for their graduation classes, and we saw several performances, including Ulyana Lopatkina, and when you see it in their home base, with their whole company, it reminds you of what ballet is supposed to be. I owe a great debt to Fernando because he put me on the road to teaching. I developed a painful infection, and I would take weeks off to let it heal, so Fernando asked me to do some teaching. I had done a little bit in the school, and studied with the Russians. He told me, "I'd like you to take the company men's class." I was a little reluctant. I had to pay close attention to my new role. I was a soloist and a good dancer, and so I had the credentials, and I was using Vaganova, and getting good results from the guys who were struggling. I was very gratified that Fernando thought enough of me that he asked me to do that work, and I was sitting on the Artistic Advisory Board, and had the title of ballet master and took some rehearsals. We made all the decisions and were at the top level of influence. I consider him a master, and I hardly ever use that term. I don't confer that title on many people. I considered it a privilege to work with him, and go there.

In your observations of other companies and schools, what is it that they lack that they might benefit from learning from Fernando Alonso and the habits and practices of the Cuban National Ballet? What could the Cuban school and ballet learn from other companies?

I always enjoy having discussions with Ramona because we're two serious teachers who can have disagreements and talk them through. Subtle nuances of épaulement, or when to introduce complicated steps; how long to stay with certain elements in épaulement. How can you argue with the success of the school? For example, there's the Cuban way of teaching pirouettes. Cubans place the foot high from the beginning with a lot of torque. We used to have pirouette classes to analyze what everyone was doing. We were planning to go to the Soviet Union, doing the peasant pas in *Giselle*. When it came time to do our double tours, which we did pretty well, we were going to knock the socks off these Russians, and he was serious. We all got to the point where we could do them. You had to do them simultaneously four times in a row, and we couldn't all do it simultaneously. Fernando said, "I'm really disappointed, but I can see that you can't."

What do you most admire about Fernando Alonso?

In my personal experience, he's the best standout ballet master I've ever had. He had a perceptive eye for details to make a corps de ballet work as a unit, to get the best out of people without intimidation, because he put out the maximum effort himself. He was a role model. He was integrated into the revolution, in the militia, standing guard duty all night, teaching class in his uniform, a pistol in his holster. He would take the holster off and he didn't miss a beat. I owe a lot to him; he was a role model for me. I worked for a year daily with Antony Tudor, William Dollar, first-rate people. None of them rise to the level of Fernando's balance.

Lorena Feijóo and Lupe Calzadilla

Born in Havana, Lorena Feijóo trained at the National School of the Arts. She began her career at Ballet Nacional de Cuba. Prior to joining San Francisco Ballet as a principal dancer in 1999, she danced with Ballet de Monterrey, Royal Ballet of Flanders, and the Joffrey Ballet. Feijóo received the 2003 Ensemble Performance Isadora Duncan Dance Award, and has danced as a guest of the Royal Ballet.

Lupe Calzadilla says she owes everything she knows about ballet to Alicia and Fernando Alonso. After having graduated from the National Ballet School, Calzadilla danced with Ballet Nacional de Cuba for eleven years. She then taught at the school while raising her daughters Lorena and Lorna Feijóo (principal dancers with San Francisco Ballet and Boston Ballet, respectively). Having taught children and adults for more than thirty-four years, she is now a master teacher at City Ballet School in San Francisco and regularly travels to teach in South America, as well as to Cuba. I was able to interview Lorena Feijóo and Lupe Calzadilla at my home in Oakland, California, on July 22, 2009.

What are your first memories of Fernando Alonso?

Lupe: I began dancing at the Lyric Theater. My first teacher was Joaquín Banegas, whom I admired, and as his students we presented ourselves at an audition for the Cuban National Ballet Company. Alicia and Fernando wanted to merge the ballet with the opera. I was very nervous when I saw Fernando, but always was a little gutsy and very expressive, and I think that helped me. They took me, and that is how my entrance exam for the Cuban National Ballet went, and my first encounter with Fernando Alonso.

Lorena: It was a school festival where he watched a performance. Of course I had seen him fleetingly as a child. But at this festival he had just seen me in my first big role, Almendrita (who lived in an almond shell, a bit like Thumbelina). I thought, "Oh my God, this man I admired so much is watching my first big role"—I was thirteen at the time! Seeing him backstage was memorable. He had a conversation at the theater with my mom after the performance, in which he told her that he had seen only one other person dance like that at that age with such facility: Alicia Alonso. It was not about how everything went perfectly, but how I dealt with the imperfections that occurred that night, the problems, like a professional, and that he was most taken by my response, my ability to solve whatever problem presented itself. At my graduation, he called me over: "Come here, you tropical beauty! Your exam was flawless. Now I have an exercise for you." I was expecting a foot exercise or something for the arms. Instead he said, "You know, you have this little space between your nose and your mouth that needs to be stretched. Here is an exercise." He was such a perfectionist, paying attention to the details that could make you better. He is the epitome of striving for perfection.

What stood out about his demeanor that was different from your other teachers?

Lupe: He had a special way of doing and saying things. He was very strict (perhaps at times too much), but I learned huge lessons that I will value for a lifetime: discipline, respect, love for what one does, the requirements to be met. He left no stone unturned. As for his requirements, he preferred that we not take class while injured because we could not work full-out, and would risk hurting other parts of the body, which carried additional consequences that further delayed recovering and contributed to a lack of discipline in class, where we would work one side, but not the other, not jumping, turning, nor going to relevé, etc. He felt it would be better to take it easy and rest.

He couldn't understand leaving class without finishing. One day, my best friend asked permission to leave class because she was feeling sick, and he said, "Make an extra effort, and see if you can do it." She continued, but I saw that she wasn't at all well. So, I interrupted the class and said to him, "Maestro, Osilita is going to pass out!" and that was that. At the end of class I apologized to him, and he said, "The problem is that one commits an offense publicly, but asks for forgiveness privately." I promised to apologize in front of the group, and did, but it did me no good, and I received the first and only note in my work evaluation for having taken the liberty of interrupting class. The following were not permitted in class: leg warmers or body wrappers. He had to be able to see the body with knees extended, the muscles, and the abdomen held. They were allowed only when it was very cold, and then only during the first exercises.

Using a methodology that was nearly mathematical, and knowledge of the human body, he offered explanations that made the students understand, for example, centrifugal force in turns (comparing the dynamic to a washing machine), that to move the head very quickly allows one to avoid dizziness, how to turn with the body on its own axis in one stable piece, how to do exercises with breathing patterns such as those used by asthma sufferers, and much more.

Even though he was a man, he more enjoyed giving class to the women, transmitting feminine gestures quite well, even showing off a bit, in a somewhat brash way, but he knew that he knew how to get across the concept of what he wanted (his famous "little kiss" port de bras). I enjoyed each class with great satisfaction, learning something new each day.

There was something inborn in him that made him a good teacher. He had a thorough knowledge of the human body, was always well dressed, and changed from street clothes to practice clothes to let us know "I'm not just going to teach this class in my Guayabera; I'm going to be with you here fully." You had to be in class or recuperating from an illness or injury. He would never teach a class halfway. He transmitted his wishes to his students. It was infectious. He always used the mot juste to give you an image or direction. It was accurate and planned in those days, with not a lot of room for changes. There was less freedom for the corps de ballet, which was the picture of symmetry and exactitude. There was more for the principals. You went onstage knowing exactly what to do.

Lorena: My direct experience with Fernando was more in his capacity as a coach, because I didn't have him as a teacher at the school. He was working with the ballet company in Mexico City at the time. In 1992 he invited me to dance *Swan Lake* at Chapultepec Lake. Act 1 was on an island close in, and the Black Swan on an island further away. I was twenty. He was both my teacher for class and coach, and would give me notes for performances. It was an unforgettable experience. I was then able to understand why in the famous film of Alicia's Black Swan, she does six or seven pirouettes. For him, two or three were not enough. I would say: "It's OK, I've done five," and he would say, "No, you can do six. If three are comfortable, then push for four. If you do four in the studio, you'll do three onstage." He pushed her, drove her, worked with her to go further. He has this boyishness and tenderness, and yet strictness, reinforced by his pale skin and blue eyes. He's an amazing man, full of love for what he does, love for women. With respect and charm, he'll tell you, "You look beautiful this morning." He does his exercises each day. To this day, when I see him, I'll say: "Maestro, you look so handsome," and he will flex his arms and say: "Feel this; I do pushups each morning. You have to maintain yourself." I wish I had had much more, because what he has to offer is so enriching. Today it serves me as well, because at the fast pace we work, when you try to put together *Giselle* in a week and a half, you unwind your tape and go back to what you were taught. He would say, "When your technique is correct, there are no ghosts." Even now in his later years, he is striking and kind at the same time, so charming, always wearing a smile, so elegant, and a true gentleman, possessing such amazing wisdom! Always ready to work for no money, just pure love for what he does, and full of fascinating anecdotes to recount. Last year, while visiting him at his home with my sister, we spoke with him for more than three hours, and we regret that we didn't bring a camera, because it would have been amazing material for a documentary.

Tell me three things you remember from him about performing.

Lupe: In rehearsals he would tell us to keep our eyes wide open, looking to the side, ahead of us, and at the front line. He taught us how to create a perfect line, the dancers equally spaced, establishing what delineated the feeling of depth on a diagonal. The right hand gives, the left hand takes the partner's in a circle or in a line, as in the grand pas de quatre in *Les sylphides*, and other works.

How to place your head, the gaze, exactly the same, angled in various positions, the hands, the wrists, as one does for the Cygnets in *Swan Lake*, the reason for each hand placed here or there, what it means in each instance. The Wilis' hands in the second act of *Giselle* are crossed in front at waist level because that is how they are in death. Many dancers do it and don't know why; everything had an explanation because if the dancers understand why, then the audience will also understand it better. In pantomime the goal is to support the action taking place around the dancer, and it was understood that we meant support with not only gesture but by its inclination, with regard for the hierarchies: kings, queens, princes, the fear or distrust of evil characters, or to create an atmosphere on the stage supporting the lead roles. Alicia was a specialist in this element of pantomime and stage movement and had us invent stories for each of our characters. When the company was onstage at performances, no warming up was allowed in the dressing room, no eating, drinking, or sitting on the floor in costume. Onstage, you are not there to watch the show but to contribute to or support what is happening onstage, or as part of the scene, all of which is to say that all observers are seated in the audience!

We were expected to check to make certain that nothing would fall onstage, head accessories, or props, etc., so that nobody viewing the show would be distracted, nor attention shifted from the key focus. We had to be alert for the unexpected, to have a plan for solving problems, including an injured comrade. Fernando saw the corps de ballet as he saw the frame of a portrait. It either enriches or impoverishes the portrait. Badly executed corps work can ruin the entire performance for the principals. On tour, always carry everything you need in your handbag, along with your toothbrush. If the baggage gets lost, you can still take class and rehearse. His having been so demanding was what enabled us to win the Paris Grand Prix. We received various very important prizes, including one that was specially awarded to the corps de ballet that wasn't even among those in the award ceremony. At each performance, Fernando had a *regisseur* at his side, someone who noted errors. The notes would appear posted on a board the next day, so that the dancers could review what needed to be fixed or improved. It was not just about technique, although he was striving for perfection in this area. The message was that this was really to feed the soul, you were there to transmit the emotions and feelings, and it was not just about the steps. Love for the art was contagious, thanks in great part to his discipline and knowledge.

Lorena: It's hard to add anything, because it all comes down to that.

What was the most dramatic moment that you remember him having been part of?

Lupe: It was in Paris. We danced in the Fourth International Champs Elysées Festival, and some dancers left the company just a few hours before the beginning of the performance. It was a very dramatic moment for us. We had to cover the vacant spots without making a big to-do. Alicia and Fernando didn't want anyone to know. The male students had to cover various roles, and Fernando had to dance Hilarion. Because of the tensions, Alicia had a serious problem with her retina, but never would anyone have guessed that they were living out such a real-life drama, filled with anguish and repressed feelings, and exercising the utmost restraint. When this madness finally burned itself out, we were all sobbing. All the while, Alicia was on the proscenium in front of the curtain as it opened and closed, with the audience in a standing ovation. In spite of all this, we were honored with the Grand Prix of the City of Paris, and various prizes for our "Four Jewels," and a special one for the corps de ballet for its exemplary work, and I imagine that Fernando experienced one of the most painful moments of his life because of what had just happened to Alicia, and that the role he had to dance was unforeseen.

What was the most comic or pleasant moment with him?

Lupe: It was in Cuba. My two daughters Lorena and Lorna had chosen this same career as mine, and Lorena, who is the eldest, had participated in national and international competitions, and won prizes of every kind. Fernando knew her, as she was born when I was still dancing. Lorna also danced and did extremely well, and had leanings toward becoming a choreographer, and choreographed several pieces, and had won awards. Fernando and his brother Alberto went to see a school competition, but had never seen Lorna dance before. Afterwards, as they were coming downstairs, they asked me, "Why didn't you just keep on having children?" So I said, "Why? Were you thinking of creating a company named after me?" We all laughed, and I will always remember that moment as the warmest one with Fernando. In addition, I would like to take this opportunity to credit those who are seldom mentioned: all the teachers from the Alejo Carpentier Elementary School, the Middle Level High School and all the ballet schools in Cuba, directed and supervised by Ramona de Sáa, ballet adviser. Thankyou to everyone, each and every one of our principal dancers in the best companies in the world: This is a great honor for the Cuban school of ballet.

Jorge Esquivel

Jorge Esquivel danced with the Ballet Nacional de Cuba for eighteen years, most of them as Alicia Alonso's partner. They traveled the world, and he also partnered other outstanding ballerinas from Cuba and other nations. He received the Laureates Festival Medal; Diploma of Honor Katia Popova, Pleven, Buglaria; Order of Merit Rubén Martínez Villena from the Cuban Union of

Young Communists; the Italian international art prize, Il Sagitario de Oro; as well as many other prestigious awards. He currently teaches at the San Francisco Ballet School. I was able to interview Jorge Esquivel at his home in Novato, California, on April 3, 2010.

When did you begin to study ballet, and with whom?

I started to study ballet in 1961, when I was eleven years old, at the provincial ballet school, where I remained for five years. My teachers were Michel Gurov, Anna Leontieva, and then Joaquín Banegas. I went on to the National School of the Arts for two years, where I had several other teachers, but Joaquín Banegas was always my principal teacher. I graduated in 1968. We were the first graduates of the revolution. My parents were still alive, but I was raised at La Beneficiencia orphanage from around the time I was five years old. My mother got pregnant, gave birth, and at some point I got lost, and the police took me to the orphanage. My parents stayed in contact, and my dad would come and visit me. It was better for them, because at La Beneficiencia they gave me everything. My parents had eleven children. The eldest died when I was four and he was five.

I didn't know what ballet was, but they got a bunch of boys together. And in Cuba, there was machismo. Parents of kids who wanted to study ballet would say, "Study anything *but* ballet!" We were the first ones, and the most disciplined of the Beneficiencia group. We had no idea of what ballet was, but we wanted to get out of that orphanage and open a path to get to know other worlds, other people, and other ways of life. As I studied ballet, I developed an appreciation and liking for it. They took us to shows. It was nice to hear the music, see the paintings, performances, or the ballet. All of it got us excited. It reached the point that there were about thirty in the group, but only seven graduated; the rest stayed behind. When I was at the National School of the Arts, I participated in a competition in 1968 and was awarded second place. I graduated in October. I danced in *The Sleeping Beauty*, but prior to that I participated in the Varna Competition with Ámparo Brito, who would become my first wife and the mother of my daughter, Yoira. I started to know and work with professionals. That's where I really learned a lot, more than I did in school. It was the maximum experience. There was Alicia Alonso, Fernando Alonso, the choreographer Alberto Alonso, and also many principal dancers. It was a source that truly enriched me technically and artistically. Afterwards, I began to work technically with Fernando Alonso, who was the director of the National Ballet.

What did Fernando Alonso contribute to your development?

I can tell you that he was the teacher of teachers. Fernando is like the encyclopedia of ballet. Truly, he knows it all. He has worked with different people, choreographers, in many places around the world, having been brilliant in directing the National School of Ballet. To speak of ballet in Cuba and not include Fernando Alonso is like speaking about ballet without Alicia Alonso, or Alberto Alonso. They were the three cornerstones of the foundation for ballet in Cuba. Alicia was the ballerina; Fernando, the director; and Alberto was the choreographer. All the requirements were there. What was missing? The support and funding that the 1959 revolution provided for ballet. And that was what took place. The revolution became the fourth cornerstone. Ultimately, the Cuban ballet would represent Cuba, and Fidel Castro would represent communism. And in that way, the school developed along with the company. It was greatly enriched, little by little, by the graduating classes in the years 1968, 1969, and 1970. Before that, there had been girls but not men. The artistic and technical level was very low at first, because the men were cabaret dancers, but they got to be first-rank dancers due to their strengths, drive, and self-sacrifice. Little by little, the men's level rose higher and higher. Fernando would spend time with us, talking, having coffee. Fernando, for me, was a huge figure, not because he was the director, but because when he taught, he spoke a lot about muscles, conditioning, and tissue! He knew the human body so perfectly that he could have graduated in medicine; so perfectly. In the San Francisco school I apply the knowledge I received from Fernando to my students. I didn't study medicine, but his inspiration is there. The dancer cannot dance without knowing his or her instrument, which *is* the body. He practically gave us anatomy class while giving ballet class! For me it was enormous, not only the artistic part, but also to have the background in anatomy, the musculature, and to know and understand the body. People dance to dance, but they don't always know what they are doing. People do turns, pirouettes, jumps, but by that alone you don't achieve the artistic quality. A simple movement has to be understood in terms of common sense. That movement has an expressiveness, a meaning, a definition; it isn't just "move for the sake of moving," but a feeling! And at the same time, he prepared me for the competitions. He was my personal coach, and my coach within the company. We lost men in Paris and in other places, so we had to push the male dancers out from among the graduates to move into those vacancies. I sincerely never thought of becoming a principal dancer, of ever being Alicia Alonso's dance partner. I just worked and worked without worrying about criticism. One knows when one has danced well or not. At that time, they were meticulous. Not only technically, but it was like the military. As Lorena told you about the corps de ballet, everyone must move with exactitude. That's why it was one of the best companies in the world. We had as examples Alicia and Fernando, who were so rigorous.

What were the high points of your career?

One of the biggest things was graduating and dancing with the Cuban Ballet Company. I have danced in more than fifty countries, and so many times. My first U.S. tour was in 1975, when Alicia and I went and broke the cultural blockade. They gave us diplomatic passports! We had police escorts, motorcades! We were in Central Park, and stayed at the Waldorf-Astoria, as if we were heads of state, presidents! Whatever we needed, we could just sign for it! Also, to work personally with Alicia, when I first danced with her in 1969—it was in the second act of *Swan Lake* in Havana, and little by little, I began to dance with her more often. I was a young boy, but so anxious to learn. I did a lot with her around the world, not just with the company. We were the point of the bayonet, Alicia and I, when we came to the U.S. in 1975. Then, little by little, more dancers danced at festivals like Spoleto, with different figures in the dance world. I was almost Alicia Alonso's exclusive partner. I began officially in 1972, and was promoted to principal. We danced to Alberto Mendez's *Edipo Rey*. It was a privilege to have experienced those huge mentors who led us to fight and keep going. When Alicia and I arrived in Paris after a long flight, she said, "OK, Jorge, we have to take class." "We have to take class?" I asked. "Look at my foot. It's swollen!" I had circulatory problems because of an Apollo costume that compressed my legs. There was no studio available, but she got them to find a terrace and I thought "Oh my God!" What could I say, except "Of course"? Afterwards I felt better, and when Alicia was feeling poorly I think that taking class was a remedy, like taking an aspirin.

I have heard Fernando give a student a correction and then say, "Make a habit of it." What habits did you acquire as a result of your training with Fernando?

Fernando generally gave us technical classes and, at the same time, paid attention to our work as professionals. Everyone makes technical mistakes that we work on constantly, every day, until we wipe them out. Even artistically—because in working you absorb many good things, but also bad ones. If you work and don't correct mistakes, they turn into bad habits. One must have discipline and begin on one's own to erase them little by little. Otherwise, your teacher would have to be there all the time to tell you what to correct. There comes a point when you are even dreaming about the correction. In Cuba it's very healthy: you can ask students to repeat something and you won't hurt their feelings. They *expect* a surgical approach to corrections.

In observing other companies where the dancers are not Cuban, what would you say those dancers don't get in their training that they would get if they had trained in Cuba?

Many students from other countries go to Cuba, and Cuba doesn't have the ballet tradition Russia has. Fernando, Alicia, and Alberto received support from the revolution so that the ballet could thrive and tour the world each year to show our work and accomplishments in the United States, Europe, Mexico, or Latin America. There is an atmosphere of healthy competition there. The *compañeros*-dancers there have danced for decades, thirty, forty, some even fifty years! Many new dancers are second or third generation, like my daughter, the Feijóos, the Sarabias, the Carreños—so beautiful! Not like here, where they tend to give it up after three or four years. There's a passion to improve.

Not only do they study, they practice all the time. You can take class, but if you don't practice it comes to nothing. When they finish class, they keep going, engaging in healthy competition, not based on ego, but on helping each other. After the revolution there were several good ballerinas like Josefina Méndez, Aurora Bosch, Loipa Araújo, but no guys. The guys came afterwards. It gave the company much more to select from. The men got to be better and better. This was a necessary period for the acceleration of ballet. To be a good dancer, you have to have technique, artistry, be a good partner, but above all, passion! Carlos [Acosta]! One of the best in the world and so humble, so nice, so beautiful! It's amazing when he's onstage. I am so proud because that *is* Cuba!

What were your most memorable personal times with Fernando?

He helped me a lot when I went to Camagüey; I had been with the BNC for eighteen years and wanted a change. I am grateful for what I was given in Havana, but I had worked so hard and didn't want to be obligated for my entire life. In 1985, I wanted to leave, and approached the Ministry of

Culture. They encouraged me to wait a year, and one year later, in 1987, I went to Camagüey to guest. I knew the sacrifices they were making there, and wanted to help, only for a year, not a lifetime. I loved being there with Fernando.

If you could turn back the clock, what role could you imagine him playing today?

You are not king because you wear the crown; you are king because of *who* you are. He doesn't need a title to be a leader. His will, effort, experience, knowledge, wisdom, authority, and modesty make him who he is. It would be so good for Cuba if he could go on forever. He has produced so many good teachers, and I stand to the side and say, "Keep on going for the next generation!"

Why did you leave Cuba?

I left Camagüey to teach in Spain for Lola De Avila. Armando Hart from the Ministry of Culture saw me there and said, "It's good you are teaching here, but we need you in Cuba!" The important thing is that I teach, and give my best to the students. It doesn't matter where, whether they are Japanese, Cuban, American, Chinese, or Spanish. I have something they need, the best of me. In Cuba they already have it, and sharing it with others doesn't betray my nation. It is beautiful there. I will never speak against my country to those in power here. I will never betray the nation that gave me these medals from the Cuban Armed Forces [he retrieves a collection of medals from a display case]. I received this People's Medal—the highest one; my image was on postage stamps. People ask me, "Why don't you open your own school?" I don't want to work that hard. I just want to give my best to these students. Don't push me now, because after all, I worked so hard when I was sixteen, seventeen, and nineteen and had huge responsibilities—a principal at twenty-one! There was only one of me, and if I was dancing with Josefina, Loipa, and another one, I'd dance with Josefina and she was done, but *I* still had two more to dance with! I'm not complaining; I just don't want to work at that pace now! All my respect goes to Alicia Alonso, to have put together what she learned from the time of Mordkin. I'd hoped to see Fernando in Canada, but wasn't chosen by San Francisco Ballet to go to the Assemblée Internationale there. I was not only his student—he was my friend. He was not only a maestro, but he was a father to us. He took such great care of Alicia and would say to me, "Jorge, look out for her."

Lorna Feijóo and Nelson Madrigal

Lorna Feijóo, described as "stunning with an exceptional attention to detail" by the New York Times, *studied at the National Ballet School in Havana and became a principal dancer while with the Ballet Nacional de Cuba. She has performed on world tours, and won critical acclaim for leading roles in classical and contemporary ballets. She has received numerous awards, including gold medals at the Vignale-Danza Competition and the Positano Competition of Young Talents in Italy. She has danced with Cincinnati Ballet and been a guest artist with the Royal Ballet, Rome Opera Ballet, La Scala and Zurich Opera Ballets, and has performed at international festivals and ballet galas in Cuba, Europe, Canada, and Japan. A principal dancer at Boston Ballet, Feijóo is married to Boston Ballet principal dancer Nelson Madrigal and is the mother of their daughter, Lucia.*

Nelson Madrigal trained at Cuba's National Ballet School and joined Ballet Nacional de Cuba in 1994, where he was a distinguished premier danseur. Madrigal was a principal dancer with Cincinnati Ballet in 2002 and 2003. He joined Boston Ballet in 2003. He is married to Lorna Feijóo and the father of their daughter, Lucia. I was able to interview Lorna Feijóo and Nelson Madrigal at the Boston Ballet building in Boston, Massachusetts, on November 10, 2009.

What are your most vivid recollections of Fernando Alonso?

Nelson: We didn't work that closely with Fernando because at the time we were studying he was in Mexico [1989–94] and no longer able to play a role in the Cuban National Ballet. We were so lucky to have known him because he is the grandfather of ballet in Cuba.

Lorna: With me it's a little different, because I knew him through my mother [Lupe Calzadilla] and sister [Lorena Feijóo] and worked with him in Italy. Even though he wasn't around, his legacy was established, transmitted to us generation by generation. I was in Italy in 1991 when I was a student at the ENA [National School of the Arts], three years before my eighth and final level. The first five levels are considered elementary, and then the last three are pre-professional, the final year of which is called "the graduating year." Fernando was on the jury at the Vignale Competition in Italy, and he was coaching Cubans and non-Cubans, whoever needed help. That is the kind of person he is. There is a nice photo of *Don Quixote*, with me as Kitri, in *attitude*, where I am just slightly touching Fernando. At that moment I felt like I was touching a god. He possesses a kind of warmth that makes you feel that you've known him all your life. He shows so much respect. Chery [Ramona de Sáa], Fernando, and I were together at Vignale Center. There was a wonderful feeling of collaboration and respect there.

How did your dance education and career begin?

Lorna: I was playing a game of jacks while the exams for the school were taking place, and told my mother that I wanted to take the exam just to see if I could get in. I passed, and began the first year. They evaluate you every two months, and you have to pass each subject with the minimum requirement or you don't advance to the next level in ballet. The other subjects are, French, piano, modern dance, character, music, folkloric, etc. We had repertoire in class to test our ability to perform, so when I finished that first year, after experiencing rehearsing and performing, I told my mother, "I want to dance ballet."

When did you advance to pointe?

Lorna: We don't go on to pointe until we are eleven years old. You have to be old enough to be able to focus, and it used to be ten years old in my mother's day, but by ten or eleven it is believed that the children are ready to decide, focus, and concentrate. You also have to have the technical foundation. So we begin pointe in the second part of second year at eleven years old, with just barre exercises in the beginning. There might be five to eight students in a pointe class.

You learn just a few steps each year; you don't do *entrechat six* [six criss-crossing leg beats in the air] or double pirouette until fifth level. If the teacher sees that you can do a double before that level, she might let you do one extra, just to encourage you and the rest of the group. The student is kept in a certain space to perfect a few steps, but when she shows the capacity to do more, she is allowed to. It's a way of saying to the class, "Look, if you work as hard as she does, someday you will do one more too!"

Nelson: When a guy is very talented, sometimes he can go further, as with Carlos [Acosta] or [Rolando] Sarabia.

Lorna: Ramona and Fernando met regularly with teachers from each city to compare their impressions of the students and evaluate the curriculum as it applied to each student's needs. What can they bring together? What doesn't work? The goal is to have a uniform pedagogy throughout the island, and so all the teachers from everywhere meet together to discuss the curriculum, as well as each student's individual development measured against it. The student-to-teacher ratio is about fifteen to one, but sometimes as low as eight to one. There are more students in character class because boys and girls take it together. Each teacher has her script, but we know that the step is the same. You don't hear one thing from one teacher and something different from another, as so often happens in the U.S. Chery consults with everyone in order to reach an agreement, instead of teachers disagreeing and confusing students with contradictory instruction. They put their trust in Fernando because they are harvesting the fruit of his work. It is fifty-fifty. Half is the talent the student brings, and the other half is the support that Fernando's methodology provides, implemented by the current pedagogical team led by Chery.

Please say more about the everyday life of the Cuban-trained ballet student, such as those who attend the Encuentro de Academias?

Lorna: They come from everywhere, not only Cuba. In the Cuban system, you do not start with grand plié, but with tendu, so that you do not work certain large muscles before developing other smaller ones; otherwise you risk overworking them and sustaining injuries that will affect you for your whole life. Fernando consulted doctors to perfect this progressive method.

Nelson: He studied methodology like someone studying medicine.

Lorna: My parents thought that if I were to study ballet, it would provoke conflict between my sister and me. When I was in third level Lorena was in fifth, and had won a prize. They were worried that I wouldn't reach that level. One reason they were worried was that I liked to eat chocolate. My father used to say that I would make a fantastic modern dancer: "Lorena will be first in classical, and Lorna in modern dance." I said "No. I want to dance classical ballet."

We started at 7:30 a.m. with ballet class, and then at 2:30 we had our academic classes, which went until 7:30 p.m. If we were to perform, we'd be at the theater until midnight. It is very important to have repertoire class from the beginning, because you are performing onstage right away, and you won't have stage fright. You are right in the element that you will be in for the rest of your career.

To qualify for the pre-professional level you have to take an exam in the fifth level. All the schools from all the cities go to Havana to take the exam. It works like this: Every school sends students, but maybe as many as fifteen or as few as four will be chosen out of as many as five hundred. By the fifth level, maybe an outlying school will have ten in Level Five to send to the exam. From all of those schools, each with its ten or fifteen or five, they pick the best. When you go into the first year of pre-professional (Level Six), you have partnering class (adagio). Fernando was insistent that once you are in that class, you leave your sexual preferences at the door: women in front, men behind. The male dancer must always be a gentleman; he has to support the woman to show her off. That relationship is intended to emphasize his masculinity and virility, and places a contrasting spotlight on the woman's femininity.

What details did Fernando make you more aware of?

Lorna: I met Fernando in my seventh year of training. I was in the corps de ballet but was doing principal roles. It's very important to do the corps work because the corps is where you pick up the company's style. When Fernando set up a diagonal to be wide or narrow, he taught us that it was always the second dancer, not the first, who is crucial to the integrity of that line. The second one has to correct any error that the first one may make because of having no other dancer to follow, and all the other dancers will set their course on her. He taught Alicia this, and Alicia taught it to Josefina, and it was passed all the way down to the rest of us. The first dancer must breathe deeply as part of a big preparation. This is a signal to the others. The great dancers who followed Alicia—Loipa, Mirta, Josefina, and Aurora—had high standards. They were perfect models for what to do. It is part of the tradition that you don't get those leading roles right away; you have to go through the corps, and then follow those who went before. The steps are there to follow, not jump into. It's a gradual replacement process. New ones replace older ones when their time comes. I was lucky because I joined when Lorena left, and it was time for a new generation. I worked with Loipa and Josefina on the role of Giselle. They taught me all that I know.

I had seven years with the company, and then Nelson and I went to Zurich and went back to Cuba on tour. We thought we would go to Zurich for only six months and then continue to dance in Cuba, but we stayed in order to avail ourselves of the European tradition and make it part of who we are as dancers. While on tour in Cincinnati they offered us a contract. We raised it with Alicia, and she asked us whether we were sure that was what we wanted to do. We knew she'd say yes because we had good relations with her. We felt that Zurich and Cincinnati were a bridge to various opportunities. We were very young, and wanted to dance Forsythe and some other contemporary choreographers' work in order to move to another level.

Nelson: I had never thought about the United States, but the welcome we received made me realize that there was something to take advantage of here.

Lorna: I had a chance to dance *Ballo della regina* in Cuba. It opened us up to Balanchine, and in the U.S. there are more of those kinds of chances— Forsythe, Kylian, etc. We loved Victoria Morgan, the Cincinnati Ballet artistic director, but wanted to move to a city with a big company, and so we joined Boston Ballet.

How did you begin your training and career, Nelson?

Nelson: I was riding my bicycle one summer afternoon, on my way to my grandfather's house. He was a bookseller. I was going around to the garage, and Micaela Tesleuano, a ballet mistress for the Cuban National Ballet, was on her way into my grandfather's, because she was a customer of his. She noticed me, and wondered who this boy was, and what he was up to. She also noticed that I had a well-conditioned body. I used to play basketball and ride my bike. I knew little or nothing of ballet, except what I saw on TV. But she saw something in this street kid. Normally, kids of school age go to the countryside for two months each summer to a work-study camp. Two weeks after we arrived at the camp, there happened to have been a hurricane, and so we were sent home. Michaela showed me books from Paris Opera and videos, and asked me if I was interested in studying ballet. I asked, "Do I have to go back to the countryside?" She said, "No, it's in the city." Classes for boys my age had already begun, and I was already thirteen, so she took me to the school herself. I probably never would have ended up a dancer had it not been for the hurricane, her taking me to the school, and me having a ballet body, but I still had problems. They took me right away, but asked me, "Would you prefer to start with girls your own age or in the ten-year-old boys' class?" I was thirteen, and so there was no question: "I'll go with the girls." I didn't know any better, so I wore my tights the way the girls did, with leotards over them. It wasn't a bad life: I could stay in the city, and spend my days in a studio full of ballerinas!

Because I had no idea what they were talking about in class, I decided to take my work very seriously. My mother asked the teachers whether I really had talent. She didn't want me to have illusions. So, in that same year, I was promoted to the appropriate level for my age, with the boys. I ended up doing five years in three. I was taking first- and second-year classes in tandem each day. Even though I was missing some steps, they kept checking to see if I still wanted to continue. They wanted to make sure that when I reached that fifth level I had all the required steps. I had many teachers. Usually you keep the same teacher for five years for consistency, and stay with the same group, but that wasn't the case for me when I reached fifth year, even though my earlier teachers were still checking in with me. "You came late, but don't get discouraged," they would tell me. "The others will be a little ahead of you." But then I graduated with the maximum grade. A jury of five or six judges from the company artistic staff, and the school faculty, gives you a grade. The grade range is 72–100. I got 100 [as did Lorna and Lorena].

Lorna: The school is very hard. You lose your childhood, but there is nothing like it, and in the long run you appreciate it.

Nelson: It's different for men and women. For a girl it's a dream, a fairy-tale Cinderella story. For a boy it's more like training for a sport, to be a boxer or baseball player. Eight guys might compete for three places. The boys from my neighborhood would all come to see me dance, and a few of them gave me a hard time. If it had been Brazil, I'd say you could compare the Cuban National Ballet School to a soccer training school.

Lorna: In Cuba, being a dancer is considered a higher calling than being a doctor. It's a point of pride for everyone in Cuba to know the name of every single principal dancer.

Donald Saddler

Donald Saddler was born on January 24, 1918, in Van Nuys, California. A founding member of Ballet Theatre (subsequently re-created as American Ballet Theatre), he has been a choreographer, director, dancer, and producer. He taught at Juilliard School of Music, and today performs ballroom dance with Marge Champion. They recently appeared together at Jacob's Pillow Dance Festival. I was able to interview Donald Saddler by telephone on January 11, 2010.

At what point were you in your career when you first met and worked with Fernando Alonso?

I arrived in New York on Saturday morning of Easter week, 1939. I knew only one person in New York at the time, and that was Paul Godkin. He had given me a ticket to see *Stars in Your Eyes*, and pointed out the stage door to me, so that I could meet him after the matinee. So I went back after the show, and out came Nora Kaye, Maria Karnilova, and Alicia and Fernando Alonso! All of them! So I met Fernando on my first day in New York in April 1939. Then we all auditioned for Ballet Theatre in September 1939, and were accepted into the company as corps de ballet dancers. I danced with the company for two years, and then was overseas in the service for two years beginning in 1942. By the time I returned, Fernando and Alicia were in Cuba.

Can you describe what it meant to be the first members of Ballet Theatre?

We were all eager because it was the first American ballet company. We were so fortunate because we got to work with Michel Fokine, Adolph Bolm, Bronislava Nijinska, Antony Tudor, and the young Eugene Loring. So it was an extraordinary opportunity for a young dancer to work with dancers of the past and future.

What did Fernando contribute to the company?

Well, onstage, he danced Peter in *Peter and the Wolf*. He had a major role in *Billy the Kid* as the Red Cowboy, and we all danced in *Aurora's Wedding*. We had a great time offstage! We both loved classical music. When we were in the dressing room, he'd start whistling the theme from some classical symphony and I'd join in, or one of us would begin whistling a classical piece and the other would have to finish it. We bonded around music. It was a joyous period. We were young and carefree, and so fortunate to be working with the masters. We were the fortunate ones.

What distinguished Fernando from other dancers you knew at the time?

He had a gift for comedy, both onstage and in life. We laughed a lot. We were good buddies.

Were you able to dance with Ballet Alicia Alonso or Ballet de Cuba in its first years?

Alicia did a gala performance, and sometimes I was her partner. We were all in *Giselle*, but sometimes her eye would move and she wasn't sure where she was going, and under my breath we would whisper "Alicia" and take her where she was going. Fernando really worked with her and tutored her, and turned her into the ballerina she was. He worked with her every day, and was her master. I'm sure she would agree with that.

What indications were there that he would become an accomplished ballet pedagogue with an international reputation?

He did a lot of coaching in Cuba and went to Paris and other countries to teach. Unfortunately, I lost track and only saw him for short intervals after the war. I'm terribly fond of him, as he is of me. He's so very intelligent and well educated. The Alonsos, his family, were very fine people, very nearly the First Family of Cuba. His mother started the dance school there, as part of Pro-Arte Musical. The family members were "doers" and had among them many accomplishments. Fernando had beautiful manners, as well being educated in both music and dance, and had he been taller, he would have had more and different roles, but he was a beautiful dancer. I mostly remember him in *Billy the Kid* and *Peter and the Wolf*. I think he was the first to do the role after Eugene Loring, whose ballet it was. Yes, when I met him the first day I came to New York, I learned that they were all studying with Mme Fedorova, and so naturally, I went and studied there, and then we went to Mordkin and studied there, and then Mordkin started Ballet Theatre.

Grettel Morejón

Grettel Morejón was introduced to ballet thanks to the efforts of her mother and grandmother. When she was still very young, they emphasized to her the necessity of expressing one's theatrical ability through use of the body. They prepared the foundation that started her down the road that led to her advanced dance education at the Cuban National Ballet School. It's a road she continues to follow today as first soloist with the Cuban National Ballet Company. Having seen the company's 2010 London tour, New York Times *dance critic Alistair Macaulay wrote of Morejón: "Gretel [sic] Morejón, delivering ballet bravura in toe shoes of unusual softness, shared Mr. Acosta's happy exuberance." I was able to interview Grettel Morejón by e-mail on July 28, 2009.*

When did you begin to study ballet? Tell me about your career since then.

I began to study ballet at ten years old at the Alejo Carpentier Provincial School of Ballet. I had magnificent teachers there, such as Sara Acevedo, Moraima Martínez, Marta Bosch, and the counsel of the master teacher Fernando Alonso in the fourth and fifth years mostly, among others.

During my fourth year they chose me to participate in the Seventh International Competition for Ballet Students, which took place every two years during the International Meeting of Academies for Ballet Instruction. I won third place in the first of three categories in this event.

After five years in the elementary level, a jury composed of outstanding individuals in Cuban dance, including such teachers as Ramona de Sáa and Fernando Alonso, selected me to study at the National Ballet School. For three years in a row I took first place in the eighth and ninth competitions in the second category: fifteen- to sixteen-year-olds, in variations, and in the third category, with the pas de deux from the third act of *The Sleeping Beauty*. My most outstanding teachers in that level were Adria Velásquez, Marta Irís Fernández, Mirtha Hermída, and, certainly, Fernando Alonso. These years were essential for my technical and artistic development. During this time I consolidated what constitutes dance, as well as the importance of working intelligently, indicated by the details and different styles that each choreographic piece requires.

In order to become a member of the Cuban National Ballet, students must pass an exam in their third year, adjudicated by the ballet masters, as well as a state exam, where students appear in a rehearsed program that includes pas de deux, solos, and choreography from the classical and contemporary repertoire. In that test I danced the pas de deux from the third act of the ballet *Don Quixote* and the first act of *Paquita*. This resulted in my being one of the dancers chosen to spend six months as a pre-professional in the BNC, and in 2007, I was accepted into its corps de ballet.

After finishing the three years in intermediate level, dancers selected for the BNC, as well as Ballet de Camagüey and other national companies, complete six months of pre-professional practicum, and if after that the companies hire them, they must complete two years of social service, and then they are promoted.

During the six months of pre-professional practice, I danced important works and original choreography presented for the first time at the Twentieth Havana Ballet Festival, such as *Nocturno* by Igal Perry, a neoclassical piece for three couples to music by Chopin, and *Danzas de Mozart* by Eduardo Blanco. I also danced *Rara avis* (second movement), with choreography by Alberto Méndez, and the Flower Festival of Genzano pas de deux. Additionally, I participated in the Women's Dance Festival in Ecuador, where I danced the pas de deux from *Flames of Paris*. In the same year that I joined Ballet Nacional, 2008, I was chosen to dance the pas de six from the third act of *Napoli*, which premiered in Cuba, and was staged by the guest artist Frank Andersen from the Royal Danish Ballet. At the Twenty-First Festival we debuted the entire third act of this work, together with two stars of that company, Diana Cuni and Thomas Lund. At the same festival, which took place in October 2008, we danced two pieces by Alicia Alonso which were a landmark in my career, *Lucía Jérez* (inspired by a novel by the same name by José Martí), a ballet with great dramatic content, where I was given the role of Sól del Valle, and also the role of Elisa in *The Magic Flute* (a one-act ballet), with principal dancer Yoel Carreño as my partner. Among other roles of importance that I have danced are the Blue Bird pas de deux from *The Sleeping Beauty* (Alicia Alonso's version based on the original), *Muñecos*, by Alberto Méndez, and the pas de trois from *Swan Lake* (Alicia Alonso's version based on the original).

This year I was promoted to first soloist after completing the two years of social service.

When did you begin to study with Fernando Alonso?

I remember that when I was an elementary student, he observed classes, and the majority of the time, ended up giving them. He gave us exercises designed to overcome our deficiencies and to teach us how to learn to feel the dance, giving us very eloquent corrections based on very practical theories from everyday life. For example, he would say to us, "Girls, those knees have to be straightened as tight as when a door closes, so that they don't bend; locked, they must be like a tree trunk, you must feel as if they are about to break."

I remember that he insisted a lot on correct alignment of the knees from *en dehors*, but above all, the pleasure with which one must perform all dance movements. "Dance is the poetry of movement," he emphasized to us.

Many times, he arrived at the school when we had already finished class, but we had to take advantage of the opportunity; so we took class again! In those days, I saw him as a luminary and held him in the highest regard.

Besides, it seemed incredible to me that there was someone so capable of having his students perfectly "get" what he was saying and correct it. His corrections came across in a surprising manner, in the sense that, as he was speaking, different images would pass through my mind, and I would suddenly change what I was doing as I began to understand how to correct the error. It was incredible!

Then, when I joined the National Ballet School, he continued to coach us at closer range. I was lucky that he was the teacher with whom we concluded our training during the first year of my group's career (no other group after that enjoyed that privilege), and I was excited. He gave us as many as three hours of class per day, but he took pains with each poorly formed tendú, with each port de bras and each head that showed no feeling. I remember that I improved a lot with his classes, because I began to assign importance to each step, to value every movement.

During my second year, with the assistance of the teacher Mirtha Hérmida, he taught me the pas de deux from the third act of *The Sleeping Beauty*. One day, at the beginning of class, Mirtha, who was the ballet mistress to whom I was assigned, invited him to the rehearsal. After that day, he visited us almost daily. He took over the pas de deux rehearsals and worked us, "cleaning" to the most minimum detail. I continued to work with "el profe" up to my graduation. I worked with him mostly on the pas de deux from *The Sleeping Beauty* and the third act of *Don Quixote*. He also visited and assiduously participated in the adagio and technique classes, because these were the bases for learning and developing all the techniques, so that both partners could correct the flaws that often accumulate, mostly for lack of an expert eye, and because the human body is a continuous generator of flaws—as Fernando Alonso would say—so it generates them without our realizing it. It is for this reason that the dance student needs the rigorous eye of his or her teachers every moment, and their patience with those who are in their first stage of apprenticeship.

What impressed you most about him?

I think it was the incredible capacity for re-creating anything through his explanations, including the nuanced details of a bird's movement: I can see it, feel it in my body, and fully become it. Whenever I listen, I can imagine an entire ambience, epoch, an individual, each detail of the place, a sense that forms part of the story; it's impressive. Then everything is more visible through the movement and the music.

On the other hand, his perseverance and constant struggle to reach perfection, as well as the unflagging battle in search of styles, emotion, dance. He always told me: "The story must excite you to be well told; the results, truthful; the audience has to feel it, it has to result in an explosion; that starts with the whole of you. If you don't believe what you are doing, the audience will be less likely to believe it; dance has to make it come to life." His enormous knowledge of physics, history, and the arts, and how they are all related, is amazing.

Also I admire the tremendous respect and passion for his work that he demonstrates on a daily basis. He has never come to a rehearsal without having previously studied each detail of the choreography, the music, the style, or the history. He asked us every day who our characters were, and about their characteristics. He sought intelligent results for each step, and when the partnering came off perfectly he would rehearse it with us over and over. We perfected it, purified it, and it was unimaginable how one could identify any movement, including of the head, that didn't correspond to the style, or whatever accent of the feet that didn't respond to the music. He had an incredible musical ear! He told me: "My little one, you must feel that phrase as it builds into a crescendo; for each note, in each musical phrase, there comes a movement which must carry forward the character of the melody you are dancing."

He taught us to translate what we were dancing, because each movement has its own meaning. In the variation, for example, I told the story of Aurora: when she was growing up, when her finger was pricked, the one hundred years that went by afterwards, and finally, he taught us to make sense out of all of it. I remember that one day we began the rehearsal practicing the steps which were giving us the most difficulty as we had been doing each day, and he made me repeat the developpé from the first pas de deux for approximately one hour, because he said that it had to be perfectly executed, with the required en déhors, and the knee stretched to the limit, to infuse it with a sensual light. It was very funny, because I repeated it so many times that the point of my shoe came apart, and we hadn't yet begun the actual rehearsal! Our teacher Mirtha always told this story to her students when they grew tired from repeating steps more than twice, because as Fernando put it, "Repetition is the source of perfection."

Never were we bored from the successive hours of rehearsal, because each day we discovered something new, and his pedagogy of giving us corrections little by little, without hurrying through them, without them piling up and accumulating, is one of his great virtues. However, I believe that what has always blown me away about him, besides the certitude of his opinion, is his teaching style that made dance come alive through the rhythm, the details, the glances, and the soul.

What distinguished him from your other teachers?

It's his struggle to conquer, and wanting to know the history of all that surrounds him, and besides his patience, his great intellectual capacity and knowledge of each style and epoch, and the broad cultural dominion he inhabits.

There is also his unceasing battle to preserve the values and forms of the Cuban school of ballet, and the immense concern for his students, as well as the ongoing connection he maintains with them, forming an inseparable relationship of confidence and respect. I have never known a teacher more attentive to problems of his students, just as much for the personal as the professional ones, and besides that, a constant counsel and a trusted confidant. He is well versed in psychology, and utilizes it all the time, and with all people—and his memory, the capacity to remember everything, up to the most elusive of details, and finally, there is his unremitting perseverance.

What did he do that made you realize that he recognized your potential as a dancer?

He has always been untiring, dedicated, persevering, happy, and proud when you achieve something that he puts forward, and it arrives onstage as it is supposed to, or when his students have reached a point where they call attention to and awaken the feelings and enthusiastic applause of the audience. I simply tried to make my own any detail he shared to bring me closer to internalizing as precisely as possible all the corrections he gave me. I think that he sensed from the very beginning the love that I have for dance and the passion that I try to bring to all that I do. I always felt that he responded to me as if this were the case. For my part, I am as particular and stubborn as he is.

In one of Fernando's master conferences in an Encuentro Internacional de Academias, when I was in my second year, he showed a compilation of videos to demonstrate the development of the Cuban school across the various generations shaped by it, and several of *Sleeping Beauty*, danced by Josefina Méndez, Mirta Plá, and others who were among our greatest ballerinas, and at the end, he showed one of us: the one in which my partner Dani Miguel Hernández and I had danced the night before in the

Gran Teatro de La Habana. He felt extremely proud of the arduous work that he had done with "his couple." Also, he is a teacher who knows what to say when things are not going well, without hurting you, but he has the capacity to demonstrate it, and make the dancer think about how much to give and how much one can achieve in one's career. He has never been interested in achieving something in a highly gifted person if that person doesn't seem to really want it. In terms of what he gives a dancer, the dancer's enthusiasm carries more weight than the innate conditioning or ability of that dancer.

What was the best advice you received from him?

I was a bit nervous when I joined the Ballet Nacional because it meant I would have to leave my student days behind and become a professional, and that would mean a radical change for me, not to mention the uncertainty that arises with such a change, and as I was speaking with Fernando about this he said something which I will never forget: that never should I tire of working, and that never should I become depressed if at any moment things aren't going well; because the sun cannot be covered with one finger and talent always rises to the top, that what one must do is persevere and learn everything for oneself.

What was the funniest experience you had with him; what was the most exciting?

Really, to have Fernando Alonso as your teacher and feel that you can tell him anything at any time is so moving. His immense gallantry, lost to those among us in the generation of the present era, and his brilliance—to work side by side with such a person—is an experience, the impact of which marks you for life.

One time, at the Ballet Nacional de Cuba, they had me study the second movement of *Rara avis* so that I could dance it in a concert program that the company would perform at the Gran Teatro de la Habana. In the piece I had to dance a hummingbird, and the truth is that I was getting pretty worried about being able to get the steps, choreographed at a much greater speed than usual, and on the very day of the opening I mentioned to Fernando that though I had done quite a bit of work, I still wasn't feeling sufficiently at ease and comfortable with the character. He, in response, gave me a lecture on birds, an explanation in which he contrasted each of the species and the peculiarities of the hummingbird. He mentioned how fast they could fly. In the end, his little chat brought magic to my interpretation. It was exciting and funny all at the same time, because I realized that at times, you can expend too much effort to achieve something, and lose sight of the origin of that very same thing in its most simple form, which often contains the one element that is key to its success.

Tell me a story about him that reflects the true character and personality of Fernando Alonso.

During my state exam I had to dance the pas de deux from *Don Quixote* and the pas de deux from the first act of *Paquita*. We had been working on *Don Quixote* over and over, and everything was going pretty well. Fernando appeared satisfied with the results. But the day of the test, we were under pressure and nervous about what was in the exam. In spite of that, we danced well, controlled and without showing off too much. Many of those in attendance at the theater on that day congratulated us on the performance, among them the teacher, Aurora Bosch, who was one of the members of the jury, and who spoke to me of her excitement at seeing some original steps, lost over time, that had been retrieved by my ballet master, Fernando. Additionally, she congratulated us on how well we had danced. Believing at first that I could have done much better, at hearing such praise I forgot my hunch and felt good. When I arrived home, I received a big scolding from the ballet master by telephone. He argued that you might now and then fail at doing some step completely right, but you must never lose your own self, your personality, and you must always enjoy dancing. Luckily, the next day we triumphed over nervousness and returned to our true selves.

Fernando as a teacher is highly unconventional. The majority of the time, when he has a conviction he is guided by his instinct and not by outside commentary. If he sees that something could be better, he requires that it be achieved.

What things will you always carry with you from your many hours of study with him?

Absolutely everything: especially, the unconventionality, the certainty that everything is perfectible, that perseverance and conscientious work are the only path to achieving a goal. He has taught me and inculcated in me all that I amount to. He made me feel the music in the movement. I still continue learning and extracting from this ever-flowing abundant source.

It is rare that a teacher can awaken great technique, artistry, and theatricality in his students. How did Maestro Alonso manage to bring forth all those things?

He teaches you to make dance come alive as a way of life. He offers you, besides that, the great confidence needed by each person, to express dance as he or she feels it. He studies each student as an individual, as much physically as mentally, and with just a sentence, hits upon the point that is key to an understanding and the reason. This is because he is a true pedagogue and everything he does is suffused with love.

Appendix A

Dance Magazine Interview

The following interview with Fernando Alonso took place on July 21, 2007, at Centro ProArt, in Querétaro, Mexico, and appeared in Dance Magazine, *Copyright April 2008. Reprinted here with permission.*

Teacher's Wisdom (by Toba Singer)

Fernando Alonso, 93, is a founding member of Ballet Nacional de Cuba and, with his ex-wife Alicia Alonso, formerly co-artistic director. He created the curriculum offered in the national ballet school system throughout Cuba. He danced with American Ballet Theatre (then known as Ballet Theatre) from 1940 to 1948. Toba Singer recently asked him about his ideas on ballet training.

How does your varied background enhance what you bring to the studio?

I bring what I absorbed from all the teachers, choreographers, and dancers who came my way—from the Italian, French, Russian, and Danish schools, even from musical comedy. I learned rhythm, timing, and the importance of not wasting time. Dancing with Ballet Theatre was like attending a university and getting a Ph.D.

Contact with orthopedic surgeons helped me understand anatomy. My great-grandfather, a professor at the University of Havana, gave me a wonderful sense of observation and taught me that there's a scientific explanation for everything. Psychologists helped me study the characteristics, idiosyncrasies, and behavior of the Cuban people. I always had a strong sense of the Cuban way of feeling.

What is "the Cuban way of feeling"?

The Cubans inherited from the Spaniards a virile sense of dance, with a hint of toreador-like aggression. From the Africans, we inherited a readiness to demonstrate those feelings with repetitive rhythms, plus a pronounced masculine sexuality in the men and natural charm in the women. We develop these characteristics to lend contrast to the pas de deux. We teach classical ballet; it's the male and female elements that create a "Cuban" way of dancing.

Many Cuban dancers are amazing turners. How do you explain the dynamics of a pirouette?

We use all the key physical laws when we dance: inertia (a body at rest), equilibrium (balance), centrifugal force (causing the body to fly outward), and centripetal force (causing the body to move toward the center axis). To start, you must be balanced on the standing leg so as not to totter forward and back. Let's say that you turn from second: You have to break the inertia by using your front arm to push. Even though you need extra force at the start of the turn, if that force remains excessive and you don't shift immediately yet slowly into centripetal force, you will be in trouble. Shifting too quickly will cause you to expend all your energy and you will lose the force to get you around.

The foot of the standing leg must be on high relevé to have the least amount of contact with the floor, or else the friction will stop you. And start not only with your arms, but also with the working foot from demi plié before it goes to that high, turned-out passé to get you around. But to be "art," a step must say something. When you pirouette, you must consider what steps came before and come after. Are they dramatic, romantic, or hateful? What is the rhythm?

How does one avoid sacrificing artistry for technique?

Quality is more important than quantity, but quality with quantity is best. Dancers must study acting—Stanislavski is the best—and music. And be aware of your timing so that you don't rush. When Giselle begs Myrta, "Please let him live!" and Myrta says, "No!" there is a connection. Let the other dancer finish "saying" what she has to say before you respond. Don't anticipate!

How do you advance students through the curriculum? Learning ballet is like learning geometry. You begin with the first theorem, master it, and then go on to the next. If you haven't learned to solve the first problem, you won't be able to tackle the one that follows.

I teach slight head movements as early as possible so that students can use the body more fully. The head is the heaviest part of the body and the part that leads, for example, in a *soutenu* turn. If you don't spot, the middle ear fluid, which determines your balance, will not keep up with the rest of the body. Spotting tricks the fluid, so that it doesn't retard you and throw you off balance.

What are the makings of a good teacher?

Teachers are like priests: You must be the servant of the goal. A good teacher should tailor choreography to the needs of her students and design steps as teaching tools, rather than show off what a good choreographer she is. The teacher's role doesn't stop in the studio. You must be accessible to your students—show them books, paintings, exhibitions, architecture, clothing, costumes, makeup, teach them how to eat properly and comport themselves in public.

How do you train a corps de ballet to synchronize as perfectly as the Ballet Nacional de Cuba?

To me, the corps is the prima ballerina of the company. The corps is the measure of the company's value. The principal is not dancing alone. The corps de ballet is helping her by giving the necessary dramatic background.

The coryphée (front corps dancer) determines the direction of the lines. The dancer who follows, the second in line, determines the focus. You must watch the coryphée's foot because if it goes to the wrong place, the second dancer must compensate or at least not move until the first dancer corrects herself. You must have very good eyesight for a wide optical view, eyes everywhere to quickly see where the mistake is and how to correct it. When Alicia began to lose her vision, we worked on all the other senses to capture the line. When you are promoted to soloist, you must remember all you have learned in the corps de ballet and think of the corps as the dancer who has the secret to the ballet.

Appendix B

La danza eterna Interview

The following interview with Fernando Alonso was recorded in the National Capitol of Havana, Cuba, on September 18, 2008, and aired on October 8, 2008, as one episode in a three-part series called Patriarchs of the Cuban Ballet. *The other two episodes were devoted to the work of Alberto Alonso and Alicia Alonso. The series was presented by* La danza eterna [Dance for All Time] *on Televisión Cubana's Educational Channel, as a tribute to the founding of the Cuban National Ballet on its sixtieth anniversary.*

La danza eterna *is a one-hour weekly program that, since its inception in the summer of 2003, airs every Wednesday evening, broadcast by the Educational Channel of the Cuban Institute of Radio and Television. Reprinted here with permission.*

Ahmed Piñeiro: What a pleasure it is to welcome the ballet master Fernando Alonso.

Fernando Alonso: It is a tremendous pleasure to be here with you tonight, as we leave everyday dance for dance for all time. And then as I look at my surroundings I remember this place as it was when I was three years old, when I used to come to visit the construction work being done on in this beautiful Capitol building of ours. It gives me great pleasure to be here with all of you and to remember those times in my life, so many, many years ago, but here we are still, with cyclones, hurricanes, everything . . . But we keep going forward with everything we have.

AP: Maestro, here we are in the Capitol. And I have been given to understand that your grandfather and an uncle of yours were very much involved in the construction of the National Capitol building.

FA: That's right. My grandfather proposed a whole series of plans regarding the construction of this Capitol, because they wanted it to resemble the Capitol in Washington, up to a certain point, but also to maintain a special characteristic with a somewhat Italian touch to it. There were many Italian visitors in those days, a wave, we might say, of Italian architects, and among them was my uncle Eugenio Rayneri, who was one of the principal builders of the Capitol. We came here quite often. And we would meet here, and we would see how this architectural marvel was emerging.

AP: So the child Fernando who dreamed to the tune of the Triumphal March from *Aida*, because his mother Laura played it on the piano, also felt like a warrior in these rooms?

FA: Well, what I basically wanted to be was a fireman, because my grandfather was captain of the volunteer fire department. In those days, it was a very important position. And so I, by way of imitation, put on his helmet, and began to march, wanting to be a fireman, not a dancer. I knew nothing of what it was to be a dancer in those days.

AP: So, maestro, at what point in his life did Fernando Alonso decide to devote himself to dance over and above everything else?

FA: After I saw my brother dancing in a ballet and looking so elegant, looking so virile. I liked it very much and I'm telling you, it was stupendous! In those days he was already dancing with Ballet Russe de Monte Carlo, and it seemed to me that studying ballet, learning ballet, dancing ballet, and traveling to different countries was a career that attracted me as if I were marching around in my fireman's helmet. But later I went to the United States to pursue a career, because I was supposed to be a public accountant and I didn't want to be that. So then I needed to look for some other way out somewhere else. I left for New York, no less, and there began to study ballet, and when I was already dancing with a professional company, then I sent for Alicia to come. I went first, and then I brought Alicia there. But whenever we had vacation we came back to Cuba to help our fellow ballet dancers at Pro-Arte Musical, which was becoming a place where there were many students interested in studying ballet. The number of students at Pro-Arte Musical kept growing, and they were always giving end-of-course performances, and we would go. We would join the groups, dance the principal roles, and that represented an enormous boost for the Pro-Arte Musical group, which wanted to be professional. And they put on many very interesting ballets, and achieved an entire history that is difficult to dispute.

We accomplished a lot for ballet in Cuba.

AP: Essentially, maestro, those were the years during which your mother, Laura Rayneri, was president of Pro-Arte, and that was precisely the period when Pro-Arte had its golden age in relation to choreographic artistry. Let's remember, for example, that in the year 1945—June 5, 1945—Alicia had already triumphed as Giselle in the United States—she came to dance Giselle for the first time in Cuba with the Pro-Arte Ballet in the theater's auditorium, and Albrecht, in this performance, was Fernando Alonso. Now I would like to introduce a subject that is perhaps less familiar to Cuban audiences. We all know Fernando Alonso the teacher, the great teacher, the teacher of teachers, and this is no idle distinction, as the Benois Prize that he recently received demonstrates. But Fernando Alonso began his dance career with Ballet de Pro-Arte, then went to the United States, where he danced with various companies, such as the Mordkin Ballet, Ballet Caravan, and Ballet Theatre, which he joined in 1940, the same year it was founded. [General] Director and dancer with Ballet Alicia Alonso, today the National Ballet of Cuba. I want now to refer for a bit to this lesser-known Fernando Alonso, the dancer.

FA: Well, Fernando Alonso, as a dancer, danced quite a bit! He danced a lot. First he started to study professionally in New York. I went to New York to study. I was taking classes there with a very nice lady named Julieta Méndez. One day Mordkin saw me, that was Michael Mordkin, a great choreographer and ballet director who was also a great dancer—and he said: "And this boy, who is he?" "Fernando Alonso." "And this Fernando Alonso, who is he?" "He's a Cuban." Tell him to come to see me. And I went to see him, and he proposed that I become part of his group—which was being reorganized. And so it was that I became Fernando Alonso, dancer. Fernando Alonso the dancer felt such great pleasure in gaining mastery over his body. Because Fernando Alonso had been a gymnast in school—rings, parallel bars, horizontal bar—all those things that they do—really—not as good as the Olympics, not even close, but I did have the sensation of pleasure of mastery over my body. It's an almost sensual pleasure to have mastery over the body, and the interpretation of the characters lends an added flavor to what one is doing. From there we went to Ballet Caravan, which was a ballet company organized by Balanchine, and supported by Lincoln Kirstein, and then that ballet . . . it's very interesting, doing things from American ballet: *Billy the Kid*, *Filling Station* . . . a whole series of American ballet programs that they were teaching us, so that we were getting closer and closer to incorporating Cuban ballet into ballet.

AP: And then comes . . .

FA: But before American Ballet Caravan, let's go to musical comedy. Two musical comedies that we enjoyed a lot because in those musical comedies, we had to sing and dance. And in the beginning, in the first of them, *Great Lady*, there was ballet. But in the second, *Stars in Your Eyes*, in which we appeared with Jimmy Durante and a whole series of movie personalities, and we danced with them . . . Ethel Merman was a singer who liked ballet a lot. And she would pick up Laurita, our daughter, Alicia's and mine, and put her on her makeup table, and make her up, and they were the best of friends, and she wanted us to bring her along every day [to the theater]. That's how we began . . .

AP: Maestro, you were speaking with me earlier of Lucia Chase, Lucia Chase and Oliver Smith created Ballet Theatre in 1940 . . . today ABT . . .

FA: Richard Pleasant . . . But I want to tell you that there was a gentleman named Richard Pleasant . . . Ricardo Agradable the correct [Spanish] translation . . .

AP: And he was as pleasant as his last name?

FA: He was Richard Pleasant, yes, and he was one of the people who helped me a lot, gave me scholarships so that I could take my classes there and it wouldn't cost me a cent. Richard Pleasant was a person who was truly "pleasant." But it was his idea to create as great a company as Ballet Russe, as they had Russians in their company, but with an American ballet company. So he convinced Lucia Chase from Mordkin Ballet to turn it into the great American Ballet Theatre. It was he who created it, organized it and succeeded in founding it: the great ballet company, American Ballet Theatre that was then Ballet Theatre.

AP: You debuted very many works by Balanchine, Agnes de Mille, Robbins . . . as a member of Ballet Theatre . . . By Antony Tudor . . . *Lilac Garden*, OK, it wasn't a debut specifically, but yes, you danced in it. And other ballets by him. *Undertow.*

FA: *Undertow,* that I did debut in.

AP: And there were very important works, very interesting, and historical things, also, such as those of Agnes de Mille . . . *Fall River Legend.*

FA: *Fall River Legend,* exactly. So, all that, had something in it that produced . . . that meant something.

AP: Balanchine's *Theme and Variations.*

FA: *Theme and Variations.* Yes, that one.

AP: In which Alicia and Youskevitch danced the principal roles and you were one of the soloists.

FA: One of four soloists. And I danced with Melissa Hayden, a principal, who was my partner and danced with me. Many, many ballets of many different kinds. And I was surrounded by such great artists, and had learned so much with them because there had been great choreographers, great teachers, great male dancers, great female dancers, and all this leaves one with something here, inside of oneself. See, I had so very much enjoyed the roles that I did. Not only the classics, the purely classical, but the corps de ballet roles as much as the principal ones that I had to do. I danced the role of a truck driver in one of Lew Christensen's ballets—*Filling Station*. And so we played around with it. We danced a ballet in which we danced various steps that we made up together. I placed my hands here, and he grabbed me because Lew was very tall, very tall, and he had me like this, and one time he knocked me down so my head hit the floor and I ended up with my hands on my head. And we laughed a lot and enjoyed ourselves a lot.

Then he made *Billy the Kid*, for example, in which there was a fight between the two gunmen from the American West, because I was The Cowboy in Red, who was a friend of Billy the Kid. So there was a fight, and in the gunfight I got shot, and fell to the floor. And everyone was struck by the extraordinary killing of The Cowboy in Red. There were reviews and everything.

The Three Virgins and a Devil. I danced the role of The Devil, who was supposed to take away the three virgins. Each one of them had a weakness, and there I went taking each of them except the last one. The last one was very strong and she wanted to take me to the convent. And there was a struggle . . . But at the end I succeeded in sending her to Hell, and I played a bass violin. There were roles that I enjoyed very much because they had something to say.

AP: *Peter and the Wolf* . . .

FA: *Peter and the Wolf*. Even my daughter was screaming at me from the audience! And the kids shouted at me: "Peter! Peter!" And I waved to the kids. Oh well. I very much enjoyed the roles that I played. Because I made the most of them from the bottom of my heart. Enough.

AP: Maestro, I suggest that we take a break in our dialogue and introduce some camera shots, perhaps the oldest ones of you that have been preserved from the time that you were a dancer. This one is from an advertisement that was shown in the Havana movie theaters in 1940 as part of the Newsreel that Héctor Alonso directed, and which invited audience members to attend the debut of the ballet *Dioné* with music by Eduardo Sánchez de Fuentes at the Teatro Auditorium and in which Alicia Alonso and you starred.

FA: Oh, *Madre mia*, and where did you get hold of that? Because that was lost. Please!

AP: OK, so we're going to see it now on *La danza eterna*.

FA: Because honestly, to see me dance, there are few people who have seen me dance. And principal roles, and supporting roles . . . Many have already passed away. But here it is!

AP: Okay, then, so, Fernando Alonso and Alicia Alonso in this promotional clip from *Dioné*.

[*Dioné tape runs*]

AP: Maestro, another surprise. I have amassed in my personal archives a series of documents from the Cuban National Ballet that seen in today's context prompt in me a mixture of emotion, affection . . . I brought some of those documents especially to share with you. Prompted by holding these programs, what memories come to you now? How do these programs in which you are sharing the stage with Alberto and Alicia make you feel? What does Fernando Alonso think about these marvelous documents that I have here in my hand now?

FA: I am amazed, I am profoundly amazed by what we have achieved. Because honestly, one sees that we gave our entire life for that work, to construct the ballet here. We devoted our entire lives to it. And look at what has been achieved. The other day, I was watching some ballet classes, a group of kids, a boys' class, all with good physiques . . . And I wondered: "but from where did all these people come?" . . . And the girls, so many, so many, so many. How is this possible? What happened? OK, the same thing happened during the French period, when one of the Italians married the King of France. She brought her ballet teacher and he began to establish ballet in Paris. It had emerged in Italy, the Italians had made it their own. It went to France; the French made it theirs. From there it went to Denmark, from there on to the Russians, who added their own essence, their way of feeling and interpreting. And then after that it came to Cuba, and the Cubans did the same, and that is what we have today.

AP: Now we will take another break in the discussion to see the other existing film document about the dancer Fernando Alonso: Hilarion from *Giselle*, in Enrique Pineda Barnet's film.

FA: Ah, yes.

AP: You danced Hilarion in this film, an artistic work in ballet cinematography, but it wasn't originally Fernando Alonso; I have heard that Hilarion was to have been danced by Carlos López.

FA: Ah, yes, a Mexican.

AP: You had not danced since 1956. It is certainly important to remember that in 1956 you danced *Les sylphides* with Carlota Pereyra in that historic performance . . .

FA: in which I danced with trousers on—for the simple reason that I wasn't going to dance and I couldn't contain myself and said: "I will dance in any case," because we were doing this performance to support the ballet, but more than anything else in order to oppose Batista.

AP: So that you ended up dancing in this performance without prior notice.

FA: To dance with Carlota Pereyra. A ballet that I had already danced and that I had rehearsed a lot, but that nonetheless we were putting ourselves at risk for because we were putting ourselves on the line in those shows.

AP: So, returning to Hilarion in *Giselle*, after 1956, Fernando Alonso did not dance. He decides then to devote himself to directing the company. I would like for you to tell me about that filming (of *Giselle*).

FA: [*Laughter*] There was a very nice scene that Enrique wanted to do so that it came off more like a staged version. And a trampoline was put in the orchestra pit, so the Wilis took Hilarion and threw him into Hell, which was a lake, right? The lake is where he drowned. And we did many takes because each time I fell, I would bounce back up again, and the camera kept missing me, missing me. I repeated it several times. People were saying more than thirty. It wasn't that many, because by then people liked to turn just a few into 32 *fouéttés*. Finally the problem was solved once and for all with a boy named Luis Alonso, who threw me up in the air from one side, and so I avoided jumping and coming back up again. It was all very nice, because we had to do the entire routine just so they could toss me and, well, we got it done.

FA: OK, so let's see the Hilarion scene in the second act of *Giselle* with Fernando Alonso.

[*Hilarion Scene*]

AP: Was it traumatic for you to have interrupted your career as a dancer?

FA: No, because I had already realized that one couldn't keep doing both. And that transition from one thing . . . that time of switching over, you know, to teaching—teaching brought me so much pleasure, mastering how to go about forming that image, enabled me to fully appreciate painters. I can completely appreciate sculptors, above all. How I can create that image, that figure, and at the same time, that figure moves, and it is double the pleasure at the same time.

[*This foot turned outward*]

FA: So I began to teach class and the pleasure that I began to feel of *Pygmalian and Galatea*, let us say, if I may make the comparison . . . That pleasure of seeing how one goes about creating these ballerinas, and above all, the girls, because I worked more with them, even though I worked with the boys as well, because I gave plenty of classes to [Jorge] Esquivel. And so on it went. The same with Azari Plisetsky, himself, when he worked with us. Anyway . . .

AP: What is, in your opinion, the trait most characteristic in the formation of the Cuban dancer, relative to ballet students in the rest of the world?

FA: The most extraordinary thing, you know, the most extraordinary thing, no, what is most extraordinary is the characteristic of the boys' virility and the girls' femininity. That combination when they collide on stage can work wonders, so rich, so delicious, no? Because of the emotions that both are able to produce. That is one of those characteristics.

AP: Why do you think that the virility, masculinity in a man, is one of the characteristics of the Cuban school of ballet?

FA: Because of the heritage issuing from Spanish ballet, the Spanish heritage and African heritage. That feeling of rhythm and strength. And that is present. Look, just the other day I was at a stop sign. And my driver and other people were with me. And there was a girl hitchhiking. And the girl who was hitchhiking was standing, but she was not still, she was dancing, and I said: "Look, this is the Cuban school of ballet. Look at her there!" So when they go walking down the street, you see them walking and that is the Cuban school of ballet.

AP: Remember what Alejo Carpentier said, that dance is inseparable from the human condition.

FA: Yes sir! Absolutely. There is no greater truth than this.

AP: Now I want to pose a question that is slightly polemical. We are in the presence of the so-called globalization. We are witnessing the death of some historic schools. I believe that one can no longer speak of an Italian school, of an English school. Aren't you afraid of losing the Cuban school of ballet? How can we avoid this taking place?

FA: Oh, Ahmed, what a danger this is . . . And it lies beneath the surface, like the Sword of Damocles over our heads. What a danger it is! Because we are constantly being visited by by personalities who come to learn from us and we learn something from them. And this is very dangerous because we have to know what we can accept, because neither can we deny evolution. We have to accept certain things that won't shatter our style, our way of being, our way of dancing. How dangerous this is! What shall we do? So we want to keep the essence of what Cuban ballet is, not let it be influenced, as happened with Danish ballet. What happened with Danish ballet? Danish ballet kept itself pure, virginal, and how nice, how they danced, how they danced as in that epoch! Then they were infiltrated by other elements and now it's globalization! That is the word that worries me most. Globalization.

AP: I was mentioning to you just now that there has always been a concern on your part about the grafting of the world outside onto Cuba, as [José] Martí said. For example, I cannot forget when you and Alicia went to the former Soviet Union for the first time. You were put in contact with the Russian-Soviet school. You took some important things, but never losing the Cuban perspective, or that of the Cuban school of ballet, a phenomenon that did not yet exist from a theoretical point of view, but did exist from a practical point of view.

FA: But, however, seeing Alicia dance, they realized that there already was a Cuban school. And so they asked me whether I would give a demonstration class, and I gave no more than one class in Leningrad [St. Petersburg], in front of all the great teachers of that epoch. In Leningrad. It was a class for the principals and Alicia was among them, lucky for me, because I put her in front of the them and they were able to copy her. Afterwards, they liked it so much that when I went to Moscow, Moscow asked me as well, but I was shaking when I arrived at that studio and saw the teachers seated on the floor, and above in the balcony all the ballet dancers from the Kirov. The boys, the girls were below with Alicia, who was with us to give class because of the style. And so I began to remove my clothing and they were dying of laughter, because it was 40 below zero. A terrible cold snap. And I began to take off my clothing little by little, because I was warming up, you know, the enthusiasm and doing the variations . . . Listen, but standing there in front of those people was a problem.

AP: It makes me happy that you are stressing the Kirov. Let's remember that the Kirov represents the heritage of the old St. Petersburg Mariinsky. Mariinsky, Petipa and the great classicism. In the seventies, when the ballet company made the grand tour of the socialist countries, the encounter with Irina Tiormimova and the exchange of experience between you, Irina Tiormimova, Alicia . . . The classes given by Irinia Tiormimova to the company in the seventies. But I repeat, always taking care to not lose the Cuban perspective.

FA: Clearly, this is what we could not lose. [*Pause*] Even though I don't want to belabor this point, but I have to say it, we learned a lot with Alicia. Because the way in which Alicia lost her vision and the help she required and my having studied all the problems having to do with vision loss and the reinforcement of the other senses. Because we succeeded by closing her eyes and giving her the exercises with eyes closed. That is how we developed our auditory sense and sense of balance which compensated for vision, because there are three: vision, the auditory canals of the inner ear, and the brain's kinesthetic sense, that tells you—I'm in the right place, I'm fine. And with Alicia we achieved the most extraordinary thing in the world, [sensory] compensation, and this is what enabled Alicia to dance so long. Because honestly, Alicia is truly a phenomenon. She is an extraordinary phenomenon, because no one in the world would have been able to achieve what she did, with her vision. No living person could have achieved it. We would place a red light, a green light, a blue light onstage so that she would know where she was, right? We kept on inventing, and this helped us a lot. For us in our teaching careers.

AP: Maestro, to end up, I would like to ask you two questions: What is in your opinion Fernando Alonso's greatest merit?

FA: What a problem this is to think about! Well, discipline is one of the things, this is very important. Obstinacy.

AP: Thank heaven for obstinacy!

FA: Insistence on achieving things which take a lot of work and which we cannot do and we end up surmounting them. This has been my ongoing theme. Something that I have achieved through my effort, and that of others who worked with me. But above all, discipline. Love. Love. And, how can I say it?—my power of absorption, of comprehension, the personality I lead with when I am teaching class, giving classes.

AP: OK, now that answer inspires a third one. Does Fernando Alonso have . . . is there any paradigm for the male or female dancer?

FA: Well, I have always had an image of the male dancer and of the female dancer in my mind. I've had it in my mind. It has been building and changing. It's difficult . . .

AP: OK, now, yes, I promise you that this is the last question. In the program for the *First end of year Ballet Alicia Alonso and Academia Conchita Espinosa party, held in the Auditorium Theater on June 21, 1951* . . .

FA: Ah, hold on, this is very important. You have it here and you are going to read it?

AP: Yes, maestro, that's what I want to ask you about. You wrote on this program: "Our aspirations are that Cuba be the place in the Spanish-speaking Americas where one can go from everywhere else in 'Nuestra America' [Our America] to acquire instruction in dance. We dream of being the center of ballet in Latin America. That is the goal of our national ambition." Fifty-six years after that statement, I ask you, "Do you consider yourself having achieved this dream?"

FA: I am going to ask YOU a question. Some years ago, we, those of us here prepared a document to be presented in Santiago de Chile, at a Cultural Congress held by the Chilean Communist Party, and we explained it in great detail, and it was read by Nicolas Guillén, who was the one who traveled there. This dream came true, Cuba has achieved it, and we are in the presence of that accomplishment by [virtue of] the acclaim we have received from the Latin American countries. Now we have Cuban ballet teachers that are teaching classes all over the world. Laura, my daughter, a ballet teacher who is giving classes everywhere: Denmark, Russia, everywhere . . .

AP: Loipa Araújo . . .

FA: Loipa Araújo is teaching classes everywhere . . . And so on. But among the good teachers, because now Cuban teachers are showing up all over the place. And an enormous number are popping up, but the real ones, the good ones, the great teachers, who are Aurora, Laura, Loipa . . . they are out in the world giving and receiving in turn.

AP: That is to say that what Fernando Alonso put forward in 1951 has been achieved.

FA: Yes, and what is the question you were going to ask me, because now I do wish to remain in the position of the interviewee, not the interviewer.

AP: [*Laughter*]

FA: No . . . It's just that the only thing I want to wish for you, Ahmed, is that you keep going with the work you are doing, which is very important, with all, how does one put it, [the] enthusiasm and veracity in what you are seeking and trying to do, and I wish you the best for that.

AP: Thank you so very much.

FA: This is the one thing I want to say to you, and that is long live dance, now and for all time.

AP: Maestro, we haven't finished. We haven't finished, because now I have a gift for you. We are going to end today's program, your program; I want to do it with four of your most outstanding students. Four emblematic, indispensible figures of Cuban ballet, shaped primarily by you and by Alicia. Of course I refer to "The Four Jewels." Mirta Plá, Josefina Méndez, Loipa Araújo, and Aurora Bosch. It's a historical and rather curious recording of the Grand Pas de Quatre. Mirta Plá appears dancing the Mme Taglioni character and Josefina Méndez dances Mlle Cerrito. That was for sure the only time that Méndez danced this character onstage. The recording was made in the Gran Teatro de La Habana, on October 16, 1983, during the 30th Anniversary Gala of the professional début of Mirta Plá.
[*Take Two*]

AP: What is in your opinion Fernando Alonso's major achievement?

FA: I think the sense of discipline, order. Obstinacy, certainty of victory over the obstacles that presented themselves. I think that not long ago we saw some of them here.

AP: Farewell

FA: Thanks so much, so very nice. The one thing that I can say again is long live dance now and dance for all time. And keep working just as you have up to this point. Congratulations!

AP: I promise you I will. And to you, friends . . .

Appendix C

Address to the Assemblée Internationale, Toronto

Fernando Alonso delivered the following address to the National Ballet School of Canada–hosted Assemblée Internationale, Toronto, Canada, November 22, 2009. Translation by Maiensy Sánchez. Edited by Maiensy Sánchez and Michael Mahoney.

Dear Friends:

In my few years of existence, I have seen heard about, learned and questioned a few universal premises both in theory and practice. Out of the many aspects of such premises I could share with you today, I have chosen the one that, perhaps, to this day, continues to make the most sense to me. It is also one that has proven to be a decisive point of reference in the art of teaching. I am referring to the marriage of art and science; the notion that higher art must rely on the benefits of scientific inquiry at its base, just as much as a building must require some foundational support. How my personal journey into such understanding began, and how it developed, is a little story I would like to share with you.

Although my ballet studies did not begin as early as most, my interest in physical preparation, and the importance of discipline and cultivating the spirit and the body, started at a very young age. I became an athlete during my years at Spring Hill High School in Mobile, Alabama, and later on, while studying at Blanton Business College in Asheville, North Carolina. I was able to practice, on a regular basis, sports such as gymnastics, American football, swimming and weightlifting. I remember how the exposure to each specialty was coupled with the discovery of new techniques of muscular development. For instance, in order to acquire speed and strength, we had to tow a boat while swimming. We were using its weight as a catalyst. My background in weightlifting became instrumental years later, as I was faced with the need to calculate, measure and distribute my muscular efforts as a ballet *partenaire*. The gymnasium practice prepared me to carry ballerinas in a controlled manner. Moreover, since the ballet classes were mostly developing my lower limbs, I kept lifting weights in an effort to maintain a balanced figure. As a result, my overall physical condition was constantly improving.

At that point in time, as we all know, ballet was not a socially respected discipline. In addition, there were many prejudices involving the concept of a male dancer. There was very little appreciation from any perspective. Going to the gym on a regular basis and becoming close friends with other young men who were invested in rigorous training was essential. Eventually, we managed to involve some of them in projects by Pro-Arte Musical. This cultural society led by women, brought to the Cuban stage the finest and most internationally acclaimed artists of the time. By 1931, Pro-Arte Musical was offering ballet classes in Havana. It was through this collaboration that we began to foster a more dedicated audience. This, eventually gained acceptance, and the growing prestige of male dancers, were the impetus for a new generation of passionate Cuban ballet dancers and ballet aficionados. My curious eyes, always ready to learn something new, detected a difference in the muscular work between the practice of weightlifting and ballet training. Evidently, in both cases it was necessary to use muscles in order to fulfill the physical requirements. However, while weightlifters were using all of what was available, ballet dancers had to be much more selective for the movement to carry an artistic sense, an aesthetic meaning.

I was studying the human body from the perspective of kinesiology. I was invested in creating an awareness of human movement: what it entails and why; what meaning or meanings can we attach to it . . . I was seeking a higher ground of bodily consciousness in which to explain, from a structural perspective, which muscles were necessary for each movement, and when it was unnecessary to add support to such movement from other complementary muscles. For example, upon raising the arms, do not use the elevators of the shoulders. Instead, use the grand dorsal and the external and internal oblique muscles to keep the shoulders low, and thus maintain a better posture.

During the period of time in which I was analyzing how to improve the methodology of the Cuban School of Ballet, we concluded that the most favorable way to begin a class would be with *demi-plié* exercises. They are best for warming up the knee joint, so it is not forced, nor rushed into a *grand plié*. We frequently arrived at this type of conclusion after experiencing classes beginning with *grand plié* exercises. Such was the case in the early years of our School. Back then, ballet dancers were having a more difficult time reaching the technically correct body posture. Of course, in addition, it was simply too difficult to attempt a nice *grand plié* from the *en dehors* [turned out] position. After consulting and listening to orthopedic specialists, personal friends of this humble speaker, and friends of the ballet, we came up with a more favorable sequence of steps. This way, we changed for good the way to deliver a class within the Cuban School, by commencing with *demi-plié* exercises that will better prepare the dancer to reach the *grand plié*.

My grandfather, a scholar at the University of Havana, was very passionate about science. He taught me from an early age that everything has a logical explanation. (Well, almost everything. After all, as Blaise Pascal once said, and I will paraphrase, "the heart has reasons unheard by the mind!") As a committed scientist, my grandfather was always addressing the importance of finding the cause of each effect. It is a philosophy I have treasured ever since, one I have always supported as a teacher.

Once I took notice of my students having trouble with a specific step, I would analyze its mechanics right from the start. I would first identify the problem and then the cause of the flaw, in order to correct it. As I previously mentioned, everything has its logic. I can think of many examples of the implementation of this understanding. As I grew in experience, I could sometimes lead a class and address the most frequent mistakes without looking. It was easy for me to decipher them, because I knew each of my dancers well; I knew where their limitations were. The solution to the troublesome step forced them to change their conditioned reflex. It was necessary to begin correcting them from the prior step, then ask them to perform the step with the mistake and finally the following movement. This is the ideal route to the creation of a new reflex or habit: place the mistake in a small sequence. It is very important, however, to remember that the repetitions are necessary, just as long as they do not become boring clichés. It is also crucial for the teacher to create a class that caters to the specific needs of the student, keeping in mind his or her positive development, and not a self-fulfilling choreographic forum that disregards the most basic teaching premise: to help.

Speaking of premises, one of my most fundamental premises as a teacher has been the use of the laws of physics to reinforce students' awareness of movement. Laws such as that of inertia, balance, centripetal and centrifugal forces—especially during turns, from pirouettes and chaînés, to fouettés— laws of gravity, of point of support—they are all insiders' elements that can enhance students' perspective, their knowledge and understanding of the process underlying the aesthetic delivery. As artists—whether dancers, teachers, and/or choreographers—we all owe a scientific approach to our work in order to solidify it. Science is inseparable from art.

Among the technical achievements in ballet over time, we have the *en dehors* and the maximum extension of the legs. The latter serves as a support. It is indispensable in order to avoid the augmentation of the thigh muscles, not to mention how frankly beautiful and sensual a well-extended leg looks!

Too often I observe dancers having difficulties with the support of the heel on the floor. Such a problem can lead, in time, to the shortening of the Achilles tendon, which will prevent the execution of a deep plié, especially in jumps. Thus, we must work daily to avoid the atrophy of that precious Achilles tendon. I know of the unfortunate cases of many young dancers who had to undergo surgery or have suffered regrettable accidents because they did not work correctly from the base, in the ballet class.

I have always said that human beings are generators and seekers of comfort, and that ballet is about insisting on the correction of the body and execution. In order words, ballet is about pain, a joyful one, I can assure you! I advocate the idea that, in order for a dancer to stay active for many years, he has to go beyond the maintenance class. He or she must seek the adequate warm-up, a class structured to develop new skills, and a daily iron discipline. Only in this way will his technique be flawless, his vocabulary grow on a consistent basis, and his overall performance be the best it can possibly be.

We should also pay attention to the Classical Duet partnering class, in which male dancers learn to control and use their strength appropriately, and both dancers learn to balance their strength as a unit. The pas de deux should not be a war of the sexes; to the contrary, what matters in this duet is the contrast between the virility of the male dancer and the sensuality of the woman. Male virility enhances the femininity of the woman and vice versa: her femininity increases his sense of virility onstage. In addition, the ballerina must feel taken care of by her *partenaire* at every moment.

Another detail in classical dance regards the impulse we use to perform a step. It is a subtle effort that should go unnoticed. Let us not forget there is a difference between an artist and a gymnast. Neither should we forget that every performance matters, because it is through that process that a dancer will become better. And, mind you, we never know who could be sitting there, watching us. Every audience has a specific sensitivity through personal history, cultural background, and origins. We must know how to deliver to all audiences.

One essential element in classical ballet is the sense of tradition, meaning the transferring of a legacy from one generation to the next without losing its original value, its beauty. I am an honest advocate of such quality. I was fortunate enough to work with some of the greatest figures of all time, among them, Michael Mordkin, Pierre Vladimirov, Anatole Oboukhov, Enrico Zanfretta, Alexandra Fedorova, Michel Fokine, George Balanchine, and Anton Dolin. I also worked with more contemporary icons such as Leonid Massine, Anthony Tudor, Agnes de Mille, Jerome Robbins, and Eugene Loring, among many others. Time and time again, they all demonstrated their love and high respect for art, which to me is the maximum expression of the human condition. I have made every effort to pass on to my students everything I have learned, and the knowledge I have consolidated in my long experience as a teacher. I hold in the highest respect the original variations I once learned, and always make the greatest effort in trying to remember each of their details. The discipline they taught me, the corrections they gave me . . . I was fascinated, for instance, watching and listening to Fokine rehearse *Les sylphides*. I remember the beautiful, ethereal image I still carry with me in which the ballerina is not lifted by her *partenaire*, but rather flies, as he attempts to keep her from escaping. To me, *Les sylphides* is one of the most beautiful ballets of all time. It is one I enjoyed tremendously when I had the opportunity to perform it.

During the beginning years of my career as a shaper of ballet dancers, I would follow up my teachers' legacy with serious care. In time, I gained my own experience. I learned from observation, by monitoring my students' progression. I watched how their bodies changed and became sculpted by the training. Thus, by the time we designed our first academic program in 1950, I made every effort to complete the methodology with every single necessary ingredient that, to me, would secure the development of future talents. The academy had students with a range of physical aptitudes. Among them, there was a select group of students under scholarship. We invested a great deal of effort into their development. I am referring to internationally accomplished artists such as Mirta Plá, Josefina Méndez, Margarita de Sáa, Ramona de Sáa (current director of the National Ballet School in Havana), Loipa Araújo, Aurora Bosch, my daughter Laura Alonso, Ménia Mártínez, Joaquín Banegas, and Jorge Lefebre, among others. I think that initial experience was very interesting in its results.

Later on, in 1959, once we established the National School of Ballet with official support, those students eventually became teachers as well as ballet dancers. Those were intense years. They were also truly beautiful. I would add, they were also very fruitful. We had our first, grand graduation in 1968. These were the first ballet dancers shaped under an academic system based on its predecessor, but prolonged from five to eight years of training. Among them were Jorge Esquivel, Orlando Salgado (both principal dancers of the Cuban National Ballet), Rosario Suárez, Ofelia González, and Ámparo Brito. They won awards at various international ballet competitions and are well loved by the Cuban audience. New generations followed, including a greater number of male dancers, attracted by the growing success of our ballet company and the equally increasing prestige of our dancers.

We do not lack male dancers anymore, as once we did. In contrast, we are proud of the contribution new generations of male dancers make to the ballet world. Every day continues to present new challenges, and we are ready to face them. I help with what I can at my young age of almost 95— that would be in December, by the way, for those of you planning to send congratulations. Yet, it is up to the young generation to respectfully follow up on the legacy of everything we have worked for, to enrich it with new insights, and to enjoy it. Only a sense of history can deliver the finest artistic product.

One last thing: a dancer has to cultivate his mind, his heart and his soul. His or her aesthetic sensitivity, degree of sophistication and level of education will show onstage. It is a perceivable weight that has no substitute, for it grants the right to ultimate artistry. Moreover, those pursuing a teaching experience will be able to share such a value and pass it on to others. So, educate yourselves, every single day of your lives: the future of ballet depends on you! Thank you very much!

Appendix D

Prizes Awarded to Cuban National Ballet Dancers, 1964–1974

Loipa Araújo and Aurora Bosch received the Gold Medal in Bulgaria; Marta García and Rosario Suárez received First Prize in the youth category, Mirta Plá, Josefina Méndez, and Mirta García received the Silver, and María Elena Llorente received the Bronze. The 1966 Paris International Dance Festival honored Alicia Alonso with the Grand Prix of the City of Paris and the Anna Pavlova prize; Aurora Bosch received the Paris Critics' Award and the Anna Pavlova prize. In 1970, the same event again recognized Alicia Alonso by awarding the Cuban National Ballet the Grand Prix. Araújo, García, Méndez, and Plá were recognized with Gold Stars as the best festival ballerinas. In addition, Mirta García received special mention by the jury.

In Moscow, Araújo was honored with the Silver Medal, Marta García with the Diploma of Honor (1969), and Ámparo Brito with the Gold Medal (1973). The Katia Popova Laureates Festival in Bulgaria conferred medals and diplomas of honor on Araújo, Marta García, Méndez, Plá, Aurora Bosch, Llorente, and Suárez.

Appendix E

Selected BNC-Commissioned Repertoire Works, 1959–1974

Among the most outstanding were *Carmen*, *El guije* (1967), and *La rumba* (1968), and *Primera conjugación* (1970) (changed to *Conjugación*) by Alberto Alonso; *Tarde en la siesta* (1973) and *El rio y el bosque* (1973) by Alberto Méndez; "Rítmicas" (1973) by Iván Tenorio; *Sinfonía latinoamericana* (1959) by Enrique Martínez; and *Calaucán* (1962) by Patricio Bunster.

Other pieces were *El sombrero de tres picos*, by Rodolfo Rodríguez after Diaghilev, *Majísimo* by Jorge García, *Espacio y movimiento* by Alberto Alonso, *Bach por 11 igual a cuatro por A*, *Plásmasis*, and *Nos vemos ayer noche Margarita* by Alberto Mendez, *Edipo rey* by Jorge Lefevre, *Canto vital* by Azari Plisetsky, and the four-act Mary Skeaping version of *The Sleeping Beauty*.

Appendix F

Elementary, Middle Ballet, and National Arts Schools

The elementary schools included, but were not limited to, the following: Vocational School of Art Raúl Sánchez in Pinar del Rio, Vocational School of Art Juan P. Duarte in Havana, Elementary School of Art Paulita Concepción in Havana, Elementary School of Art Alejo Carpentier in Havana, Vocational School of Art Alfonso Pérez in Matanzas, Elementary School of Art Manuel Saumell in Cienfuegos, Vocational School of Art Olga Alonso in Villa Clara, Vocational School of Music Ernesto Lecuona in Sancti Spiritu, Vocational School of Art Luis Casas Romero in Camagüey, Vocational School of Art El Cuclambé in Las Tunas, Vocational School of Art Raúl Gómez García in Holguín, Elementary School of Music and Dance Manuel Muñoz in Granma, Elementary School of Music Manuel Navarro Luna in Granma, Vocational School of Art Jose Maria Herédia in Santiago de Cuba, Vocational School of Art Regino Botti in Guantánamo, and Vocational School of Art Leonardo Luberta in Isla de la Juventud (formerly the Isle of Pines).

The following is a list of the national arts schools: National Conservatory of Music, National Academy of Ballet, National Academy of Dance, National Academy of Theatre, National Academy of Musical Theatre, National Academy of Circus and Variety Arts Yuri Mandich, and National School of Documentary Bibliology and Technique.

The following is a list of cities and towns with National Schools of the Plastic Arts: Pinar del Rio, Havana, Matanzas, Villa Clara, Sancti Spiritu, Camagüey, Las Tunas, Holguín, Santiago de Cuba, and Isla de la Juventud.

Appendix G

Proposal on Ballet

Proposal presented by Fernando Alonso at the Continental Congress of Culture, Santiago de Chile, April 1953, read by the poet Nicolás Guillén

The ballet in Latin America and worldwide

From the beginning of this century, the ballet, like the opera and the theater, has suffered a huge crisis. The political and social reforms taking place in the world, eliminating kings, courts, and patrons, apparently struck a death-blow to the performing arts.

The new social system confers upon the state the guardianship and protection required by those arts, but such a brand-new system hasn't succeeded in breaking down, in many cases, the indifference and tepid outlook of present-day governments, impeding the compliance with this official function in most countries. That explains why art and artists lead a precarious existence, teetering on the brink of decay from the inside out.

Moreover, film, television, and other such entertainment, whose production offers the economic perspective of easy money, have been favored with huge investment, depriving the arts of an audience composed in its majority of wage earners, who cannot buy a seat priced high enough to cover the expenses incurred by a theatrical production.

Many times, this gives rise to cases where—and this is not new—even a full house may result in the promoters sustaining losses.

The ballet, specifically, faces problems along the same lines, as the opera and theater, but with the added exacerbation that dancers can do nothing else but ballet to survive. Given that one's body is one's instrument, and since it requires years to sculpt it, maintaining it via intense and exhausting physical exercise, since one can lose in a very short time the technical mastery acquired only through long years of dedication, and since one's professional career is shorter than that of the singer, actor, or any other artistic genre career, the dancer is prevented from doing any other kind of professional work, for which he or she has not prepared.

For other artists it is possible, even though it is cruel, to divide their time between their artistic calling and a job that allows them to subsist, but the dancer can only do it at the expense of his art, his technique, his virtuosity. Even though we know of many cases of such a double life, in which a ballet dancer looks for some routine job that provides him with the economic resources that his profession denies him, but such self-sacrificing artists will never be good employees, nor halfway dancers, because one's life is negatively marked by frustration, an intimate tragedy, very common and prevalent among those of our epoch.

This worldwide artistic problem is more serious among the populations and cities of "Our America," where the education is less extensive and our governments' concern is less intense.

Recent ballet boom

Since 1929, the year that Diaghilev, the last great individual ballet promoter, died, it appears that this art seems to have completely died out.

Colonel Basil, with his heroic troupe, sought to keep a votive candle burning, but that individual effort wouldn't have been sufficient had Russia and England not, with a scrupulous vision directed at their obligations to the state, taken under their wing this venerable art form, becoming patrons of classical dance academies, which have taken on an official character.

This example, which has produced such optimal results for the culture and artistic credit for those countries, is beginning to spread, and today several governments are beginning to imitate them, resulting in an international ballet boom and stimulating even more competitive spirit. In the U.S., tours are sponsored and subsidies granted to various companies. The City of New York, along with private patrons, supports both a dance and an opera troupe. Mexico, Argentina, Chile, Cuba, and some other countries in Latin America help to sustain some of these activities. And thanks to this initial and correct approach on the part of government figures, the ballet, born in the Italian and French courts, an elite art par excellence, begins to take root in townships, to extract indigenous essences of different nationalities, to tint itself with new colorations, to reinvigorate itself with new currents and help the average man and the humble man gain artistic and intellectual knowledge. Ballet will never again be the art of kings and potentates, but an art of and for the people, just as times demand.

That is what we must work for.

The need for knowledge and domain over classical and modern dance for the preservation, mastery, and sharing of national cultures

Classical ballet, the ballet of the academy, with its traditional canons and intellectualization, rather than blocking popular expression in every town, as it has done somewhat, the genuine and spontaneous expression, distinctive to every nation, wrenched from its own roots, might now tend to favor its development, extracting from such folkloric expression its richest lode, its own essence, studying them, explaining them, mastering them, rendering them universal, removing them from the narrow boundaries of a single country, and giving the world the opportunity to get to know them in their purest form, preserving it for posterity.

But if classical or modern dance offers the opportunity to gain mastery of folk dance, thereby raising the level of authentic universal art, folkloric dance, in turn, brings to dance of the academy its vigor, its color, its rhythms, its gestures, its conceptions, archaic or modern, but always different and novel.

Complete familiarity with history and dance techniques as universal art is necessary and healthy for the study and development of the folk arts. From the joining together of what is spontaneous and traditional from each nationality with what is intellectual and found in the academy of dance overall, there always emerges the branding that tempers a style into something all its own. Ballet is tinged in each region by the rhythm and color of each locale. It is today easy to distinguish Spanish ballet from Russian ballet, and we Latin Americans should aim to create a ballet with all the virility of the *pampa gaucha*, a Mexican ballet with the ferocity of its own indomitable people; an Indian ballet full of color and the sadness of lineage of heroes subjugated by a civilization that enslaved it; a Cuban ballet with the cry of the black slave, the heat of our tropical sun, and all the softness and sweetness of our landscape.

If the language and customs become universal, if the way of life is made communal and the governments join together, if we aim to be citizens of the world, then Latin American artists must do our best to make sure that at least Our America, the one that Martí located between the Río Bravo and Patagonia, is known, better admired and recognized, joined together and better loved.

Formal proposal to this Congress

Considering all of the above, before this Congress, let me propose the following:

The creation of a professional Latin American ballet company that tours the world, bringing to every country on the globe our most genuine native dance forms, not as an exotic and novel show but as a pure art with our own protocol and style, so that we may assume our rightful place as the civilized nations we are, in the continuum of universal values.

This company will make its home in the designated Latin American country that will operate as a great ballet school, where classical and modern dance will be taught at the academy level, as well as the wealth of folkloric dance, traditional American dances, Creole, indigenous, African, etc. Although special emphasis will be placed on the folkloric aspect, the student must master classical ballet technique.

The faculty will be composed of teachers from all Latin American countries, chosen via competition. If necessary, classical ballet would be taught by a European teacher who is a qualified and recognized authority on the subject, brought in to transmit his knowledge and experience.

In addition to pure dance instruction, the school will teach those other disciplines which in the end are indispensable to the creation of great choreographic works, such as music, aesthetics, dance history, art history, etc.

Each government will subsidize its students, the form and amounts of these scholarships to be determined at a later date.

The school shall have its own small local company, which will serve as a laboratory for dancers and choreographers, and which, after a designated training period, would become a professional company, ordained by the merit of its work, and all things being equal.

The different Latin American countries, through their ministers of education, will contribute in a form and quantity to be determined to sustaining this dance institution with fixed and permanent annual subsidies, additionally sponsoring the professional company's tours.

An annual festival will take place in a different Latin American country each year, to which guest companies from Europe and other countries will be invited jointly with the Latin American ballet company.

On these occasions, the government of the host country will make available to the participants all manner of facilities in terms of hotels, visas, promotion, and such.

Finally, I would like to address the Congress about the achievements of Ballet Alicia Alonso, which it is my honor to direct. This company was founded in 1948 with the goal of creating links among dance artists in Latin America. That's why Ballet Alicia Alonso is largely composed of dancers from nearly all Latin American countries.

We count among our stars Carlota Pereyra, prima ballerina from Argentina, Víctor Álvarez from Uruguay, Vicente Nebrada from Venezuela, José Parés from Puerto Rico, Julián Pérez from Costa Rica, etc. We have also created a company school in which there are a large number of students from a broad representation of our sister countries.

The education provided in that school has been planned in collaboration with teachers from the Sadler's Wells, George Goncharov and Mary Skeaping, both of whom carry great international prestige, León Fokine from the Russian Imperial Ballet, and other outstanding personalities who play a role in our classes as guests or as permanent faculty.

The work achieved by this company in its three Latin American tours has contributed on a huge scale to the increase in popularity of this art form over the past three years in the countries it has visited.

Appendix H

Revolutionary Government Statute
to Guarantee National Ballet and Law 812

Revolutionary Government Statute to Guarantee National Ballet of Cuba Activities

OSVALDO DÓRTICOS TORRADO, President of the Republic of Cuba, Be it Known: That the Council of Ministers has resolved and I have sanctioned the following:

Whereas: "Ballet" is, undoubtedly, one of the loftiest and most beautiful artistic expressions counted as a long-standing tradition in our country, owing to efforts carried out by private institutions, principally the "Ballet of Cuba," that over long years of patient and tenacious work has sustained reverence and admiration in the dance culture, embodied in its most distinguished exponent, the Prima Ballerina Alicia Alonso, remarkable triumphs that honor our country.

Whereas: To date, the state has not provided the support required by that beautiful art form so it may attain constant perfection and put its best foot forward among all the popular sectors.

Whereas: Since taking power, the revolutionary government has adhered to the standard that culture cannot be the property of the few, but, on the contrary, must be scrupulously planned and oriented so that all social classes of this nation, preferably the working class and all the other popular sectors, can claim it as theirs.

Whereas: The cultural program that the revolutionary government has just executed, through the Ministry of Education Cultural Bureau, comprises all aspects of cultural expression, and moreover, "ballet" has been included in that general program, with the concept in mind of achieving its broad and effective promotion and stimulating the creation of works in this genre on a national scale.

Whereas: A technical and economic standard makes it advisable to consolidate such cultural activities as music, theater and the "ballet," and having created the National Symphony Orchestra, to be constituted shortly, awaiting only the remodeling and installation of the "La Avellandeda" National Theater, which will meet the need for a center to train, rehearse and, hold performing arts events, the revolutionary government for reasons set forth the foregoing "Whereases," believes that "Ballet of Cuba" must be subsidiary to the Ministry of Education Cultural Bureau in order that, with the required state support, it will be possible to accomplish the official plan with regard to dance to achieve the proposed goals.

Therefore be it resolved: Acting in accordance with the powers vested in it, the Council of Ministers issues the following order:

Law No. 812

Article 1. That the association called "Ballet de Cuba" be a subsidiary of the Ministry of Education Cultural Bureau, which shall exercise governance, direction, administration over it, and regulate its operation in accordance with this Law and rules pertaining to it.

"Ballet of Cuba" shall be used in all official activities related to "ballet," in its different styles.

Article 2. The "Ballet of Cuba" shall make an effort to offer the widest and most exemplary promotion of this artistic genre, throughout the Republic of Cuba, producing ballet performances inspired by the finest historical, national folkloric and musical traditions, both inside and outside the country, in order to stimulate works created by Cuban choreographers and musicians.

Article 3. The "Ballet of Cuba" shall have as its headquarters an assigned location at "La Avellaneda" National Theater once it is deemed adequate for its needs.

Article 4. The "Ballet" Board shall be constituted as follows: The general manager of the Ministry of Education Cultural Bureau, or the person delegated by him; chief of the Music and Dance Department of the Ministry of Education Cutlural Bureau "Ballet of Cuba" general manager, its musical director, and prima ballerina.

The regulations applying to this law will provide for amplification, reduction or substitution of "Ballet" Board membership when the "Ballet" Board of directors itself agrees and recommends that it is necessary.

Article 5. The "Ballet" Board shall be responsible for all aspects of the technical functioning of the "Ballet of Cuba," its performance calendar, general activities, length of season, number of performances each season, determining the number of performances per month, the staging of new productions from the overall repertoire, as well as choreographers, set designers, and musicians.

Article 6. As concerns the "Ballet" Board of Directors, the Ministry of Education Cultural Bureau shall recruit all "Ballet of Cuba" staff, both technical and administrative.

Said recruitment may be open and competitive, specifying in this law's rules the number of technical and administrative personnel and what form the competition for positions will take.

Article 7. The Ministry of Education Cultural Bureau remains solely authorized to execute the powers and duties stipulated in this law and its rules, such that in the Ballet de Cuba's governance, functioning, and administration any act, valid under the law, can take place with support for that purpose by whatsoever public or private documents are required, pending approval by the "Ballet" Board of Directors.

With reference to money orders and checks attendant to the needs of "Ballet of Cuba," the general manager of the Ministry of Education Cultural Bureau or the person delegated by him will sign said drafts, along with the administrator.

All "Ballet of Cuba" personnel shall receive the wage stipulated in the contracts on a monthly basis, charged to "Ballet of Cuba" funds.

Article 8. The Ministry of Education must include in its budget the amounts necessary for "Ballet de Cuba" to meet its goals and accomplish all assigned activities in annual amounts no lower than 200,000.00 Cuban pesos. Above-referenced amounts shall be made available to the general manager of the Ministry of Education Cultural Bureau for the exclusive use of attending to the needs of the "Ballet of Cuba" as follows: One half of the total in the first month of each semester of each fiscal year, therefore exempting it from the usual twelve-installment plan, in consideration of the nature of the expenses and peculiarities of the activities that the "Ballet of Cuba" is obligated to carry out.

Amounts obtained through "Ballet of Cuba" performance box-office receipts or other such revenues shall be for the exclusive use of attending to the needs of "Ballet of Cuba."

All amounts referenced in the foregoing paragraphs shall be deposited in an account under the name of General Management of Culture—"Ballet of Cuba." The account must be opened in a Cuban bank in the City of Havana.

Article 9. Within sixty days of the passage of this law, the Ministry of Education Cultural Bureau, jointly with the "Ballet of Cuba" Board of Directors, shall draft the regulations pertaining to this law, and submit them for approval by the President of the Republic via the Ministry of Education, maintaining the power to order the number of resolutions deemed necessary for the best execution and compliance with this law and its regulations.

Transitional Provisions

First: Until such a time as the "Ballet of Cuba" has an assigned place at "La Avellaneda" National Theater, the Ministry of Education Cultural Bureau must provide adequate space for its activities.

Second: In a term not exceeding ninety days, counted from the implementation of this law, the general manager of the Ministry of Education Cultural Bureau may ratify all or part of current "Ballet de Cuba" contract personnel or terminate them, pending approval by the "Ballet of Cuba" Board of Directors.

Final Provisions

First: The education and finance ministers, insofar as each is concerned, are responsible for compliance with this law.

Second: The legal and regulatory provisions in opposition to this law are repealed when this law takes effect, upon publication of this law in the Official Republic Gazette.

Therefore: I order compliance with and execution of his law in all of its parts.

Sworn in the President Palace, La Habana, May 20th, 1960.

OSVALDO DÓRTICOS TORRADO

Fidel Castro Ruz
Prime Minister

Armando Hart Dávalos
Minister of Education

Chronology

December 27, 1914	Fernando Alonso is born in Havana, Cuba
June 1936	Began ballet lessons with Cuca Martínez at Society Pro-Arte Musical
1937	Began studying at Spring Hill College Preparatory School
1937	Left for New York to study ballet
1937	Married Alicia Martínez
1938	Joined Mordkin Ballet
1939	Joined Ballet Caravan
1940–48	Danced with Ballet Theatre, where he achieved rank of soloist
1941	Guest artist with Ballet Russe (Col. de Basil)
1948	With Alicia Alonso and Alberto Alonso, founded Ballet Alicia Alonso, later renamed Ballet de Cuba, today called Ballet Nacional de Cuba. Served as general director of those companies from 1948 to 1975
1948–56	Campaigned for company recognition and support of the companies, promoting them as pillars of indigenous Cuban culture
1949	Directed, taught, and danced in extensive tours of Latin America, beginning at the Mexican Palace of Fine Arts, during which time he began to teach company class on a regular basis
1950	Founder of Alicia Alonso Academy of Ballet, where he anchored and established his lifelong career as a ballet pedagogue and master teacher
1959	The Cuban Revolution opened the road to ballet through government financial support on a grand scale

1959	Founder of the National School of the Arts at Cubanacán, and director of the School of Ballet (1962–68) while continuing as general director of the Ballet Nacional de Cuba until 1975
1964	Ballet Nacional de Cuba, under the general directorship of Fernando Alonso, was awarded Order of Work, First Class, by the Democratic Republic of Vietnam
1965	Ballet Nacional de Cuba, under the general directorship of Fernando Alonso, was awarded the Order of the People of Mongolia
1968	Fernando Alonso was awarded the Order of Thirty Years of Dedication to the Arts by the National Union of Theatre Arts, Cuba
1968	Fernando Alonso received the Bolshoi Theatre Bicentennial Commemorative Medal in Moscow
1968	Ballet Nacional de Cuba, under the general directorship of Fernando Alonso, was awarded First Prize at the Berlin Theatre Annual Festival and the Silver Medal at the Mexico City Cultural Olympiad
1970	Ballet Nacional de Cuba, under the general directorship of Fernando Alonso, was awarded the Paris Grand Prix at the Paris International Festival of Dance
1972	Ballet National de Cuba, under the directorship of Fernando Alonso, was recognized in the Resolution of the Second Congress of the Union of Young Communists of Cuba
1974	The Ballet Nacional de Cuba was recognized at the Sixth Biennial Ballet Festival at Lubliana, Yugoslavia
1975–92	Director of Ballet de Camagüey
1981	Order of Felix Varela First Rank, Counsel of State, Cuba
1984	Honorary Doctor of Advancement of the Arts, conferred by the Higher Institute of the Arts, Cuba
1986	Designation as member of the UNESCO International Counsel of the Dance
1986	*Opina* magazine poll Crystal Sunflower Prize, Havana

1987	Annual Revolutionary Armed Forces Prize (replica of the machete of Cuban national hero Máximo Gómez)
1988	Designaton as member of the UNESCO International Counsel of the Dance
1988	Vice-president of jury at International Moscow Competition, and served on similar juries in Varna, Bulgaria; Vignale, Italy; New York; and Trujillo, Perú
1989	Municipality of Nicea, Greece, Medal
1992–94	Director of the National Dance Company of Mexico
1995	Director of the National Ballet of Monterrey
2000	Municipality of Ionia, Greece, Medal
2000	Socialist Emulation Medal Prize, Union of Soviet Socialist Republics
2000	Order of the First Class of Workers of the United Soviet Socialist Republics
2007	Homage and Recognition Award at the First International Festival Iberica Contemporánea in Querétaro, Mexico.

Notes

Chapter 2. Pro-Arte Musical, Yavorsky, and New York

1. Ruíz, *Fernando Alonso*, 37.

Chapter 3. Alicia, Fernando, and Laura

1. Siegel, *Alicia Alonso*, 37.

Chapter 6. Challenges and Pilgrimages

1. Ruíz, *Fernando Alonso*, 57.
2. Ibid., 59.
3. Ibid., 61.
4. Ibid.
5. Ibid., 62.

Chapter 7. Autumn in New York, and a Dawning in Havana

1. Ruíz, *Fernando Alonso*, 63.
2. Ibid., 85.
3. Ibid., 67.
4. Ibid., 70.
5. Ibid., 71.

Chapter 9. Ballet Alicia Alonso

1. Ruíz, *Fernando Alonso*, 80.

Chapter 10. El Maestro de Maestros, the Father of Cuban Ballet

1. Ruíz, *Fernando Alonso*, 82.
2. Ibid., 83.
3. Ibid., 86.

Chapter 11. Crafting a Curriculum, Sculpting a Style

1. Ruíz, *Fernando Alonso*, 89.

Chapter 12. Legends and Lessons

1. Terry, *Alicia and Her Ballet*, 39.

Chapter 13. A Revolutionary Proposal

1. Ruíz, *Fernando Alonso*, 95.
2. Ibid., 96.

Chapter 14. Batista's Blackmail Bid

1. Ruiz, *Fernando Alonso*, 104.

Chapter 16. Cuban Revolution Triumphs—and Invests in Ballet!

1. Terry, *Alicia and Her Ballet*, 53.
2. Ruíz, *Fernando Alonso*, 114.
3. Bosch, "Desarollo de la danza en Cuba," 90.
4. Ibid., 91.
5. Ruíz, *Fernando Alonso*, 115.

Chapter 17. Constructing Ballet Schools, Extending the Revolution

1. De Gámez, *Alicia Alonso at Home and Abroad*, 184.

Chapter 18. International Recognition Abroad, at Home, on Film, and in Print

1. Ruíz, *Fernando Alonso*, 121.
2. Ibid., 122.
3. Ibid., 123.
4. Ibid.
5. Ibid.

Chapter 19. Camagüey

1. Ruíz, *Fernando Alonso*, 122.
2. Ibid., 123.
3. Mesa, *Camagüey*, 385.
4. Hernández, "Memorables *willis* del Ballet de Camagüey."
5. Mesa, *Camagüey*, 386.

Chapter 20. Révérence

1. Ruíz, *Fernando Alonso*, 131.
2. "Fernando Alonso 90 años de un príncipe."

Bibliography

Acosta, Carlos. *No Way Home*. London: HarperPress, 2007.

Atkinson, Margaret F., and May Hillman. *Dancers of the Ballet*. New York: Knopf, 1955.

The Ballet Theatre, 1946–1947 [souvenir program]. New York: Hudson Press, 1946.

Bosch, Aurora. "Desarollo de la danza en Cuba." *Revista de la Biblioteca Nacional José Martí*, No. 2, Havana, 1979.

Cabrera, Miguel. *Orbita del Ballet Nacional de Cuba/1948–1978*. Havana: Orbe, 1978.

De Gámez, Tana. *Alicia Alonso at Home and Abroad*. New York: Citadel Press, 1971.

English, T. J. *Havana Nocturne: How the Mob Owned Cuba—And Then Lost It to the Revolution*. New York: HarperCollins Publishers, 2007.

"Entrevista realizada por Francisco Morán." *La Habana Elegante*, www.habanaelegante. com/Spring2000/Pasion.htm, accessed May 16, 2010.

"Fernando Alonso 90 años de un príncipe." Entrevistas, Librinsula: La Isla de los libros, www.bnjm.cu/librinsula/2005/febrero/57/entrevistas/entrevistas142.htm, accessed September 18, 2007.

Hernández, José Manuel Cordero. "Memorables *willis* del Ballet de Camagüey." *La Jiribilla*. www.lajiribilla.co.cu/2006/n254_03_13.html, accessed May 20, 2009.

Laws, Kenneth. *The Physics of Dance*. New York: Schirmer Books/Macmillan, 1984.

Livingston, Lili Cockerille. *American Indian Ballerinas*. Norman: University of Oklahoma Press, 1997.

Loomis, John A. *Cuba's Forgotten Art Schools: Revolution of Forms*. New York: Princeton Architectural Press, 1999.

Mesa, Aurelio A. Horta. *Camagüey: Una razón en puntas*. Universidad de La Habana, No. 227. Havana: Dptdo de Actividades Culturales, 1986.

Payne, Charles, and Alicia Alonso. *American Ballet Theatre*. New York: Knopf, 1978.

Roca, Octavio. *Cuban Ballet*. Layton, Utah: Gibbs Smith, 2010.

Ruíz, Raúl R. *Fernando Alonso: Danza con la vida*. Havana: Editorial Letras Cubanas, 2000.

Sarabia, Nydia. "Medicos guerilleros: Testimonios." *Cuadernos de Salud Pública*, No. 64. Havana: ECIMED.

Siegel, Beatrice. *Alicia Alonso: The Story of a Ballerina*. New York: Frederick Warne, 1979.

Singer, Toba. "Fernando Alonso." *Dance Europe*, no. 135 (December 2009): 48–49.

———. *First Position: A Century of Ballet Artists*. Westport: Praeger Publishers, 2007.

———. "Teacher's Wisdom: Fernando Alonso." *Dance Magazine* 82, no. 4 (2008): 74–75.

Terry, Walter. *Alicia and Her Ballet Nacional de Cuba*. New York: Anchor Books, Anchor Press/Doubleday, 1981.

Index

Page numbers in *italics* refer to illustrations.

—partnered by: Alberto Alonso, 13; Andre Eglevsky, 157; Azari Plisetsky, 63, 95, 122, 131; Donald Saddler, 179; Fernando Alonso, 16, 30, 32, 37–38, 95, 196; Igor Youskevitch, 35, 157, 195; Joaquín Banegas, 127; Jorge Esquivel, 122, 167, 169–70

—problems with vision, xii, xvii, 33, 131, 146; don't stand in her way, xii, 100, 155, 191; Fernando Alonso's help with, xvii, 29, 118, 146, 179–80, 200–201; has eye surgery, 29, 118

Alonso, Fernando: addresses Assemblée Internationale in Toronto, 204–9; on Alicia Alonso, 100, 200–201; and Alicia Alonso Academy of Ballet, 54–56, 78, 91, 223; Alicia Alonso on, xv–xix, 116; and Alicia Alonso's vision problems, xvii, 29, 118, 146, 155, 179–80, 191, 200–201; artistic collaboration with Alicia Alonso, xvi, xvii, 57–58, 126, 134, 148, 172; attention to detail, 132, 136, 139, 154, 161, 163, 183–85; and Ballet Alicia Alonso, xviii, 44–46, 54–55, 73, 223; and Ballet Caravan, xvii, 18, 22–23, 26, 44, 126, 194, 223; and Ballet de Camagüey, xiv, 100–107, 128, 140–41, 145, 147, 156, 171–72, 224; and Ballet de Cuba, 75–77, 84, 86, 218–21, 223; and Ballet Russe (Col. de Basil), 29, 223; and Ballet Theatre, 24, 25–28, 29, 33, 34–35, 39–42, 44, 179, 189, 223; begins ballet lessons, 13–14, 193, 204–5, 223; birth of, 3, 223; and the Continental Culture Congress, 70, 202, 213–17; courts Alicia Martínez, 12–13, 16; and Cuban National Ballet, ix, x–xi, xiv, xvi–xvii, 75–77, 87, 89–90, 156, 224; as Cuban patriot, 27, 28, 44–45, 46, 118; and Cuban Revolution, 75–76, 80, 83–85, 130, 162; on dance, 24, 142, 153, 182, 209; and daughter Laura, 18, 21, 65–67, 124, 145; divorce from Alicia Alonso, ix, x, xiv, xv–xvi, 100–101, 128, 148; and Eugenio Rayneri (maternal grandfather), 3–5, 8, 11, 192–93, 206; family history of, 3–4; father of Cuban ballet, 129, 130, 146–47, 173; father of (Matías Alonso), 4, 6; favorite choreographers and dancers, 115; and Fidel Castro, 85–86; and gay male dancers, 158–59, 176; gift for comedy, 179; on globalization, 199–200; honored by International Festival of Iberian Contemporary Dance, 110, 117, 225; international reputation of, ix, x, xix, 101, 104, 180; on jury at Vignale-Danza Competition, 173–74, 225; knowledge of psy-

chology, 185–88, 189; love for music, 4, 6, 67, 147; love for women, ix, 100, 118, 165; marriage and collaboration with Aida Villoch, 101, 104–6, 118, 147; marriage and collaboration with Ana Yolanda Correa Cruz, 108, 113, 118; marries Alicia Martínez, 17, 223; masculine style of, 67, 142, 158–59, 190; medals and awards, 224–25; meets Picasso, 94; and Mordkin Ballet, 18–20, 24, 44, 223; mother of (see Rayneri Piedra, Laura); and National Ballet of Canada, 112–13, 117–18, 204; at National Ballet School, 91–93, 182–88; and need for discipline, 138, 163, 166, 171, 201, 204, 207; in New York, xv, 16, 17–29, 33–35, 40, 127, 193, 223; not motivated by financial gain, 28, 44, 45; participation in demonstrations against Machado, 7–8; perfectionism of, 63, 125, 136, 163, 166, 184; photos of, 57–60, 108–13, 149, 151; and physical exercise and sports, 6, 8, 114, 165; and Pro-Arte Musical Society, 10–11, 13–14, 16, 23–24, 28–32, 33–38, 193; relationship with brother Alberto, 4, 5–6, 57, 193; and religion, 5, 8; retires from dancing, 76–77; and social issues, 7–8, 13, 14, 16, 17, 40, 74; in Soviet Union, 63, 78–79, 159, 200; at Spring Hill College Preparatory School, 8–9, 10, 13, 204, 223; on This Is Your Life, 74; and UNESCO International Council of the Dance, 106, 224, 225; visa to travel to United States withdrawn, 70, 74

—as choreographer, 30, 71, 78, 87, 97, 116, 127; of Divagaciones, 78; of Pelleas and Melisande, 30

—as dancer, xviii, 32, 194, 196–97; in film of Giselle, 95, 97; in Les Sylphides, 32, 33, 35, 37–38, 76, 197; in musicals and operas, 19–20, 22, 24; partnered Alicia Alonso, 16, 37–38, 95, 196; in Peter and the Wolf, 28, 33, 45–46, 179–80, 196; in Swan Lake, 26, 27, 35, 37, 45, 73

—as director of ballet companies and schools, 145, 223–25; of Alicia Alonso Academy of Ballet, 54, 73; of Ballet Alicia Alonso, 45, 194, 217; of Ballet de Camagüey, 101, 105, 107, 171–72; of Ballet de Cuba, 84, 87; of Cuban National Ballet (BNC), 89–90, 100, 134, 168–69, 174–75, 181; of National Ballet of Monterrey (Mexico), 117, 173, 225; of National Ballet School, 92, 116, 134, 137, 208–9, 224; of National Dance Company of Mexico, 117, 164, 173, 225

Centro Pro-Danza, 64–65, *109*, *111*, 117, 118, 124, 145

Chase, Lucia, 18, 22, 25, 27, 34, 37, 40, 147, 195

Chauviré, Yvette, 94, 115

Chile, 51, 70, 74, 87, 202, 213

China, 128, 159

Choreography, 99, 115, 191, 206

Christensen, Harold, 22–23

Christensen, Lew, 18, 22–23, 196

Cienfuegos, Camilo, 84

Concerto (The Concert), 31, 36, 38, 44, 46, 50, 115

Conrad, Karen, 18, 25

Contemporary, The (Bucharest), 89

Continental Culture Congress (Santiago de Chile), 70, 202, 213–17

Copland, Aaron, 23

Coppélia, 13, 46, 47, 50, 53, 76, 87, 102, 106, 145, 157–58

Corrales, Manuel, 48, 87

Correa Cruz, Ana Yolanda, *108*, *113*, 118

Costume design, 29, 31, 39, 65, 71, 95, 105, 191

Covarrubias, Adriana, *110*, 117

Cuba: African influence in, 68, 128, 189–90, 199, 215–16 (*see also* Afro–Cubans); Chinese influence in, 128; Lebanese influence in, 128; Spanish influence in, 54, 128, 189. *See also* Cuban Revolution

—pre-revolutionary: attitude toward culture, 46, 48–49, 50, 51; under Batista (*see* Batista, Fulgencio); deepening political polarization in, 73; fight against Spanish rule, x–xi; under Machado, 7–8, 16, 83–84; Ministry of Education, 48–52, 53, 68; position of women in, 3–4, 16; protests in, 7–8, 10, 16, 73–76, 83–84; social class in, 14, 16, 17, 36–37, 43, 49

—revolutionary government, 83–85; and education, 83, 86, 102, 136; expropriation of U. S. holdings, 123; as inspiration internationally, 87, 89, 106; and medical care, 136; Ministry of Culture, 86, 148, 172; Ministry of Education, 86, 218–21; support for art and culture, 83, 86, 91, 95, 102–3, 107, 136, 143, 172, 218–19; support for ballet, x–xi, xiv, xx, 80, 83–90, 91–93, 99, 101–2, 116, 124, 169, 171, 208–9, 212, 218–21, 223; television under, 144–45

—and United States, 180; domination by, xi, 7, 13, 16, 73, 83, 123; Guantánamo Naval Base, 95; missile crisis, 95; trade embargo and travel ban, 64, 88–89, 92

Cuba, rumba de Albeníz, 15

Cuba en el ballet, xix

Cubanacán. *See* National School of the Arts at Cubanacán

Cuban Armed Forces, 172

Cubanismo, 23–24

Cuban National Ballet (BNC): and Ballet de Camagüey, xiv, 101, 117, 128; corps de ballet of, x, 61, 191; entrance exams to, 181; expanding repertoire of, 91; founding of, xiv; has dancers from around the world, 86–87, 132; important cultural institution, x, 146; national tours of, 94–95; prizes won by its dancers, 210; scientifically constructed, 89 (*see also* Ballet, science of); signature work of, xi; 60th Anniversary Festival of, ix; unified pedagogical system of, 89 (*see also* Alonso, Fernando, as pedagogue); for working people, 89, 146, 218; world tours of, 87–90, 159, 170. *See also* Ballet Alicia Alonso; Ballet de Cuba; Cuba: revolutionary government: support for ballet; National Ballet School

Cuban Revolution, x, xx, 55, 80, 83, 123, 143

Cuban school of ballet, 98, 138–39, 185, 199–200; African influence on, 128, 189–90, 199; and *Antes del alba*, 36–37; and Ballet Alicia Alonso, 44; built collectively, xvi, xix–xx, 98; classical style of, 70, 89, 131; and Cuban folk dance traditions, 54, 92, 99, 131, 215–16, 219; and Cuban traditions, xvi, xviii–xix, 68–70, 86, 223; development of methodology of, xvi–xviii; and *Dioné*, 23–24; and femininity, 67, 159, 164, 176, 190, 199, 207; José Manuel Valdés Rodríguez on, 35–36; and Latin culture, x, xvii, xix, 138–39; and masculinity, 131, 143, 158–59, 176, 189–90, 199, 207; and Pro-Arte, 36; rebellious nature of, 35–36; Spanish influence on, 128, 189, 199; synthesis of other schools, xvi–xvii, 19, 28, 98, 128–29, 155–56. *See also under* Ballet: schools of

Dance, 24, 142, 153, 169, 182, 199; in Cuban culture, xviii–xix, 68–70, 86, 99; folk dance, 54, 92, 99, 131, 174, 215–16, 219; modern, 92, 115, 174; and pantomime, 54, 165–66; and sports, 114–15, 156, 177–78, 194, 204–5, 213; tap dance, 20. *See also* Ballet

Dance Europe, 129

Toba Singer, author of *First Position: A Century of Ballet Artists*, was senior program director of the Art and Music Center of the San Francisco Public Library and its dance selector until her retirement in 2010. Raised in the Bronx, she graduated from New York City's School of Performing Arts with a major in drama, from the University of Massachusetts with a BA in history, and from the University of Maryland with an MLS. Since high school, Singer has been actively engaged in a broad range of pro-labor, social, and political campaigns. She has lived, worked, organized, and written in Baltimore, Boston, the Bronx, Cambridge, Charleston (West Virginia), Jersey City, Richmond (Virginia), San Francisco, and Washington, D.C., working in steel mills, chemical refineries, garment shops, and as an airline worker; also editing, teaching, and as an office worker. Singer has contributed articles to the *Charleston Gazette, San Francisco Chronicle, Dance Magazine, Dance Europe, City Paper, California Literary Review, Provincetown Advocate, Voice of Dance, CriticalDance.com, Dance International, InDance*, and *Dance Source Houston*.

Singer returned to the studio to study ballet after a twenty-five-year absence, and in 2001 she was invited to become a founding member of the board of Robert Moses's KIN dance company and currently serves as a member of the San Francisco Museum of Performance and Design's Center of Documentation and Preservation. Singer studied ballet with Svetlana Afanasieva, Nina Anderson, Perry Brunson, Richard Gibson, Zory Karah, Celine Keller, Charles McGraw, Françoise Martinet, Augusta Moore, E. Virginia Williams, and Kazako Zmuda; and modern dance with Cora Cahan, Jane Dudley, Nancy Lang, Donald McKayle, Gertrude Shurr, and Zenaide Trigg. Her son, James Gotesky, is a soloist with Houston Ballet. Singer lives in Oakland, California, with her husband, Jim Gotesky.